ALSO BY THOMAS R. VERNY, M.D.

Nurturing the Unborn Child:
A Nine-Month Program for Soothing, Stimulating,
and Communicating with Your Baby
(with Pamela Weintraub)

The Secret Life of the Unborn Child
(with John Kelly)

Parenting Your Unborn Child:
A Practical Guide and Permanent Keepsake

Inside Groups:
A Practical Guide to Encounter
Groups and Group Therapy

EDITED BY THOMAS R. VERNY, M.D.

Gifts of Our Fathers: Heartfelt Remembrances of
Fathers and Grandfathers

Pre- and Perinatal Psychology: An Introduction

———— ∾ ————

Pre-Parenting

———— ∾ ————

Nurturing Your Child from Conception

Originally published as *Tomorrow's Baby*

Thomas R. Verny, M.D.,

and Pamela Weintraub

SIMON & SCHUSTER

New York   London   Toronto   Sydney   Singapore

SIMON & SCHUSTER
Rockefeller Center
1230 Avenue of the Americas
New York, NY 10020

First Simon & Schuster trade paperback edition 2003

Originally published as *Tomorrow's Baby*

SIMON & SCHUSTER and colophon are registered trademarks
of Simon & Schuster, Inc.

For information about special discounts for bulk purchases,
please contact Simon & Schuster Special Sales at
1-800-456-6798 or business@simonandschuster.com

Designed by Katy Riegel
Manufactured in the United States of America
1   3   5   7   9   10   8   6   4   2

The Library of Congress has cataloged the hardcover edition as follows:
Verny, Thomas R.
Tomorrow's baby : the art and science of parenting from conception
through infancy / Thomas R. Verny and Pamela Weintraub.
p.   cm.
Includes bibliographical references and index.
1. Child care.   2. Parenting.   3. Child rearing.   4. Parent and child.
5. Children—Care and hygiene.   I. Weintraub, Pamela.   II. Title.
RJ131 .V47 2002
649'.1—dc21   2001054959

ISBN 978-0-671-77524-7
0-671-77524-3 (Pbk)

Contents

Introduction

Over the past decade, revolutionary discoveries in neuroscience and developmental psychology have shattered long-held theories of early development, toppling our most vaunted traditions of parenting. The news from the world-class laboratories at Yale, Princeton, Rockefeller, and elsewhere is breathtaking in scope. Starting from the moment of conception, a child's brain is wired by his or her environment. Interaction with the environment is not merely one aspect of brain development, as had been thought; it is an absolute requirement, built in to the process from our earliest days in the womb.

When it comes to early development, scientists outside the field of neuroscience—including those who teach at universities and influence public opinion—often maintain more traditional views. Most geneticists, for instance, still think that genes overwhelmingly determine the way the brain develops. And until recently, most psychologists agreed that prior to age three, experience had limited influence over intelligence, emotions, and the structure of the brain. The latest discoveries in neuroscience, however, prove such notions false. The brain is sensitive to experience throughout life, but experience during the critical periods of prenatal life and early postnatal life organizes the brain. Our brains and, consequently, our personalities emerge from complex interplay between the genes we are born with and the experiences we have.

We now know what has always seemed intuitively true—that separating the mind from the body or nature from nurture is impossible. Every biological process leaves a psychological imprint, and every psychological event changes the architecture of the brain. In short, early experience largely determines the architecture of the brain and the nature and extent of adult capacities. A secure relationship with one or two primary caretakers leads to more rapid acquisition of emotional and cognitive skills. Such interactions confer not just temporary advantages but permanent ones because they are evolution's number one tool for constructing the brain.

These findings emerge against erroneous concepts of child development that have led us astray for years. No longer can we invoke abstract developmental timetables suggested by the likes of Freud and Piaget, who attributed scant perception or cognition to the child under three; tantalizing though their theories seemed for many decades, they simply do not hold up against the rigors of modern brain scans and double-blind studies of the very young. No longer can we point to Darwin's theory of evolution as proof that humans are mindless automatons driven by their genes to mercilessly propagate the species and survive; the social nature of brain building means this can't be so. And no longer can we view our children through the lens of economics—asking how exposure to poverty or crime will affect their lives—unless we factor in the more important elements of mothering and fathering, too.

I have written *Tomorrow's Baby* to bridge the polarities—to make a connection between the troublesome ideas of the past and the truths gleaned from science, between the influence of experience and that of genes. I'll describe the interface between psychology (how a father holds his baby) and biology (what happens in the baby's body and brain).

Ten years ago, I could only have guessed at this. Today, backed by hundreds of reliable and verifiable findings from the world's leading universities and labs, the answers are certain and bound to change the way we parent and teach the young. By taking the concepts of psychology and translating them into concrete, measurable, and observable phenomena, neuroscientists have uncovered the inner human timetable for the acquisition of many capacities, including those for social relations, empathy, and love. When and how can parents sculpt the growing brain for something as seemingly elusive as basic goodness? When is it too late? Where do depression and violence start, and can parents extinguish the predispositions to these traits before they become self-fulfilling for life? The secret lessons of neuroscience and early development offer meaningful answers to these questions.

For instance, the new brain science has mounted a staggering assault on the notion that learning is more or less constant through the first three years of life. Instead, brain scans tell us, learning is actually explo-

When a mother gazes lovingly into the eyes of her newborn child, that infant's body is primed with hormones for socialization and empathy, and his brain, literally programmed (the scientific term is entrained) with the capacity to love. Throughout the early years of life, the research shows, the baby's brain is continuously tuned by his caregiver's brain to produce the correct neurotransmitters and hormones in the appropriate sequence; this entrainment determines, to a large degree, the brain architecture the individual will have throughout life. An incomplete or inappropriate tuning process may damage the neural networks of the prefrontal cortex, the seat of our most advanced human functions, producing an enduring vulnerability to psychological problems. But if the entrainment is appropriate, the child will be wired for health. The constant, often unconscious, flow of verbal and nonverbal messages sent by parents and caretakers interacts with biology to regulate the growth of the brain.

The new studies reveal that every early experience, from conception on, materially affects the architecture of the brain. From the journey down the birth canal to afternoons at the park, a child will register every experience in the circuitry of his or her brain. Whenever a mother strokes her baby, whenever a father plays with his daughter or son, those physiological acts will be instantly converted to neurohormonal processes that transform the body and wire the brain of the child. Every time a child is traumatized or abused, the integrity of the circuitry is threatened; if the trauma is powerful enough, the architecture of the brain will be permanently damaged. Everything the pregnant mother feels and thinks is communicated through neurohormones to her unborn child, just as surely as are alcohol and nicotine. Just as a computer virus gradually corrupts the software of any system it infects, so, too, maternal anxiety, depression, or stress alters intelligence and personality by gradually rewiring the brain.

The realization that genetics is not destiny, that environment is paramount to development, places new responsibility on parents but carries new opportunity as well. The lessons of neuroscience, birth psychology, and early development, still largely unknown to the general public and to most experts, will transform the art of parenting. In the past we knew that stimulation was good. But what kind is best, how much, and whom? Does a mother's tone of voice make a difference, and what, if any, should a child be exposed to in the womb?

When I was the parent of a young child, we could answer these questions only intuitively. Today parents can follow a road map based on de-sive, occurring as different regions of the brain fire up, on schedule, for the acquisition of specific skills, from language to music to math. Teach something to your child when the learning window for that skill is open, and he or she will learn it well; miss it, and the skill will be hard if not impossible to acquire later.

Every age has defined the brain in terms of its leading technologies. Thus only recently we have witnessed the shift from the old analogy of the brain as electrical circuitry to the brain as computer. Though the brain has certain things in common with computers, it is far more subtle and complex. For one thing, it is a living organism capable of growing, multiplying, and dying. For another, and this is really crucial, it is bathed in a biochemical soup of hormones, neurotransmitters, and polypeptides that allow it to establish two-way communication with far-flung regions of the body. It is these messenger molecules that enable pregnant mothers to communicate so intimately with their unborn children, and later on, these same molecules that determine whether we are prone to depression or joy, anxiety or calm. Computers lack consciousness. They feel neither pain nor joy, and unlike the readers of this book, they lack the basic desire to make a better world for the young.

A NEW PARADIGM FOR PARENTING

The new brain science proves that human emotion and the sense of originate not in the first year after birth, but significantly earlier—womb. When I first suggested this concept in my 1981 book, *Th Life of the Unborn Child*, it was considered controversial. Pe cause the research was then so preliminary, I opened myself ticism writ large from the scientific community. While scie large segments of the public, especially mothers, readi' conclusions: that pregnant women and their unborn ch each other's thoughts and feelings; that it makes a ' we are conceived in love, haste, or hate, and wheth be pregnant; that parents do better when they liv environment, free of addictions and supported ' the past ten years, dozens of lines of evidence studies have validated my original ideas, pe overwhelming role that prenatal and earl' the development of personality and the

But there's more. Based on some r' scientists have also charted the biolo

sive, occurring as different regions of the brain fire up, on schedule, for the acquisition of specific skills, from language to music to math. Teach something to your child when the learning window for that skill is open, and he or she will learn it well; miss it, and the skill will be hard if not impossible to acquire later.

Every age has defined the brain in terms of its leading technologies. Thus only recently we have witnessed the shift from the old analogy of the brain as electrical circuitry to the brain as computer. Though the brain has certain things in common with computers, it is far more subtle and complex. For one thing, it is a living organism capable of growing, multiplying, and dying. For another, and this is really crucial, it is bathed in a biochemical soup of hormones, neurotransmitters, and polypeptides that allow it to establish two-way communication with far-flung regions of the body. It is these messenger molecules that enable pregnant mothers to communicate so intimately with their unborn children, and later on, these same molecules that determine whether we are prone to depression or joy, anxiety or calm. Computers lack consciousness. They feel neither pain nor joy, and unlike the readers of this book, they lack the basic desire to make a better world for the young.

A NEW PARADIGM FOR PARENTING

The new brain science proves that human emotion and the sense of self originate not in the first year after birth, but significantly earlier—in the womb. When I first suggested this concept in my 1981 book, *The Secret Life of the Unborn Child*, it was considered controversial. Perhaps because the research was then so preliminary, I opened myself up to skepticism writ large from the scientific community. While scientists balked, large segments of the public, especially mothers, readily accepted the conclusions: that pregnant women and their unborn children can sense each other's thoughts and feelings; that it makes a difference whether we are conceived in love, haste, or hate, and whether a mother wants to be pregnant; that parents do better when they live in a calm and stable environment, free of addictions and supported by family and friends. In the past ten years, dozens of lines of evidence and thousands of research studies have validated my original ideas, particularly with respect to the overwhelming role that prenatal and early postnatal experiences play in the development of personality and the mind.

But there's more. Based on some remarkable new techniques, neuroscientists have also charted the biology of bonding and attachment.

When a mother gazes lovingly into the eyes of her newborn child, that infant's body is primed with hormones for socialization and empathy, and his brain, literally programmed (the scientific term is entrained) with the capacity to love. Throughout the early years of life, the research shows, the baby's brain is continuously tuned by his caregiver's brain to produce the correct neurotransmitters and hormones in the appropriate sequence; this entrainment determines, to a large degree, the brain architecture the individual will have throughout life. An incomplete or inappropriate tuning process may damage the neural networks of the prefrontal cortex, the seat of our most advanced human functions, producing an enduring vulnerability to psychological problems. But if the entrainment is appropriate, the child will be wired for health. The constant, often unconscious, flow of verbal and nonverbal messages sent by parents and caretakers interacts with biology to regulate the growth of the brain.

The new studies reveal that every early experience, from conception on, materially affects the architecture of the brain. From the journey down the birth canal to afternoons at the park, a child will register every experience in the circuitry of his or her brain. Whenever a mother strokes her baby, whenever a father plays with his daughter or son, those physiological acts will be instantly converted to neurohormonal processes that transform the body and wire the brain of the child. Every time a child is traumatized or abused, the integrity of the circuitry is threatened; if the trauma is powerful enough, the architecture of the brain will be permanently damaged. Everything the pregnant mother feels and thinks is communicated through neurohormones to her unborn child, just as surely as are alcohol and nicotine. Just as a computer virus gradually corrupts the software of any system it infects, so, too, maternal anxiety, depression, or stress alters intelligence and personality by gradually rewiring the brain.

The realization that genetics is not destiny, that environment is paramount to development, places new responsibility on parents but carries new opportunity as well. The lessons of neuroscience, birth psychology, and early development, still largely unknown to the general public and even most experts, will transform the art of parenting. In the past we knew that stimulation was good. But what kind is best, how much, and by whom? Does a mother's tone of voice make a difference, and what music, if any, should a child be exposed to in the womb?

When I was the parent of a young child, we could answer these questions only intuitively. Today parents can follow a road map based on definitive studies illuminating the complex web of influences essential for building a brain.

In the pages that follow I'll detail the lessons—the *secret* lessons—of parenting for the long-term health, ability, passion, mood, and character of tomorrow's baby. Maximizing the utility of this guide, I'll deliver the lessons chronologically, starting with our time in the womb.

1

—∿—

Crossing the Amniotic Sea

In what amounts to a paradigm shift in our understanding of the human mind, we now know that interaction with the environment is not simply an interesting feature of brain development but rather an absolute requirement—built in to the process as the brain grows from one cell to 100 billion, from the moment of conception on. It is this requirement for brain building, says neuroscientist Myron A. Hofer of Columbia University and the New York State Psychiatric Institute, that explains why there is so much fetal activity so early in pregnancy; interacting with the environment through movement, the unborn child's experience provides a scaffold upon which the brain can form. No one doubts that the mother's diet is important to the developing baby, but today studies by Hofer and others point to an even greater influence: incoming signals—crystallized through the mother as a swirl of behavior, sensation, feeling, and thought—immerse the unborn child in a primordial world of experience, continuously directing the development of the mind.

IN THE BEGINNING

The spark of a new life is lit when a sperm fertilizes an egg. Containing the mother's genetic contribution to an offspring, eggs are released from the ovaries and travel down the fallopian tubes (the oviducts) to the uterus at the rate of about one a month.

Although eggs are few, sperm are plentiful. Produced in vast numbers—as many as 300 million with each ejaculation—they propel themselves up the cervix and through the fallopian tubes in a race to reach the egg. Just one sperm will win that race, entering the egg and triggering the biochemical chain reaction that will most likely result in the birth of a baby nine months later.

The quest for individuality and survival starts in these earliest moments, before conception itself, when spermatozoon, one varying from the next, compete for access to the egg. While most of the contenders propel themselves toward the egg at about four inches an hour, a few speed demons make the complete journey in five minutes. In fact, biologists now tell us, sperm cells seem to fall into two groups: warriors and lotharios. The soldiers form a rear guard whose function is to prevent any unauthorized personnel—another man's sperm—from interfering with the amorous advances of their brothers.

In the recent past, experts thought that fertilization occurred when enzymes in the head of each sperm, acting like dynamite, blasted through the outer shell of the egg so that the sperm could lodge inside. Today we understand that each egg selects the sperm it mates with, making the first irrevocable decision in one's life. Indeed, rather than passively participating in this drama, the egg opens its shell and literally embraces the sperm it feels attracted to.

When maternal and paternal genes commingle in a single cell, a new entity, called the zygote, is formed. Over the next few days the zygote divides again and again, giving rise first to a morula (Greek for "raspberry") and then to a blastocyst.

After seven days the blastocyst floats down the oviduct to attach itself to the posterior wall of the uterus. But here it often runs into trouble. Because half the genetic material in the new organism derives from the father, the mother's immune system identifies the blastocyst as a foreign substance and mounts an attack, just as it would against a virus or a splinter. As a result, many early embryos are aborted. This life-and-death struggle will mark all survivors through the process of cellular imprinting, in some sense becoming the first experiential "memory" we have.

THE BRAIN MAKES A DEBUT

After successful implantation of the blastocyst, the cells grow and differentiate, forming the beginnings of the skeleton, the kidneys, the heart, and the lungs. The first traces of the unborn's brain emerge with the appearance of the "neural groove" along the growing but still tiny embryo some 17 days after conception. By day 21, ridges called neural folds develop along the groove, and by day 27 the folds have wrapped around the groove to form the neural tube, precursor to the spinal cord and brain.

When the neural tube closes off at day 27, cells from its anterior end start dividing so rapidly that they double in number every hour and a half. As they divide they also differentiate, giving rise to the major brain structures—including the cerebral hemispheres, the cerebellum, the diencephalon, the midbrain, the pons, and the medulla oblongata. In these early days of gestation, primitive brain cells continue their rapid division, migrating from the original "zone of multiplication" at the anterior of the tube to the more distant regions of the flowering brain.

It is during this migratory voyage that brain cells, guided by a still obscure string of chemical messengers, begin to forge a true network. Because the system is multiplying so rapidly and because it is so complex, it is extremely vulnerable to damage by inappropriate concentrations of hormones or toxins and a host of outside disturbances. And consequences may be dire.

In one early mechanism, primitive cells form what scientists now call cortical ladders. Neural cells use these ladders to "climb" from the zone of multiplication to the outer regions of the cerebral cortex—the center of thought. If disrupted, cells may fail to get off the ladder and move to the side, so that the path for new climbers is blocked. In the case of gridlock, developmental abnormalities may result.

Two species of mutant mice, called reeler and staggerer because of their bizarre motor behavior, are believed to result from this type of developmental abnormality, says Arnold B. Scheibel, professor of neurobiology and psychiatry and former director of the Brain Research Institute at the UCLA Medical Center. In humans, similar problems may contribute to schizophrenia, temporal lobe epilepsy, dyslexia, and some types of character disorders. Preliminary studies suggest that the most intractable sociopaths may have suffered damage during the "ladder" sequence in the development of the brain.

But "climbing the ladder" is just one challenge facing embryonic brain cells. As the young network evolves, neurons must connect with specialized "target cells" in distant brain regions. If the targets have not yet developed, then proxy target cells are spawned. Without the target cells or their proxies, neurons end up in the wrong place or simply wither and die. If things go well, the proxy cells are destroyed and the real target cells take their place in the architecture of the brain.

"This remarkable sequence of processes, culminating in a 'change of partners' and the establishment of permanent connections, is subject to error," says Scheibel, "and the results may include a number of major and minor cognitive and emotional disorders that show up at various stages in the life of the individual. We are only at the beginning of our understanding of these complex phenomena, but certain types of dyslexia may be one of the results of problems during this change of cortical connections."

THE NATURE OF THE NETWORK

Finally, after migrating nerve cells reach their destination, they commence the process of networking by growing branches, or "dendrites." The dendrites deliver messages to the nerve cell's long, slender axon, which in turn carries the information to other receptive cells.

From the middle of the second trimester—about midway through gestation—an elaborate network of neurons, their projected axons, and their lush dendritic branches start communicating through connections known as synapses. A synapse is not a point of literal connection between two nerve cells but rather a microscopic gap. One cell communicates with the next by sending a chemical messenger (known as a neurotransmitter) across the synapse. The neurotransmitter released from the first cell provokes an electrical signal known as an action potential in the second. If the action potential is strong enough, it will cause the second cell to release its own neurotransmitter, thus passing the signal on. A single neuron may have tens of thousands of synaptic connections. At the present time about 150 unique neurotransmitters and trillions of synaptic connections have been identified in the brain of an unborn child.

The profusion of primitive neurons is great: at least fifty thousand cells are produced during each second of intrauterine life. So immense are the challenges involved in brain building that at least half our entire genome (the full catalogue of human genes on all the chromosomes) is devoted to producing this organ that will constitute only 2 percent of our body weight.

The complexity of the human brain far exceeds the instructional capacity of our genes. When all is said and done, the adult human brain will consist of about a hundred billion neurons, or nerve cells, embedded in a scaffolding of up to a trillion glial, or support, cells. Although genes may provide the blueprint for basic brain development, the final location, pathway, and interrelationships of individual neurons are determined, to a large degree, by early environmental input: nutrition, states of wellness or disease, presence of toxins like cigarette smoke or alcohol, persistent sounds or movements, maternal mood and associated neurotransmitters, and intrauterine conditions, such as the presence of twins. Such input is always idiosyncratic, different for each unborn child; as surely as our genes, it accounts for the diversity of personality and style, for the unique nature of each individual on the planet today.

BRAIN EVOLUTION

This new way of thinking is bolstered by findings from evolutionary science itself. For most of the past hundred years, evolutionary biologists instructed by Darwin believed that one elegant mechanism could explain the diversity of life on Earth. According to this prevailing view, all species evolve through random mutation of the genes. Populations with new traits arise when mutations produce organisms especially good at finding food, avoiding predators, or producing offspring. After generations, these successful mutants may replace earlier organisms within their species or even form whole new species. In this view of natural selection, nature selected the organisms with the genes most likely to survive but, other than that choice, had no impact on the expression of the genes.

A convincing challenge to Darwin, however, has been made with the theory of "directed evolution," spearheaded by scientists such as the molecular biologists John Cairns and Barry Hall. Cairns and Hall are hardly creationists; instead, their research shows that the mutations driving evolution are not always random. In experiment after experiment, they find, microorganisms are whipping up mutations especially suited to their surroundings—as if some inner molecular scientist were helping the cells adjust to environmental requirements and needs. In light of such studies, scientists have come to recognize living organisms as "dynamic systems" capable of actively reprogramming gene behaviors to accommodate environmental challenges.

Now that we have cracked the human genome, we are learning that within the staggeringly long sequences of DNA, only a small percent codes for proteins. More than 95 percent of DNA is "noncoding," made up of on and off switches for regulating the activities of genes. Robert Sapolsky, professor of biological sciences and neurology at Stanford, notes, "It's like you have a 100-page book, and 95 of the pages are instructions and advice for reading the other 5 pages."

What triggers these switches? Many things, including messengers from inside the cells and the body, and external factors from nutrients to chemical toxins. Carcinogens may enter a cell, bind to a DNA switch, and turn on the genes that cause the uncontrolled proliferation that eventually leads to cancer. Through the act of breast-feeding, a mother initiates a train of events that activates genes related to infant growth.

The "malleable aspect of gene expression is an extremely important point in terms of fetal development," says cellular biologist Bruce H. Lipton. "In the uterus, the fetus is constantly downloading genetic information required for development and growth. But when compromised, it will modulate the instructions, enacting behavioral programs that enable it to stay alive."

Every living organism has two categories of behavior for survival: those supporting growth, and those supporting protection. Growth-related behaviors include the search for nutrients, supportive environments, and mates for species survival. Protection behaviors, on the other hand, are employed by organisms to avoid harm. In single cells, survival behaviors related to growth and protection can be distinguished by movement toward or away from a given target or source. But in more complex organisms—the human prenate, for instance—behaviors result when cells act in concert. There's a kind of "gang" reaction, Lipton notes, in which patterns of development are shunted toward growth or protection, depending on the environment outside. As with every living system, the selection of growth or protection programs by the unborn child is based on his perception of his environment.

Such perceptions reach developing children in myriad ways, but for the unborn child, the only channel is the mother. She serves as the baby's conduit to the outside world.

"Initially, one might think that free passage of maternal signals through the placenta represents a 'defect' in nature's mechanism," Lipton says. "But far from being a design flaw, the transfer of maternal environment–related signals to the fetal system is nature's way of providing the baby with an advantage in dealing with the world she will soon enter. The old axiom, being forewarned is being forearmed, is appropriate to apply to this situation."

In the best of all worlds, a mother's ability to relay environmental information to the developing offspring will directly affect the selection of gene programs best suited to survival. The downside of the story is that a pregnant woman in distress—whether from natural disaster or spousal abuse—will continuously relay distress signals to her unborn baby, shifting the balance of brain development in her child from growth to protection. On the other hand, signals relaying the existence of a loving and supportive maternal environment encourage the selection of genetic programs promoting growth.

"These decisively important love/fear signals are relayed to the fetus via the blood-borne molecules produced in response to the mother's perception of her environment," Lipton states. Since the offspring will spend their lives in the same or essentially the same environment as they are born in, developmental programming of the newborn by the mother is of adaptive value in species survival. This is nature's equivalent of the Head Start program. "One important part of the new credo," Lipton adds, "is turning away from the Darwinian notion of the 'survival of the fittest' and adopting a new credo, the survival of the most loving."

SEX ON THE BRAIN

One essential aspect of love and family, of course, is gender. Like so many elemental parts of our nature, sex differentiation begins the moment we are conceived. We all know the basic facts: when a child is conceived, each parent contributes a sex chromosome, either an X or a Y (so-called because of their shapes). When two Xs combine, the fetus develops ovaries and becomes a girl.

An X and a Y, on the other hand, produce a boy. The Y chromosome makes a protein that coats the cells programmed to become the ovaries, directing them to become testicles instead. The testicles then pump out two hormones, one for absorbing what would have become a uterus, and another—testosterone—which promotes development of the penis, among other things.

The Y chromosome accelerates growth of the male embryo so that testicles can be differentiated before high levels of maternal estrogen hit the baby's circulation. Male embryos thus have a faster metabolism and rate of growth than females.

Numerous studies show that this tendency is maintained throughout life: it has long been observed that masculine behavior involves forceful forward motor behavior, or propulsion. Boys are far more likely than girls to prefer cars, trucks, tools, and other toys based on propulsive movement; to use ostensibly neutral toys—including blocks and action figures—in a propulsive fashion; and to engage in physical and verbal aggression involving forceful forward motion, including football, wrestling, threatening, boasting, and so forth.

To test the relationship between propulsion and masculinity, a team of scientists from McGill University in Quebec and the University of Hartford in Connecticut devised a game of tag for children aged three to five. Studying the group over the long term, the researchers found that forceful forward acceleration was most pronounced during the tag game among children who were later evaluated as most masculine by other measures.

But speed comes at a price. From the earliest days of gestation, accelerated metabolism leads to higher risk of breakdown, emotional as well as physical. The weak sex is in fact the speedy sex, because speed increases vulnerability. It's well known that male fetuses and neonates are at greater risk from hazards of pregnancy, including preeclampsia (a form of toxemia marked by convulsions), placenta previa, and premature rupture of membranes, suffering from low birth weight, and prematurity far more frequently than female counterparts. Researchers from the University of London found that boys whose mothers were depressed during the year after giving birth have lower IQs than girls whose mothers were depressed. As if played on fast-forward, the male life span is shorter than that of the female, a universally recognized phenomenon.

Scientists now agree that such differences are reflected in "his and her" brain anatomy caused by the ebb and flow of hormones during critical periods of prenatal life. In rats, notes Rockefeller University neuroscientist Bruce McEwen, this sensitive period stretches from a few days before birth to a few days afterward. "Females given heavy doses of testosterone during this period develop physical traits and behavior like those of normal males," he says. Male rats deprived of testosterone through castration during this sensitive period, on the other hand, develop as females. "Genetically, the sexes were not altered. The males still have the male chromosome while the females do not, but the behavioral and structural attributes of sex are switched," McEwen explains. "Timing of the experiments is crucial. No hormone bombardment in adulthood will produce the change. It can only be done during the sensitive period near birth." For humans the timing is different, with the period of greatest sensitivity between the twelfth and twentieth weeks of gestation.

To learn where sex hormones operated, neurobiologist Donald Pfaff of the Massachusetts Institute of Technology injected various animals with radioactive hormones and removed their brains. He cut each brain into paper-thin sections, then placed each section on film sensitive to radioactivity. He thus made maps showing that the hormones collected at specific "receptor" sites, similarly located in the brains of fish, rats, and rhesus monkeys.

The primary site for the hormone action, Pfaff saw, was the hypothalamus, a primitive brain structure at the base of the brain stem. That made sense, because the hypothalamus is the center for sex drive and copulatory behavior. "But the most intriguing thing," Pfaff notes, "may be the receptors found in the amygdala," a part of the midbrain. During the 1960s, surgeons found that when they destroyed the amygdala, patients who had previously suffered fits of aggression became completely passive. This led Pfaff, now at Rockefeller University, to suggest that sex hormones control aggression, even fear.

Later, scientists from Oxford University showed that differences in hormonal secretions during gestation accounted for differences in anatomy and wiring patterns in the brains of male and female rats. Studying the preoptic region of the hypothalamus, thought to be responsible for the hormone that activates egg production, they found that the flow of hormones during the sensitive period induced production of a rich growth of synapses in females only. Examining brain slices in rat after rat during intervals of development, the scientists discovered these circuits were not hardwired from the start; instead they changed only during the course of sexual differentiation, according to patterns dictated by the hormones themselves.

In subsequent experiments, scientists castrated young male rats and primed females with testosterone. They already knew such manipulation would alter behavior and sex characteristics. But now they proved that the treatment altered synapses in the brain as well—castrated males had synaptic patterns characteristic of females, while testosterone-treated females had brain circuitry characteristic of normal males.

In the decades following these pioneering studies, scientists have found that the early ebb and flow of hormones render male and female brains anatomically different across a host of species, and in a variety of ways. "Experts on the brain have known for a long time that the cerebral hemispheres—the two sides of the 'thinking brain'—are almost symmetrical, but not quite," McEwen says. "It is also known today that the asymmetry is different between men and women. That may account for the observation in medical studies that injury, such as stroke, affecting only one part of the cerebral hemisphere on one side of the brain results in different losses of function in men and women." It may also account for recent findings that women, on average, appear more adept at verbal tasks and fine motor coordination while men, on average, seem better at perceiving spatial relationships and in certain areas of math.

CARE AND FEEDING OF THE FETAL BRAIN

The more we know about the requirements of brain building, the clearer it is that input determines outcome. Along with more surprising implications, the new findings underscore the importance of guidelines for nutrition, smoking, drinking, and drugs.

Nutrients and chemicals the pregnant mother eats or breathes will enter her bloodstream, travel through the umbilical cord to the placenta, and ultimately influence the development of her baby's brain. When maternal blood is rich in oxygen and appropriate nutrients, the unborn child will thrive. On the other hand, thousands of research studies now document the consequences of deficiencies in certain nutrients and vitamins, which impede healthy development in the womb.

There are hundreds of books on nutrition during pregnancy, and if you are or are about to become pregnant, I suggest that you read one of these as soon as possible, but certain basics bear repeating in thumbnail form:

- Even if your diet is already healthy, you will need some adjustments, including increasing your intake of protein.
- Be conscious of calories. Don't believe the old myth that you are eating for two. Pregnant women should consume only about 300 calories more per day than before they were pregnant.
- Talk to your doctor about appropriate vitamin and mineral supplements for the duration of your pregnancy. Usually on the list for pregnant women are iron and calcium supplements, a daily vitamin, and folic acid, an essential B vitamin; lack of folic acid has been linked to neural tube defects like spina bifida (failure of the spinal column to close).

It's obvious that there are also things to avoid:

- Foods that might be a source of bacteria for your unborn child. These include sushi, raw oysters or other uncooked seafood, rare burgers, undercooked poultry, soft cheeses like Brie and Camembert, and unpasteurized milk.

- Megadoses of vitamins, which might be harmful to a developing baby.
- Caffeinated beverages: studies show that more than four cups of coffee or the equivalent a day increases risk of miscarriage, low birth weight, and sudden infant death syndrome (SIDS). Remember, coffee is not the only source of caffeine. It can also be found in tea, colas and many other soft drinks, and chocolate.
- Dieting, which can deprive you and your baby of iron, folic acid, and other essential vitamins, minerals, and nutrients required for the growth of the developing body and brain.

Of particular note is new research into prenatal famine. A series of studies from Columbia University used psychiatric registry data to look at babies exposed to the Dutch "hunger winter" of 1944–1945. The investigators found that those exposed to the hunger winter in early, but not late, gestation had two times the risk of schizophrenia as those not exposed. Another study, using military induction data, showed that those exposed to the hunger winter in early gestation were twice as likely to exhibit schizoid personality disorder as well.

Building Brains with Omega-3

Of all the nutrients needed for building your baby's brain, scientists now say, one of the most important may be the longer-chain omega-3 fatty acids—eicosapentaenoic acid (EPA) and docosahexaenoic acid (DHA), both found primarily in fish oil.

Scientists now know that omega-3 oils were key nutrients propelling the evolution of the human brain. In abundant supply around the African lake region where our ancestors evolved, omega-3 fatty acids provided a dense, efficient source of energy that no other nutrient could supply. Their importance is documented by human physiology today: omega-3 oils are the major building blocks of membranes surrounding every cell in the body. And they are especially abundant in the healthy brain, where they imbue nerve cell membranes with the flexibility required to work optimally.

Therefore, I recommend that pregnant women pay attention to their intake of foods rich in omega-3 oils: fish, walnuts, and free-range meats all fill the bill. Please note that medical supervision should be sought by a woman considering any omega-3 fatty acid supplementation. Too much of any good thing is potentially hazardous.

SUBSTANTIAL DANGERS

Just as appropriate nutrition can forever enhance the structure of the fetal brain, so, too, exposure to harmful substances can cause damage for life. Whether inhaled or ingested, toxins and pollutants can alter genes, skewing the molecular instructions that underlie embryogenesis—including the basic structure of the brain.

Well documented in the literature are the dangers of radiation. Depending on when and how much exposure occurred, dangers include brain malformations, Down's syndrome or other forms of mental retardation, and a laundry list of birth defects.

In the past, doctors have routinely advised pregnant women to avoid alcohol—clinical observation has shown that two or more drinks a day during pregnancy can lead to fetal alcohol syndrome (FAS), a devastating disorder associated with low birth weight, growth deficiencies, facial abnormalities, and a legion of neurological problems, including mental retardation. In recent years, researchers have documented the destructive effect of alcohol on the circuitry and anatomy of the brain.

Studies of mice show that exposure to alcohol early in pregnancy reduces the number of cells in the neural tube, the embryonic structure that gives rise to the brain and spinal cord. When alcohol is administered to rats throughout prenatal development, nerve cells in the cortex (the thinking part of the brain) not only are smaller than expected but also have fewer dendrites (the structures that enable brain cells to communicate with each other).

These findings have been confirmed in humans: the EEGs (brain wave patterns) of infants born to alcoholic mothers show markedly reduced activity, especially in the vital left hemisphere, which is crucial for language, memory, and logical thought.

As with drinking, smoking during pregnancy has long been disouraged because of studies connecting it with premature birth and low birth weight. Now evidence from the frontiers of brain science shows that the nicotine in tobacco inhibits the growth of brain cells and the reabsorption of critical neurotransmitters like dopamine, which carry messages from one brain cell to the next. Such interference with normal development can have clear, long-term consequences, even when the unborn child is exposed to levels of nicotine not usually considered toxic.

In one study in Chicago, for example, researchers found that boys whose mothers smoked more than half a pack of cigarettes a day during pregnancy were far more likely than sons of nonsmokers to develop conduct disorders. Researchers at Emory University in Atlanta found that boys whose mothers smoked while pregnant retained a high risk of criminal behavior well into adulthood. Compared with males whose mothers did not smoke during the third trimester, boys whose mothers smoked at least twenty cigarettes a day during that period were 1.6 times as likely to be arrested for nonviolent crime, 2 times as likely to be arrested for violent crime, and 1.8 times as likely to be categorized as lifelong offenders. The clear-cut implication: smoking interferes with appropriate development of the fetal brain.

Also perilous is exposure to drugs like cocaine. Linda Mayes of Yale reports that as many as 375,000 such babies are born each year. We've been hearing reports on "crack babies" and victims of drug-using mothers for decades; but again, it is only recently that observations of developmental delays, learning disabilities, and behavioral disorders have been validated by brain science. The newest research shows that exposure to cocaine early in gestation disrupts migration of neurons up the wall of the cerebral cortex. Later in the prenatal period cocaine interferes with the production of synapses. Like nicotine, but more so, cocaine floods the brain with disruptive levels of neurotransmitters. Is it any wonder that babies exposed to cocaine grow up with disturbances in attention, memory, information processing, and learning as well as motor delays?

THE IMPACT OF INFECTIOUS DISEASE

Scientists at Loyola Marymount University, meanwhile, have found that maternal bouts of the flu put offspring exposed in the womb at greater risk for clinical depression. The research team, led by Richardo A. Machon, compared a group of Finnish men and women born during an A2/Singapore influenza epidemic in Helsinki with a control group of individuals born at the same hospital nine years earlier. They found that 16 percent of the men and 8 percent of the women exposed to the virus during the second trimester were later diagnosed with major affective disorder. Only 2 percent of those in the control group were afflicted. The same team also found a link between the Singapore flu and schizophrenia.

Other diseases and conditions during pregnancy have been connected to long-term brain damage as well. Individuals exposed to infectious diseases like syphilis, AIDS, and herpes simplex can experience severe central nervous system disorders and may possibly die. Pregnant women with gonorrhea or chlamydia can transmit these infections to their babies during vaginal delivery, with eye infections and chronic pneumonia the greatest risks to the infants.

Rubella, or German measles, during pregnancy has long been known to cause neurological abnormalities, including mental retardation, cerebral palsy, and deafness. But researchers have recently also traced this disease to increased risk for schizophrenia and several childhood psychiatric disorders, including autism.

MATERNAL MOODS AND FEELINGS

It only makes sense for the new brain science to validate long-held views on the developmental impact of nutritional, chemical, and biochemical inputs—foods, toxins, and destructive microorganisms that cause disease. The latest research, however, has uncovered something more subtle but equally significant: the overwhelming impact of maternal moods and feelings on the developing brain of the unborn. This is one of the most important secret lessons parents unwittingly teach their children, and I shall discuss it in depth in Chapter Three.

SUMMING UP

The physiological events that result in the conception and birth of a child leave lifelong imprints on our minds. The adult human brain weighs about three pounds and consists of a hundred billion neurons, or nerve cells, embedded in a scaffolding of up to a trillion glial, or support, cells. Despite the role genes play in orchestrating brain development, it has become abundantly clear that environmental factors modulate the process from the start of embryonic life. In a final resolution of the nature-nurture debate, we now understand that the environment acts on the genes we were born with to drastically change their expression during the formation of our personality, skills, and predilections and the circuitry of our brains.

Key Parenting Points

- Ideally, every child should be a wanted child.
- Try, if possible, to plan for the conception of your child.
- During your pregnancy eat well, avoid drugs, relax, and have fun.
- Surround yourself with people who will nurture, protect, and love you, so you can focus on loving your baby.

2

— ∾ —

The Dawn of Consciousness

A former Harvard professor, Chicago radiologist Jason Birnholz, has over the past two decades prepared more than fifty thousand fetal sonograms, pictures taken with ultrasound. One of the most striking findings for Birnholz has been that unborn babies, especially those beyond the fourth month of pregnancy, are not all that different from newborns.

"You can see emotional reactions on the fetus's face," says Birnholz. "If they look unhappy, there is probably a reason. I've seen starving fetuses cry just like newborns. They used to be considered blobs, but they are not."

In fact, the great weight of the scientific evidence that has emerged over the last decade demands that we reevaluate the mental and emotional abilities of unborn children. Awake or asleep, the studies show, they are constantly tuned in to their mother's every action, thought, and feeling. From the moment of conception, the experience in the womb shapes the brain and lays the groundwork for personality, emotional temperament, and the power of higher thought.

THE ORIGINS OF SENSATION

We've understood some things about fetal sensation for some time. At 28 days, when the embryo measures a quarter inch and the tiny blood vessel that is the precursor of the heart begins to beat, the three primary parts of the brain have already formed. At 6 weeks, and about half an inch in length, when the eyes, nose, and ears have started to form, the unborn child can respond to touch. At 19 to 20 weeks she has primitive brain wave patterns, and by 22 weeks sustained patterns similar to those of adults. By the fourth month, the unborn child's capacity to explore her world explodes. She plays with her umbilical cord and sucks her thumb. If iodinated poppy seed oil, foul to the taste, is introduced into the womb, it causes the prenate to grimace and cry; a sweet substance, on the other hand, causes her to swallow amniotic fluid at twice the normal rate. At five months the same child will react to a loud sound by raising her hands and covering her ears.

THE BEGINNINGS OF THOUGHT AND CONSCIOUSNESS

Although it is impossible to determine an unborn child's thoughts for certain, research conducted by neuroscientist Dominick Purpura of the Albert Einstein Medical College in New York shows that the baby in the womb has formed the brain structures necessary for learning and even awareness sometime between the fifth and sixth months of development. Other scientists, studying brain waves, have learned that during the last trimester unborn children experience periods of wakefulness and sleep, even exhibiting physiological measurements associated with dream sleep.

The notion that unborn children in the final months of gestation process sensory and cognitive abilities makes sense even to the most skeptical these days. But an exploration of cell biology suggests that some form of consciousness—a rudimentary awareness of the world beyond—exists from the earliest days in the womb.

The first person to publish a paper addressing the psychology of conception was the virtually unknown analyst Sabina Spielrein. Her paper, "Destruction as a Cause of Coming into Being," was delivered in Vienna in 1912 to Freud's small circle of analysts. The fusion of the two gametes engenders destruction and creation at once, she told the analysts. The male segment dissolves in the female, while the female becomes disorganized by the invasion of the male, taking on a new shape because of the alien intruder. Structural change flashes through the organism; cellular destruction and reconstruction, normally slow and cyclical, here happen abruptly. It hardly seemed possible, she declared, that an individual would not somehow sense the destructive and reconstructive crucible of his birth.

Taking the notion further, Isador Sadger declared in 1941 that the emotional circumstances of our conception matter as well. It is to the benefit of the individual, he said, if sexual congress is accompanied by feelings of sensuality and love, and if the ovum receives the sperm with "open arms."

For years, such ideas resided at the outer edge of credibility. That our conception might somehow linger as experience seemed as unscientific a notion as past lives and UFOs. Yet it turns out that these prescient theorists were ahead of their time. Today the evidence for cellular memory, covered in detail in Chapter Nine, comes from scientists at the Massachusetts Institute of Technology, the National Institute of Mental Health, and other prestigious labs.

Their collective finding—that individual cells accumulate experience-based memory even before the brain has formed—underscores the drama of embryonic life. The jolt at conception is just the start. Another critical juncture is implantation of the embryo in the uterine wall. When embryo and uterus first connect, the embryo's outer cells begin to proliferate, forming fingerlike networks of capillaries and blood vessels that infiltrate the uterine lining. If implantation succeeds, the fingers—known as chorionic villi—will infuse nutrients into the embryo and ultimately become the placenta. Recognized as foreign by the mother's immune system, the embryo comes under attack as the uterine lining swells out to engulf it and thousands of white blood cells rush in for the kill. Depending on the outcome of the struggle, the embryo either dies or succeeds in establishing a foothold, usually in the posterior wall of the uterus.

These physiological events and the many that follow, according to the new tenets of cell biology, are "experienced" by the young embryo and probably serve as forerunners of sensation, emotions, and personality. Although the details are still just conjectural, the latest theories trace our deepest sense of pleasure, pain, fear, and struggle to the earliest days of life.

As the unborn child grows, experience, both positive and negative, enters through the rapidly developing senses—hearing, taste, smell, touch, motion, and sight. The prenate starts to make movements in response to being touched at 8 weeks. He can respond to sound from 20 weeks, and discriminate between different tones at 28 weeks. Brain wave studies of preterm infants show sustained patterns of visual and tactile sensation.

Scientists have documented tactile sensitivity in the unborn as early as 7 weeks' gestation, when she has been observed to respond to hair stroked along her cheek. By 17 weeks' gestation, most parts of the fetal skin are sensitive, and by 32 weeks, skin sensitivity includes the entire body.

Vision develops in the womb as well. Although fetal eyelids remain fused from week 10 to week 26 of gestation, unborn children, aware of light and dark, respond to light flashed on the mother's abdomen.

THE SOUNDSCAPE OF THE UNBORN

Given the recent watershed of evidence, the view of our life in utero as a silent passage has been put solidly to rest. In fact, the womb is a chamber of echoes, say researchers, in which sound plays a significant role. Placing a hydrophone into the uterus of pregnant women, researchers have measured noise comparable to the background noise in an average room. Sounds include the pulse of blood flowing through the mother's veins, the rumbling of her stomach and intestines as food passes through them, and the sound of her voice, filtered though it is by the barrier of her body and the amniotic sea in which the unborn child floats.

Although the sounds are always there, the unborn child will perceive them only when he has developed the auditory apparatus enabling him to hear. As with many sensations—and the development of consciousness itself—hearing sharpens slowly as the newborn brain grows. Researchers have noted that the human auditory system is as advanced at 20 weeks as it is in the adult. Irish researchers have noted that unborn children respond to tones as early as 19 weeks; by 27 weeks, they are especially sensitive to the mother's voice.

In a series of remarkable studies, University of North Carolina psychologist Anthony deCasper showed that newborns were far smarter than anyone had realized. In one study, he asked sixteen pregnant women to tape-record their reading of three children's stories, "The King, the Mice and the Cheese" and two versions of "The Cat in the Hat." During the last six and a half weeks of pregnancy, one group of women read the first story aloud three times a day, another read the second story aloud three times a day, and a third read the last story aloud three times a day. When the babies were born, deCasper and colleagues offered each infant a choice between the story its mother had repeatedly read and one of the other two stories.

To enable the newborns to cast their votes, deCasper invented the "suck-o-meter"—a nipple on a baby bottle connected to a computer-controlled tape player. Newborns could switch between two taped stories, both recorded by their mothers, simply by changing their sucking rhythm. The findings? When the babies were tested within a few hours of birth, thirteen of the sixteen adjusted their sucking rhythm to hear the familiar story rather than the unfamiliar one, providing truly convincing evidence for prenatal memory.

In a further elaboration of this work, psychologist Robin Panneton asked two groups of pregnant women close to term to sing a melody every day for the rest of their pregnancies. Again, each mother recorded two melodies: the one she regularly sang to her unborn child, and the one the mothers from the other group sang. After birth, babies hooked up to the "suck-o-meter" consistently chose the familiar melody.

THE ACQUISITION OF LANGUAGE

As the deCasper work suggests, our brains are primed for language in the womb. That explains why, at the age of four days, infants can distinguish language from other sounds and have already begun to prefer not just their mothers' voice but also their mothers' language. Newborns can differentiate language based on properties such as intonation and rhythm. French, English, and Japanese follow distinctly different patterns: for instance, in French the duration of the vowels is fairly constant, but in English, vowels vary in duration depending on whether they are accented or not. In Japanese, rhythm is set by sounds called mora, which are shorter than the syllables they mark. No matter what the language, researchers now say, our brains are primed for native speech just once, early on.

Observations of newborns make this notion compelling. Almost immediately after birth, babies preferentially select speech sounds over other sounds. They seem to grasp intuitively the meaning of intonation and rhythm in speech, even when they do not understand the words. On contact with his environment, moreover, the human infant starts limiting attention to linguistic categories pertinent to his native tongue. At first, say researchers, the newborn can distinguish every sound of every human language, but rapid neural development in the first year after birth gradually makes the infant an expert only in those languages he or she hears.

Language heard in utero predisposes the unborn child to specific tongues and dialects. Recent neurological studies suggest that brain cells in utero grow in response to external sound, especially during the period of rapid brain maturation, from 24 weeks of gestation on. During this period, neurons in the cortex—the center of thought—react to language sounds by producing specific patterns in the dendrites and synapses they spawn.

"Even without special effort on the part of mothers, unborn babies benefit from whatever speech they can hear," says Marshall R. Childs, professor at Fuji Phoenix College in Japan. "They have the opportunity not only to internalize the sound patterns of the mother's language but also to put these sound patterns in context. The fetus undoubtedly experiences the mother's mental states, such as stress, relaxation, sleeping, waking, aerobic exercise, contentment, and anger."

The prenate forms impressions of his mother's internal state and the world outside by listening to her voice, with its changes in tone, loudness, rapidity, and rhythm. Language, after all, is used in context with situations, which include the mental state of the speaker. "Mother's language is never sterile syntax or vocabulary," says Childs. "Instead it is inextricably bound to her experiences, and that inextricable binding is what the fetus experiences and builds into the neural makeup of the brain."

Support for the connection between the structure of the brain and language heard in utero comes from its absence: after birth, children of mute mothers tend to cry in anomalous ways or not at all, in response to stress, as if some essential life lesson had been lost.

FETAL PAIN

The issue of fetal pain has remained controversial for years. Pain, after all, is a subjective experience. The prenate cannot describe what he or she feels, and in the past we lacked objective tools for measuring pain.

During the last decade, however, evidence has been mounting to show that unborn children feel pain as powerfully as those outside the womb. The most convincing evidence is anatomical, since the perception of pain depends on nerve pathways from the source of discomfort through the spinal cord to the brain.

Nature lays those pain pathways down early: connections from peripheral tissue to the spinal cord form at 8 weeks. The cerebral cortex starts to form at 10 weeks. The brain continues to lay down nerve fibers as it takes on shape and structure. By week 16 the connections for pain are in place, and by week 28 that wiring is more or less complete. In fact, anatomical evidence suggests that the unborn child is more sensitive to

pain than the rest of us; the inhibitory pathways that block incoming
pain do not develop until after birth.

Studies of preterm babies show a clear response to pain as well. At 23
weeks, preemies show distinct reactions—including facial grimaces,
clenched hands, and leg withdrawal—to stimuli such as heel pricks.
Mothers and nurses caring for preterm babies consistently report their
observation of a pain response.

It's also possible to infer the presence of pain from the stress response.
The unborn child mounts a significant stress response, measured by ac-
tivation of specific hormones and neurotransmitters, particularly cortisol,
B-endorphins, and noradrenaline, in response to trauma. Although the
stress response itself does not indicate the presence of pain, it's unlikely
for pain to be present in the absence of stress. High levels of stress hormones measured during surgery in newborns, moreover, make it likely
that stress is a reliable pain index in the unborn.

The implications of these findings are disturbing indeed. According
to Nicholas M. Fisk, professor of pediatrics, obstetrics, and gynecology at
Imperial College School of Medicine, Queen Charlotte's and Chelsea
Hospital, London, "The fetus is currently treated as though it feels nothing, and is given no analgesia or anesthesia for potentially painful interventions."

As the unborn child becomes gradually more conscious, growing
from a single egg and sperm to a fetus with all senses fully functional by
six months, it experiences the world in two complementary modes—one
through the molecular sensors in each and every cell, and the other via
the organized network of the brain. It is the second step, the establishment of mature neurological networks that make up the central nervous
system and the brain, that is required for consciousness. But the stream
of unconscious experience, coursing through our cells, influences our
beings for as long as we live. How many people, unconsciously retracing
the cellular struggle waged in the earliest days of life, strive for acceptance by a figure of authority? How many dream of wild, buffeting winds
or an oasis of calm? Such tendencies can often be understood in light of
influences after birth, but sometimes they cannot. In these latter instances, we might look for a clue to our very first moments of life.

SUMMING UP

Whether the sensation is pain or vision or hearing, it is clear that perception and consciousness emerge not after birth but long before, in the

womb. Sensation is always there: at first in the experience of the earliest fetal cells, and later in the emerging neural networks that form the organs of sensation and the brain.

I am often asked: When does life begin? What the questioner really wants to know is when, in a person's life cycle, do consciousness and self-awareness first make an appearance. The answer depends on the sort of proof the questioner is looking for.

Although the experience of the embryo remains shrouded in mystery, she nonetheless begins to record and react to events on a cellular level from conception on. Between the third and sixth months of gestation, the unborn child begins responding to a variety of stimuli and seems capable of volitional acts, such as moving away from the source of light or even attempting to push aside an amniocentesis needle. Somewhere between the fifth and sixth months of gestation, roughly at the end of the second trimester, the unborn child changes from a largely *sensate* being—one who receives, processes, and reacts to sensations—to a *sensible* being, one who is mentally alert, conscious, and capable of primitive cognition.

There is no doubt in my mind that at six months after conception the unborn child is a *sensing, feeling, aware, and remembering human being.*

Key Parenting Points

- A child conceived in love and cared for lovingly in the womb will benefit throughout life.
- To maximize an unborn child's emotional and mental development, provide an optimum amount of stimulation throughout pregnancy.

3

_—∽—_

Maternal Stressors
and the Unborn

I'm a very unhappy woman because my husband isn't supporting me in any fashion in my pregnancy. I'm in my fifth month and
feeling suicidal. I don't want to face my life as a single mother, especially if my baby is emotionally unstable or mentally disabled.
The stress in my life continues to build, I walk around on the brink
of tears. The minute I get into my house I cry. My husband is prac-
tically never home and he doesn't help with housework. I'm practi-
cally always home because I work part-time in the afternoons only.

My husband is the classic type A. He works long hours dreaming of the top VP position. After work he works out, plays squash,
and takes two MBA classes. On weekends he plays more squash.
I've asked him to reserve one day for me. He just can't do it. He
has no interest in me. My tears only make him guilty. He hasn't
touched my body in ages.

By his actions, this husband may be affecting more than his wife's
feelings, or even their marriage—he may also be wiring the brain of his
unborn child for greater risk of depression, conduct disorder, inappropriate aggression, and a host of other ills. Perhaps someone should tip
him off: in the last few years, scores of studies have documented the potential for increased risk of lifelong problems for children exposed in the
womb to excessive maternal stress, anxiety, and depression.

In just a sampling of studies, researchers have learned that

- Mothers of schizophrenic offspring are almost twice as likely to have rated themselves as depressed during the sixth or seventh month of pregnancy
- Babies with mothers under stress while pregnant are at higher risk for hyperactivity, motor problems, and attention deficits than babies of calm mothers
- Babies who undergo ultrasound as an adjunct to amniocentesis (a high-stress situation) show more fetal movement during the procedure than babies who are exposed to routine ultrasound without amniocentesis
- Emotionally disturbed mothers give birth to babies at higher risk for sleep problems, digestive problems, and irritability

These reports and hundreds of others make sense because maternal feelings and moods are linked to hormones and neurotransmitters that travel through the bloodstream and across the placenta to the developing brain of the unborn child. Prolonged exposure to stress hormones, including adrenaline and cortisol, prime the growing brain to react in fight-or-flight mode—even when inappropriate—throughout life. Maternal emphasis on joy and love, on the other hand, bathes the growing brain in "feel good" endorphins and neurohormones such as oxytocin, promoting a lifelong sense of well-being.

The old thinking held that a calm pregnancy created a favorable context for development. While true, the new findings show that maternal emotions and even thoughts directly affect the wiring of the brain.

MATERNAL STRESS

Joanne was 45 years old and the mother of two preteen girls when she learned she was pregnant. Unfortunately, one of her two daughters had learning problems and required a lot of attention. Joanne's mother was dying. And she had to work full-time to pay the bills.

Married and able to support this third child, though with difficulty, Joanne was not happy at the prospect of having another child. Her stress escalated precipitously when she learned that the medication she'd been on for a urinary tract infection before she realized she was pregnant was associated with birth defects. Her baby responded to her anxiety by moving frenetically in the womb—something Joanne had not experienced with her two previous pregnancies.

We would all agree that Joanne was stressed. Stress may be defined as a threat, real or imagined, to the psychological or biological integrity of an individual. It refers to both the internal and external demands that we face to accommodate change. What may be stressful to one individual may not be so to another. A lot depends on how an event is perceived by the person.

The primary hormonal mediators of the stress response are glucocorticoids (hormones secreted by the hypothalamus, pituitary gland, and adrenal cortex) and catecholamines (secreted by the core of the adrenal gland). These hormones have both protective and damaging effects on the body. When they act for short periods of time they serve the functions of adaptation and survival. However, if stress becomes chronic, then the hormones it generates exact a cost, including acceleration of disease.

Pregnant women have long reported excess fetal movement associated with periods of anxiety. In recent decades, researchers have validated these reports in experiments with animals and in studies of human populations and the brain. More recently, research has anchored these observations solidly in our biology and the developmental processes of the brain.

It was long clear to researchers that psychological stress might stimulate production of hormones that would pass the placental barrier and affect development. But collecting the data to prove this was difficult in humans, where so many variables seemed to be in play.

To simplify issues, the first scientists to explore the process in the 1950s and 1960s worked with monkeys and rats. In one study, female rats were trained to avoid a shock that followed a conditioned stimulus in the form of a loud buzzer. After the training the rats mated and became pregnant. During the pregnancies, the rats were presented with the loud buzz but no shock. Without the shock apparatus, they were unable to respond in a way that previously enabled them to avoid the shock, and thus experienced a period of stress. By creating stress without the shock, the researchers were able to measure pure psychological stress.

To eliminate any confusion that might result from atypical maternal styles of shocked rats, the researchers mated a control group of nontrained (that is, nonshocked and nonstressed) rats at the same time. Then, when the rats gave birth, half the pups from the anxious (trained) rat mothers were given to the nontrained mothers, and vice versa. This experimental design is known as cross fostering and is an excellent way of measuring the differential effects of genetics, prenatal experience, and parental influence.

The result was that there were behavioral differences between pups that gestated in anxious mothers and those that gestated in normal mothers, regardless of which group of mothers reared them. When placed in an open field, which arouses fear in rats, pups from anxious mothers defecated more and were less active, both signs of negative emotion.

Beyond that, the researchers observed, the stressed mothers demonstrated a different parenting style, eliciting more negative reactions in the pups they raised; pups gestated by stressed mothers, meanwhile, elicited more negative behaviors from unstressed mothers than did nonstressed pups.

In the years that followed, scientists used a variety of stressors, from handling to restraint to exposure to light. They also repeated the experiment with monkeys, obtaining similar results. All in all, work with animals across a range of species showed that psychological stress during pregnancy produces lasting undesirable changes in both mothers and their offspring. Other research has shown that these findings apply to humans as well.

For instance, Pathik Wadhwa, a researcher at the University of California at Irvine, studied 156 unborn children to measure the impact of maternal stress. First he drew blood samples from the pregnant women and asked them to fill out questionnaires on their emotional state. Then he mildly stimulated the unborn child through the mother's abdomen and measured fetal heart rate to detect the impact on the unborn child. Fetal heart rates were raised significantly and stayed high longer in expectant mothers with the highest levels of stress hormones, who reported feeling the most anxiety and the least support. Women with wanted pregnancies, good self-esteem, and sufficient social support had the calmest babies, whose heart rates returned to normal in the shortest time.

Furthermore, mothers already under stress react to new stress in heightened fashion, releasing hormones that adversely affect the fetus. Prolonged fetal heart rate reactions, it should be noted, have been linked, in other studies, to increased risk for heart disease and diabetes in later life.

In another study, Curt A. Sandman, Wadhwa, and colleagues found a significant connection between prenatal stress and the outcome of a pregnancy, including low-birth-weight and premature birth. Looking at these issues in a group of ninety pregnant women under care, they assessed stress according to five criteria:

- Life-event changes: these stressors include everything from change of job to change of marital status to change of residence.
- Daily hassles: Were subjects short of money, overworked, or imposed on by sick relatives? Little disruptions in day-to-day life add up.
- Chronic stress: those who continually feel anxious in response to daily life may have a chronic problem, as may those who reported life as unpredictable, uncontrollable, and overloaded.
- Psychological and physical symptoms: if stress has mounted to the point where it induces other symptoms, including backache, nervousness, and depression, it becomes "strain."
- Pregnancy-related anxiety: here Sandman and Wadhwa assessed maternal fears and anxiety related to the health of the baby, to the labor and delivery process, and to the obstetrician and other health care providers.

Of the five factors, Sandman and Wadhwa found that two were particularly predictive of adverse outcomes at birth. Women who reported a higher level of life-event stress were more likely to deliver low-birth-weight babies, and those with high levels of pregnancy anxiety were likelier to give birth at an earlier gestational age. When such factors as smoking, drinking, and drug use were taken into account, the researchers found, life-event stress and pregnancy anxiety significantly predicted infant birth weight and gestational age at birth, respectively. In fact, the relationships followed a mathematical progression: with each increase in anxiety, birth weight and gestational age fell by specific, consistent amounts. Because the Irvine patients were fairly affluent—and thus more resistant to certain types of stress—Sandman and Wadhwa suggest that this effect may actually be magnified in the population at large.

Drilling down into the details still further, a group of Michigan researchers found that monetary and family problems in lower income or unmarried pregnant women created so much stress that they increased risk of miscarriage. But there was an upside to their findings as well: stressed women with emotional support seemed to avoid the worst of the consequences. The impact of environmental pressure is reversible, their study indicates, through recognition of the problem and ample levels of support.

These findings are consistent with numerous large-scale studies on prenatal stress. A study of Danish women associated generalized stress, especially anxiety and depression, in the thirtieth week of pregnancy with risk of premature birth. In a study of pregnant women in Alabama, maternal stress, anxiety, and depression were associated with low-birth-weight babies. Another research group found that a change in life circumstances between the second and third trimesters of pregnancy led to low weight at birth.

STRESS HORMONES AND THE BRAIN

Such findings on the effects of stress are clearly rooted in the ebb and flow of hormones and, ultimately, the architecture of the brain. Well-documented responses to physiological stress include imbalance in the autonomic nervous system and disruption of hormones produced by the hypothalamus, the pituitary gland, and the adrenal glands—the hypothalamic-pituitary-adrenal axis, or HPA. During pregnancy, such disruption has clear implications for the health of the unborn, as documented in studies across the range of species.

When rats are restrained during pregnancy, for instance, their offspring exhibit elevated levels of beta-endorphins in the hypothalamus ten days after birth and, along with that, decreased binding of mood-related molecules to receptors in the brain at forty-two days of age. Overexposure early in gestation, it seems, creates a permanent state of insensitivity to these molecules throughout life. Indeed, when scientists gave first- and second-trimester rats excess quantities of the stress hormones—including opiates (beta-endorphins), corticotropin-releasing hormone (CRH), and cortisol—their behavior was permanently altered. Whether the rats were exposed to the hormones by stressed mothers or by direct administration, the results were the same: they weighed less at birth than control rats, and they emitted more stress-related vocalizations; learning, memory, and growth were adversely affected throughout life. Scientists were able to circumvent the problem in rabbits by pre-treating mothers under stress with opiate blockers, thus protecting fetuses from exposure to these hormones in the womb.

The latest studies show the same system at work in humans. Particularly relevant are the findings of the UC Irvine team. Working with fifty-four pregnant women, the scientists found that stressful life circumstances could increase stress hormones measured in the blood—up to 36 percent for ACTH (adrenocorticotropic hormone), and 13 percent for cortisol. In another study of fifty-four women, the team found that as levels of CRH in maternal blood rose, gestational age at delivery tended to fall. Mothers who delivered preterm babies had significantly higher levels of CRH in their bloodstream than those who delivered at term.

Excess maternal stress may also affect a child's ability to learn. Habituation to input is a vital part of learning. After all, if we were to react to the same sound or smell just as intensely time after time, our senses would be overwhelmed. Input from all corners would, eventually, become so disruptive and distracting it would be more difficult to pick up the truly novel event and to learn. The Irvine team discovered that when mothers had greater stress in the third trimester of pregnancy, the unborn child was more likely to continue to react to repeated stimuli, as measured through the fetal heart rate. Unborn children with calmer mothers, on the other hand, tended to habituate to repeated exposure to the same stimulus, reacting less strongly as time went on.

The finding makes sense in the light of studies showing that excessive exposure to stress affects the physiology of the brain. Changes measured by researchers include destruction and inhibited growth of neurons and synapses in the area of the hippocampus and a decrease in the production of certain neuroreceptors. In the susceptible individual, prenatal stress causes a real rewiring of the brain, setting the stage for stress-prone reactions, from heightened irritability to behavior problems throughout life. For the child who is already genetically vulnerable, exposure to extreme prenatal stress can increase the risk for a spectrum of developmental disorders, from hyperactivity to autism.

MATERNAL STRESS AND SEXUAL ORIENTATION

One of the most profound findings of developmental neuroscience has been that overabundance of stress hormones can influence the gender of the brain. We already know that the brain, right along with the body, assumes its sexual nature in part through exposure to the right dose of the sex hormone androgen during a defined critical period before birth.

But in fact the story is more complex. We are learning now that though male and female brains are distinct, each individual possesses the initial circuitry for both male and female behavior. The hormones of development act in concert with genes through sensitive periods in the womb, and again during puberty, to bring out sex-typed behaviors to different degrees from one individual to the next. The gradient of sexuality allows for many intermediate types within the range, and that is where most individuals fall.

In his persuasive work *Affective Neuroscience*, neuroscientist Jaak Panksepp presents the argument for the existence of not just two sexes but four, based on the flow of steroid hormones through the fetal brain. Androgen, it turns out, is just the kicker to a cascade of formative events involving two spin-off steroids, estrogen and dehydrotestosterone (DHT). Even though estrogen is popularly thought of as the female hormone, in the womb it is masculinizing. It is only when testosterone converts to estrogen that the fetal brain receives the final signal to take on masculine structure. Likewise, testosterone must convert to DHT before the fetal body can complete its journey toward femaleness. "Various forms of homosexuality and bisexuality are promoted if 'errors' occur in the various control points of these biochemical processes," Panksepp says.

Let's take it from the top: all embryos start as female in form, but the application of steroid hormones at critical points in gestation shifts development so that for embryos with a Y chromosome, the body and brain become male. If for some reason the developing male brain is not bathed in testosterone during the sensitive period, if the enzyme converting testosterone to estrogen is decreased or absent, the process can go awry. Likewise, if a female brain is exposed to too much estrogen during the sensitive period, it will assume malelike qualities. That explains the finding that tomboyishness is more common among girls whose mothers received the synthetic estrogen diethylstilbestrol (DES), given to prevent miscarriage during the second trimester of pregnancy in the 1940s and 1950s. The converse can also happen: male babies exposed to insufficient estrogen but sufficient DHT during the sensitive period can possess a male body with female-type circuits hidden in the brain.

There's no question that the balance can be tipped by factors from faulty genetics to environmental toxins. But recent experiments with rats suggest yet another destabilizing factor, maternal stress. In a normal, unstressed rat litter, about 80 percent of males become sexual "studs" at puberty, while the remaining 20 percent become asexual "duds," exhibiting little sexuality, either male or female. When pregnant rats are placed under stress, however, the statistics drastically change. Only 20 percent of male pups from stressed mothers become studs at puberty. About 60 percent are either bisexual (showing male behavior with receptive females, and female behavior with "stud" males) or exclusively homosexual, exhibiting lordosis, the female-specific receptivity posture, when mounted by a sexually aroused male. As with unstressed litters, 20 percent of males are asexual.

Scientists say the findings make sense in light of other experiments showing that stress hormones act against the masculinization of the fetal rat brain. The chain of events is set in motion when beta-endorphins released in excess by stressed-out mothers cause premature release of fetal testosterone. "Under conditions of maternal stress, the critical cascade of events is disrupted so that the peak of testosterone secretion occurs several days earlier than it should, when brain tissues are not yet ready to receive the organizing message. It is as if the organizational camera shutter had been clicked without the lens cap being removed. Although enough testosterone has been secreted, it simply comes too early, and the neural image of maleness is not adequately imprinted upon the brain."

Researchers have found a smaller but noticeable impact on female offspring. Female rat pups from stressed mothers are less nurturing than controls from nonstressed mothers. This is especially interesting because the opposite is found in males: male rat pups born of stressed-out mothers are, by and large, more nurturing than their normal counterparts.

Can we extend the rat findings to people? There is no definitive evidence, but a few controversial studies suggest a connection. Gunter Dorner, for instance, found that German males born during the stressful waning years of World War II reported higher levels of homosexuality than those born in peacetime. In another study, he found that homosexuals were much more likely than heterosexuals to portray their mothers' pregnancies as stressful.

The precise role played by stress in human gender identity requires further study. Nonetheless, the evidence is strongly suggestive: although gender is genetically determined, the sexual circuitry of the brain, as well as sexual orientation, emerges from the interplay of genetics and environment in the womb. Of course, later influences also play a part, particularly in the area of sexuality.

THE IMPACT OF MATERNAL DEPRESSION

"As a seven-month-old unborn child, I lived with my mother through the death of her three-year-old son. Under the deep relaxation of self-hypnosis, I found myself screaming one day 'I didn't want Charlie to die' over and over. I was totally unaware that I had this idea in my subconscious and that I felt my mother's guilt and grief."

If stress is devastating, it should come as no surprise that depression during pregnancy may have unwanted consequences as well. In their study of 1,123 mothers, a group of Boston researchers rated depression during pregnancy through measurement of initiative, appetite, insomnia, and feelings of loneliness. After birth, pediatricians with no knowledge of the mothers' prenatal history examined infants in the study group.

The Boston scientists found that depressed mothers were likelier to have babies who cried excessively and were difficult to console. And the more depressed the mother, the more irritable the newborn. These findings made sense to the researchers. Depressed mothers had elevated levels of the stress hormone norepinephrine in their bloodstream; like other blood-borne biochemicals, the norepinephrine would certainly cross the placenta to the bloodstream of the unborn child. In fact, another study found elevated levels of norepinephrine in jittery newborns. Finally, the symptoms of depression brought on a host of damaging behaviors: smoking, poor weight gain, and use of alcohol and cocaine.

It's often the case, note the researchers, that depression during pregnancy will continue as postpartum depression. And this condition may itself be exacerbated by an irritable infant; a depressed mother who has trouble interacting with and handling her newborn may be further debilitated by incessant crying, driving the cycle of depression and making it ever more difficult for mother and baby to bond. Unless this self-reinforcing system is interrupted, a lifelong cycle of depression and irritability, first passed between mother and child in the womb, may be set in motion.

A recent study of pregnancy in adolescence drives the point home. The roller-coaster ride of teenage pregnancy sets the stage for negative emotions, of which depression is chief. Working with a group of teenagers, scientists at Pennsylvania State University found that teen mothers who reported depression and anxiety at the start of their pregnancies were more likely to have babies who were more likely to require resuscitation after birth and had lower Apgar scores.

Interestingly, many of these depressed, stressed-out teenagers experienced remarkably successful labor and delivery, often associated with positive emotionality during pregnancy. In the midst of their trauma, what did they do right? The researchers say many of these troubled teens were in community programs that offered preterm and parenting classes. In that context they received emotional support and learned coping skills that helped them overcome their depressive feelings and improve the health of their children.

PREGNANCY AND VIOLENCE

While new studies and daily media stories now reveal the extent of child abuse in our culture, little has been said about another, hidden crime: domestic abuse of pregnant women. Several studies across a range of populations and economic brackets indicate that some 15 percent of pregnant women are victims of domestic abuse.

This insidious problem, a cause of debilitating depression and anxiety, does not bode well for the outcome of labor and delivery. Abused pregnant women are more likely to smoke, drink, and self-medicate with drugs to numb their pain and anxiety. Frequently, they suffer from an increased number of infections and anemia. Moreover, because abused women are embarrassed by their situation, they often delay seeking out prenatal care. Or they may be prevented by their abusers from seeking such care.

Babies of abused women are, not surprisingly, found to suffer the worst effects of prenatal stress, with especially high risk of low birth weight and premature birth. Evidence that extremely low birth weight is a risk factor for type II diabetes is just one indication of the lifelong influence of early experiences.

Often, abused pregnant women face continued abuse after they give birth. Since abusers are most likely husbands or boyfriends, the unborn child faces significant risk of abuse in the future, too.

If we are to deal with this pressing problem, we must take it out of the closet, as we have done with issues such as child abuse and incest. The first step is for health practitioners, as well as relatives and friends, to recognize those at risk. Research shows that interpersonal violence is not dependent on age, race, marital status, or socioeconomic class. Instead, look to such factors as a history of depression, substance abuse, frequent trips to the emergency room, and multiple unexplained injuries and bruises, especially around the head, neck, abdomen, and breasts. Bruises in various stages of healing are signs of abuse as well.

Although abuse is debilitating to the pregnant mother and unborn child, appropriate intervention, if accepted by the woman, can go a long way toward setting things right. As with pregnant teenagers, a good support network early on can help reverse damage to the baby, allowing for a positive outcome to the pregnancy.

When trying to help a friend you suspect may be battered, remember that disclosure of abuse is facilitated by an atmosphere of respect and nonjudgmental acceptance. Insistence that your friend just "get out" of the abusive situation may be counterproductive, causing her to reject any help at all.

In the short term, battered pregnant women need much support from their family, friends, and community agencies to weather the crisis in their lives. In the long term, successful interventions require a multilevel approach that should include job training, additional education, and counseling.

It may be harder to resolve a subset of the abusive situation—pregnancies that result from rape. Rape-related pregnancies amount to only a small portion of the estimated 3 million unintended pregnancies annually in the United States. But for the victims and their children, the fallout looms large. The majority of rape-related pregnancies involve a known perpetrator, including boyfriends (29.4 percent), husbands (17.6 percent), and friends (14.7 percent). Statistics show that 50 percent of mothers opt for abortion, 32 percent keep their babies, 12 percent miscarry, and 6 percent place the infant for adoption.

No one, so far, has studied the development of children conceived in rape. Nonetheless, it's fair to say that as a subgroup of those whose mothers suffered severe trauma, stress, and conflict over the pregnancy itself, these children will experience the worst consequences of prenatal trauma and stress.

UNWANTED CHILDREN

"I have for a long time felt that the youngest of our four children—thirteen and a half months younger than a brother, and unwanted by me until three months before her birth—has been trying to justify her existence. She is a Phi Beta Kappa, but in her personal life she lacks wisdom and must not think highly enough of herself. I have seen her so depressed that she cried for three days.

"I also was an unwanted child—born nine months after my parents' marriage, to a mother who forfeited her career as a pianist to care for me. She also had a grave illness at the time of my birth, and I'm sure I was neglected in the hospital nursery. Happily 'birthed' people don't understand the deep-rooted decisions a person makes as to whether this is a friendly or unfriendly world."

This woman's intuitive sense of the effect on a child of not being wanted is borne out by the scientific literature. Researchers have long linked unwanted childbearing to low birth weight, high infant mortality rates, and poor health and development. Ann Coker, an epidemiologist from the University of South Carolina, found that infants born of unwanted pregnancies are more than twice as likely to die within a month of being born than wanted children. The study subjects were married, largely middle-income women who were all receiving prenatal care.

Scientists in Prague, meanwhile, have followed the development of 2,290 children born from 1961 to 1963 to women twice denied abortion for the same pregnancy. These unwanted children were matched against a control group of wanted children and followed to adulthood. Consistently, the researchers found, the unwanted children had more physical and emotional handicaps. Over the years, these differences widened and many that had not been statistically significant at age 9 had become so by age 16 or 21.

Aware of the provocative literature on unwanted children, William G. Axinn, Jennifer S. Barber, and Arland Thornton of the University of Michigan's Institute for Social Research set out to study such children by examining self-esteem at age 23. Analysis of the results showed that unwanted children virtually always suffered lower self-esteem than wanted children.

For these children, say the Michigan scientists, lack of involvement or even abuse is likely to characterize the parental treatment they receive throughout their lives. "Parents who did not want a child," they suggest, "are probably less likely than other parents to invest their time and emotional resources in that child, resulting in lower self-esteem."

DEALING WITH LOSS DURING PREGNANCY

Snippets of conversation from two mothers:

"Every time I think of it I get scared. Those two boys that died during childbirth must have been so horrifying for my mother. The upcoming birth is frightening to me. I'd like to try to have a vaginal birth, but I don't trust my body to do it."

"I never thought of him as having lived before, but he did, and he was so strong. The doctors were surprised he hung on so long. He brought my whole life into a different relief, I've changed so much. I can hear him saying to me now, 'Go ahead, Mom, have a baby, it's okay.'"

There's no question that the family enduring the death of an unborn or newborn child suffers deep tragedy. Those who experience such loss say it hurts as much as the death of an older child, spouse, or parent. The pain of mourning an unfulfilled life is often difficult to understand for those who have not been through it. Those who say things like, "You can have another child," or "Life goes on," have simply failed to comprehend the enduring impact of the loss.

California psychologist Gail Peterson wondered whether such an experience might have an impact on subsequent pregnancies as well. Overwhelmingly, she found in her clinical study that it did.

Women who endured previous perinatal loss found it harder to adjust to a new pregnancy—they feared another loss and felt guilt about loving their new baby, Peterson says. "This not only has impact on attachment to the unborn fetus but also may precipitate heightened fear and panic states throughout the pregnancy and into labor. Women who have endured such loss," she says, "are at greater risk for future miscarriage, premature delivery, and complications of childbirth."

Perhaps more surprising, Peterson has found that such loss crosses generations. Women can absorb during childhood the impact of their *mother's* prenatal loss and are particularly vulnerable to high levels of fear during their own pregnancy, childbirth, and the ongoing parent-child relationship.

One woman Peterson studied, for instance, recalled that her mother had suffered two stillbirths before going through five cesareans. "This patient felt her mother's unresolved grief throughout her childhood," says Peterson, "and felt the need to make many of her own decisions based on her mother's fears." Ultimately, anxiety and guilt over bearing the son her mother had lost compromised her bond with her newborn son.

The positive side for Peterson was the discovery that she could relieve these feelings—and by extension, the outcome of the pregnancy—by helping her clients explore the underlying sense of loss. "Pregnancy offers a window of opportunity for healing and resolution," she says.

SUMMING UP

Emotional disturbances in the pregnant mother lead to increased production of stress hormones, particularly cortisol and norepinephrine. These, in turn, have adverse effects on gene regulation, precipitating excessive destruction of neurons and synapses, changing organization and function of the brain, and damaging the baby's future ability to deal with stress. The upside of this knowledge is that parents who are aware of the damage stress may cause can act to alleviate anxieties within their control. Pregnancy may not be the best time to move across country, risk a lot of money in the stock market, fight with your mother, or initiate a risky career change. It may be a good time for relaxing baths, uplifting music, and long chats with close friends.

Key Parenting Points

- Whether the issue is grief, stress, or depression, emotional baggage that is recognized and shared with a sympathetic person can often be lightened for the mother and her unborn child.
- During pregnancy more than at any other time in your life you need emotional support. Find someone with whom you can freely discuss your hopes and worries.
- Remember, short bursts of upset or stress are not harmful to you or your child. It is chronic, ongoing stress that is potentially damaging.
- It is important for prospective parents to do all they can to create a sense of calm and ease during pregnancy, when the ebb and flow of stress hormones may powerfully affect the architecture of the brain.

4

—◆—

The Womb
as Classroom

Where do we first experience the nascent emotions of love, rejection, anxiety, and joy? In the first school we ever attend—in our mother's womb. Naturally, the student brings into this situation certain genetic endowments: intelligence, talents, and preferences. However, the teacher's personality exerts a powerful influence on the result. Is she interested, patient, and knowledgeable? Does she spend time with the student? Does she like him, love him? Does she enjoy teaching? Is she happy, sad, or distracted? Is the classroom quiet or noisy, too hot or too cold, a place of calm and tranquillity or a cauldron of stress?

Numerous lines of evidence and hundreds of research studies have convinced me that it makes a difference whether we are conceived in love or hate, anxiety or violence. It makes a difference whether the mother desires to be pregnant and wants to have a child or whether that child is unwanted. It makes a difference whether the mother feels supported by family and friends, is free of addictions, lives in a stable, stress-free environment, and receives good prenatal care.

All these things matter enormously, not so much by themselves but as part of the ongoing education of the unborn child.

READINESS FOR PARENTHOOD

The foremost motivation for having a child is the desire to nurture and raise a child. A child may bring great joy into a family and enable a parent more personal growth, the renegotiation of relationships, and the opportunity to participate meaningfully in another's development. Parenthood also provides a chance to revisit one's own childhood experiences. If they were positive, the parent will happily share with the child. If they were negative, parenting allows one to compensate by providing for the child what the parent never had.

Both women and men often consider raising children as central to their sense of identity. Having a child ensures continuity of the generations. It satisfies the desire to identify with one's parents, one's peers, and society at large. But even the best prospective parents can fall short if they choose to have a baby for the wrong reason, in the context of the wrong relationship, or during troublesome periods of life. Indeed, prospective parents must take some time to recognize their motives for wanting to parent at all. Are those motivations pure and strong enough to power them through the joyful but arduous task of child-rearing, not for a month or two but a lifetime?

Sometimes an individual has a child to please a partner, other times to fill a void that has occurred through loss. Before we embark on the adventure of parenthood, we should seriously consider our motives for this monumental task. Parenting through the fog of internal chaos will compromise our competence as parents, not to mention our ability to love and nurture, and place our children at risk.

There's no question that "high risk" parents must postpone reproduction until they have put their house in order. Who's in this category? Those who, because of severe psychological or social problems, are confused, self-absorbed, or immature.

High-risk fathers tend to be hostile and rejecting toward their partners and toward the baby throughout the pregnancy and after birth. Commonly, they act out by having affairs or violent domestic arguments that may end in wife battering. High-risk mothers may attempt to abort their babies before birth and ignore them afterward. Studies show that their babies are at risk for prematurity, low birth weight, and the health problems that ensue. Brigitte Bardot, the French actress and sex symbol of the 1960s, typified this profile. In her autobiography, *Initials B.B.*, writing for all the world to see, she said she had hoped for a miscarriage when pregnant with a child that "fed on her body like a tumor." Emotionally volatile, unpredictable, and depressed, high-risk men and women must resolve their own problems before they can hope to nurture another life.

Those planning to have children must look deeply into themselves. If motivated by a desire to please others or compensate for a loss, they may experience feelings of resentment.

Addressing the issue, William Axinn and his research team from the University of Michigan found that although unwanted children had by far the most trouble with self-esteem, those born earlier than wanted suffered a loss of self-esteem as well. Parents who hope to put off conception, after all, often face obstacles: a degree that must be earned, an illness, professional hurdles, or instability in the marital relationship itself. Parental feelings that a child has been born too early may result in less support for that child after birth. Parental support and involvement are known to positively affect a child's self-esteem—an effect that is impressive, the researchers found in their twenty-three-year study, because it endures from childhood through the transition to adulthood.

NURTURERS AND MANAGERS

Having a baby is, for most people, an act of faith. It represents a belief in a better tomorrow, not just for themselves but for the world. But unless we actively improve our understanding and treatment of the unborn baby and the young child, that faith will go unrewarded because we may blindly pass on to our children the neurotic parenting we may have received. One key to parenting is flexibility. Those who can adapt to their baby's wants and needs will be nurturing and responsive. Those who cannot change their lives to accommodate the child—who expect the baby to adapt to them instead of the other way around—may be too rigid and uninvolved to parent well.

The task is harder than ever these days given the frequent necessity for both parents in a family to work. As parents who work, we delegate responsibilities—including the care of our children and our homes. To keep our lives afloat, to juggle all the elements, we tend to become as managerial in our private lives as we are in our jobs.

It is during pregnancy that parents—those who work as well as those who don't—must create a balance for living. I urge both partners to examine their commitments and to create a plan for increasing their time away from work so they can spend more time at home with the baby.

I know of two high-level executives who bought a Manhattan apartment with two wings—one for the husband-and-wife superstars, and another for the new baby and live-in nanny. These parents could have ensured greater future success for their child by sharing their wing of the apartment with her. Then, during those hours they were home, they would have experienced the hands-on aspect of parenting by acts as simple as changing a diaper, providing food, and singing a lullaby. This would have given their baby a better sense of self and security, a stronger feeling of love, and a greater likelihood of absorbing the cognitive skills and ethics embodied in the parents themselves. And the parents would have had the opportunity to really get to know their child.

If you work and are away from home for many hours a day, the temptation exists to delegate responsibility even during those hours when you are home. Our lives today are hectic and complex. We have families, careers, mortgages, and relationships to sustain. In the hours we are home, the tasks are endless: cooking, laundry, shopping, meetings of the PTA. It's impossible for parents who work the sixty-hour weeks required by high-powered careers to engage in true conscious parenting.

My advice is this: don't have the baby and take the promotion at the same time. If your company offers flexible work hours, avail yourself of this option for a few years. If you have the choice of hiring someone to clean the house or watch your child, have them clean the house while *you* watch the baby. If it's possible for one, or better yet, *both* parents to step back for a few years—relinquishing some income to care for a baby—that would be ideal. Contrary to the ideas promoted by popular culture, *you cannot have it all.*

Most of us are not wealthy enough to just quit our jobs and become stay-at-home moms and dads—which would be ideal, at least from the child's point of view. But we can all make the journey, in our minds, from manager to nurturer, and we can all learn to change our ways to make room in our busy lives for our precious children to grow in.

To ease your transition from manager to nurturer, I present the following tenets:

- Nurturers adapt to their babies. Managers expect their babies to adapt to them.
- While pregnant, nurturing mothers see themselves as actively growing the baby. Managers, on the other hand, perceive the baby as a separate entity, a foreign body growing inside their own.
- Nurturing parents believe in the reality of active communication and partnership with their unborn babies. Managerial parents see the growth and birth of their child as a mechanical process in which they are not involved.

The truth is that the prototypical "nurturer" and "manager" are stereo-typed extremes, the two outer points of a long continuum. As parents, most of us fall somewhere in between. Our goal, in the months before birth, is to strike a balance between being true to ourselves and achiev-ing our personal goals, on the one hand, and on the other, ensuring that our children receive the vital parental care they so richly deserve.

CLEANING OUT THE COBWEBS

Will a child's psychological and physical development be affected by the emotional makeup of the parents? To those in touch with modern re-search (not to mention personal history), the question seems rhetorical and the answer as clear as day. Still, it bears repeating: findings in the peer-reviewed literature over the course of decades establish, beyond any doubt, that parents have overwhelming influence on the mental and physical attributes of the children they raise.

Given that fact, it is the responsibility of every expectant parent to clean out the cobwebs of the psyche by airing differences with partners and resolving inner conflicts before the new baby arrives.

This "psychic cleansing" has been used to therapeutic advantage by Candace Fields Whitridge, a certified nurse-midwife who cofounded the Mountain Clinic, an innovative women's health center in the rural mountains of Trinity County, California. "With our growing knowledge of the consciousness of the unborn child, we have an unprecedented op-portunity and responsibility to improve the way we deliver prenatal care and support women and families at birth," she says. "To enhance the physical, emotional, and spiritual well-being of birth, we need to expand our attitudes and the art of our care, as well as fine-tune our technical and intuitive skills."

One of the most powerful techniques for improving the outcome of delivery, Whitridge found, was a formal "cobweb-cleaning session" at 36 weeks' gestation with the woman and her mate, or the person who would be providing primary support to her at the birth.

This came about as the result of an auspicious occurrence in my examination room one day. A very loving couple were nearing their delivery date. They had been married many years before deciding to have a child and were excited about being parents. However, the husband was acting in a peculiar manner that day and in the course of the conversation I jokingly asked him, "Is there anything Joan might do in labor that would bother you?" He didn't answer for a minute and then in a soft but serious voice said, "Yes . . . if she was a wimp."

His wife looked dumbstruck. "Go on," I said. "What does the word 'wimp' mean to you?" Slowly but steadily he replied, "I don't think that I have ever really told my wife how much I depend on her. She is the pillar in our family, and over the years I have come to rely on her constant strength. I have been talking to my male friends, and they have told me how women change in labor, how vulnerable they are and how heavily they lean on the man." He paused. "I am afraid that I will not measure up when the clutch is on, that I will fail my wife when she needs me most."

His wife's eyes never left his face as he painfully confessed his concerns. She smiled and gently replied, "I had no idea you valued those traits in me to such an extent. How wonderful to hear that. I like being strong and dependable. But I have been talking to my friends. They have said, 'Joan, labor is a primal experience. It's powerful, intense, and it is best to just surrender to the forces and go where it takes you.' The idea of that is right somehow, and it excites me.

"Let's make a deal. I am not afraid, and I want to fully experience this. The only thing I will need from you is your presence, your love, and just don't freak out." They laughed and shook on it.

Her birth was incredible. For a woman who was normally always in charge, she just let go. Her labor was earthy, noisy, wild, sensual, and short. Her husband watched her in frank adoration and kept his end of the deal. In addition to receiving a beautiful daughter, this birth dramatically changed each of their lives and their relationship forever.

Had these concerns not come up and been worked through during pregnancy, this birth could have gone quite differently. A probable scenario: she would have started carrying on, moaning and wailing and throwing herself all over the room (which she in fact did). He would have freaked out: "Somebody do something. There's something clearly wrong. She never acts this way." She would have noticed that he was freaking out and in her inimitable style would have "pulled it together." Her cervix would have shut down at 6 centimeters, and she would eventually have had a cesarean. To explain this, we call it failure to progress, when in actuality it is often just failure to take out the garbage.

In our lifetime we accumulate a lot of garbage: emotional baggage full of toxic thoughts, self-limiting and damaging notions, and negative scripts. The more aware we are of these, the more we own our own problem areas, the less likely we are to pollute our children with our mental poison. By the same token, the more empathic, caring, and nurturing we are, the more we instill in our progeny, from conception on, a feeling of self-worth, trust, and love.

PRENATAL DIALOGUE

Despite the evidence, many resist the notion that communication between parents and unborn child lays the groundwork for their relationship after birth, and in all the years to come. Freud himself, fixated as he was on the impact of later events, overlooked the importance of the relationship between parents and their unborn child. His error was never clearer to me than during a recent performance of the Greek tragedy *Oedipus Rex*. As the drama unfolded, I realized that Freud, who popularized the term *Oedipus complex*, had missed the true significance of this tragic tale.

Oedipus, as most of you may remember, was the son of Laius and Jocasta, king and queen of Thebes. Almost from the beginning of their union, the royal couple seemed doomed. Their undoing: a declaration by the oracle that Laius would perish at the hands of his son. To prevent the fulfillment of this dire prediction, he decided to abstain from sexual relations with Jocasta. But one night, in a fit of intoxication induced by the crafty queen, he gave in.

The queen became pregnant, as was her desire. Still hoping to avert his undoing, the king ordered the destruction of the child, a boy, at birth. Jocasta dutifully handed him off to a servant, instructing that he be exposed to the elements and left to die. The servant suspended the baby boy by the heels from a tree on Mount Cithaeron. There a shepherd found him and took him to Polybus, king of Corinth, who, childless, raised him as his own and called him Oedipus, which is Greek for "swollen foot."

Interpreting the myth, Freud declared that Oedipus harbored the unconscious wish to be intimate with his mother and to kill his father. But

Freud missed the obvious, neglecting to recognize the torment young Oedipus experienced before and immediately after his birth. Subject to attempted murder by his father and betrayal and abandonment by his mother, he was hung by his heels to die. Though adopted and cared for, his origins were hidden from him.

Whatever psychoanalysts may tell us about the love of little boys for their mothers, in the case of Oedipus we have a man severely traumatized by prenatal and perinatal events. In my psychiatric practice I observe the same phenomenon quite frequently. A few years ago, for instance, a young woman came to consult me about her daughter after reading my book *The Secret Life of the Unborn Child*. This is what she said:

When my daughter Marion was born she looked angry to me. I said so out loud but my obstetrician and the nurses just laughed. "Babies don't have any feelings, it's probably gas," they said. I forgot about this incident until I read your book. Marion is 12 years old now, and I thought, why not ask her? So I did. I asked her straight out.

"Were you angry when you were born?"

And she said, "Yes, I was."

"Why?"

And she answered, "Because you wanted a boy."

I was shocked but she was right. Throughout my pregnancy I wished and prayed for a boy. I don't know why, I just wanted to have a son. When the doctor told me that I had a girl, I felt a pang of disappointment, but honestly, within hours, I was in love with her. So, it's not as if she had picked up my feelings after birth. When I admitted my folly another surprising thing happened. Ever since Marion was an infant there seemed to exist this invisible wall between us. It was nothing you could put your finger on, she never gave me any trouble, but no matter what I did I could not reach her. Well, the amazing thing is that after we had this heart-to-heart talk, the wall fell away. Now I finally feel connected to her.

Marion's story is a lot happier than that of Oedipus. But both demonstrate the crucial role that prenatal communication can play in the life of a child and, later, the adult.

How are maternal emotions and thoughts communicated to the unborn child? The channels of communication are various. Right from the moment of conception, the unborn child has a dialogue with the mother and, through her, the outside world. When all the channels are active the baby receives the full message; it's like stereophonic sound.

The umbilical dialogues take place across three channels:

Channel One: Molecular Communication

Maternal molecules of emotion, including stress hormones such as adrenaline and noradrenaline, neurohormones, and sex hormones, reach the unborn child through the umbilical cord and placenta. In this sense, the unborn child is as much part of the mother's body as her heart or liver.

Channel Two: Sensory Communication

When a pregnant mother strokes her stomach, talks, sings, walks, or runs, she is communicating with her baby through the baby's senses. Newborns "speak" to their mothers through crying, and mothers can soon decipher the meaning of their cries. The sound of "Good morning, Mom, I'm awake" is very different from "I have an awful pain in my tummy." Similarly, the unborn child can communicate through kicking. For example, when she listens to music she likes, she will kick energetically but gently. Expose her to the loud, shrill noises of pneumatic drills or a rock concert, and the baby will become progressively more agitated, subjecting the mother to a series of painful kicks. Obviously, some mothers, depending on their own upbringing or circumstances, are better attuned to this kind of communication than others. If they are depressed, anxious, exposed to violence, or high on drugs, mothers are unlikely to be good listeners or good senders of positive messages.

Channel Three: Intuitive Communication

I am sure you have experienced this many times: you stand in a room speaking to someone. Suddenly, you have the urge to turn around. As you do, you meet the eyes of the person who has been looking at you. Or you have probably read or heard of the case of twins: although they may live thousands of miles apart, one is able to pick up, somehow, that the other is seriously ill or in trouble. These exchanges occur between people who are neither connected to each other's blood circulation nor touching nor talking. They happen frequently to individuals who are closely bound to each other emotionally. One might say that such people are on the same wavelength. Can you think of any two beings more connected than a mother and her unborn child? Is it surprising then that they should be able to communicate in this intuitive way? The intuitive channel transmits the mother's thoughts, intentions, and much of her emotion to her baby. The mother receives messages by the same channel from her unborn child, often in the form of dreams.

It is through this complex system of prenatal communication that the unborn child learns about herself, her mother, and the world at large.

MUSICAL LESSONS

Many years ago I received quite an amusing letter from a woman who during her pregnancy always performed her Lamaze exercises while watching M*A*S*H reruns on TV. "The M*A*S*H theme became a signal for me to relax," the mother wrote me. "I forgot the tensions of the day—including the problems between my husband and myself— and felt truly happy." As early as six months after her son was born, the mother noticed that whenever the M*A*S*H theme came on, he would stop whatever he was doing and stare at the television set as if in a trance.

One patient of mine recalled a Peter, Paul, and Mary song she had sung repeatedly during her pregnancy. After the birth of her child, that song had a magical effect on the infant: no matter how hard he was crying, whenever his mother started singing that song—and that song alone—he would quiet down.

No one questions the fact that sound and motion reach the baby in the womb. Evidence that babies recognize their mother's voice—and even words or stories she repeats—has been accepted for years. Numerous studies now indicate that the most effective means of communication may be delivered through music. Although the research is fairly recent, the technique is as ancient as motherhood itself.

In rural Uganda, for instance, women dance and sing throughout their pregnancy, then use the same songs to lull their babies to sleep after they have been born. In Nigeria, ritual dances and songs accompany the prenatal period. In Japan, the traditional practice of Taiko involved communicating with the unborn child through song.

One of the first modern researchers to study singing during pregnancy was obstetrician Michel Odent, who organized group meetings around a piano in the French village of Pithiviers. As expectant mothers in the group sang together, Odent found, group intimacy increased—and so did the bond between each mother and her yet-to-be-born child. Compared with an ordinary population of pregnant women, Odent's singing group reported easier births and more powerful bonding between mother and baby immediately afterward.

Odent's findings piqued the interest of Rosario N. Rozada Montemurro, a midwife who launched the maternal education program at the Health Center at Vilamarxant, Spain. Working with colleagues, Montemurro created a space and time for expectant mothers to sing. "Meeting to sing one day a week for two hours is now an activity we offer in addition to the basic theoretical classes, walks, picnics, games, films, and meetings with the babies' fathers," Montemurro says.

The chaotic nature of the clinic, notes Montemurro, does not encourage privacy, intimacy, and silence during birth itself, making the benefits of singing especially important to participants in her group. This environment, says Montemurro, "makes it doubly important that we create ways in which a mother finds strength which allows her to believe that she, her baby, and her husband are the principal protagonists during delivery" and that she will be able to bond with her baby and breast-feed thereafter. "Extras" like singing, she notes, increase the likelihood of success.

If singing teaches the unborn child anything, the findings indicate, it may be the basics of bonding and love. Montemurro has found that most expectant mothers have the need to link themselves together, "sharing common anxieties, fantasies, questions, fears, problems, and solutions." The connective consciousness these mothers form through singing extends to the unborn children.

The Vilamarxant repertoire includes traditional lullabies in Spanish and Valencian, the local dialect, so the mothers can sing to their newborns the songs they learned and performed during the group singing. "We included cradle songs which imitated rocking-chair rhythms," says Montemurro. "Some of our mothers could remember their own mothers and grandmothers singing small children to sleep. Some of them could remember being lulled to sleep themselves as the sounds of rocking chairs formed the rhythmic, monotonous 'tic-tac' against the wooden floor, reminding them of their own mothers' heartbeats. Participants learned the old lullabies and folk songs of their mothers and grandmothers joyfully and enthusiastically. As they learned the traditional cradle songs, their own desire to cradle their unborn babies became embodied in music and in words."

While an empirical study based on Montemurro's technique has yet to be done, the clinical findings are impressive. Montemurro reports that the pregnant women in her study could feel their unborn children participating in the songs through spontaneous and harmonious fetal movement. Among the traits that researchers have noted are especially prevalent in these children after birth are heightened awareness, ease of bonding, and, at one month of age, a propensity to smile quickly and easily. Mothers report that lullabies sung before birth are especially effective in calming babies and inducing sleep.

THE MOZART EFFECT

Other research shows that musical ability is especially likely to be nurtured in the classroom of the womb. London researcher Michele Clements, for instance, showed that exposure to Baroque music by such composers as Vivaldi and Mozart increased fetal heart rate and caused the amount of kicking to decline.

Musicians themselves often trace their talents to the womb. A few years back, Boris Brott, former conductor of the Hamilton Philharmonic Orchestra, explained the roots of musical talent on television. As a young conductor practicing certain musical scores, he told his interviewer, the cello line would just jump out at him. "I would know the flow of the piece," he said, "even before I turned the page." Brott eventually discussed the puzzling experience with his mother and found that all the pieces he "instinctively" knew had been part of the repertoire his mother, a professional cellist, played while pregnant with him.

Studies by University of Wisconsin psychologist Frances Rauscher, meanwhile, associate prenatal exposure to Mozart and other Baroque compositions with improved temporal-spatial ability throughout life. Once a child prodigy who played the cello for international audiences, Rauscher left her musical career to pursue a Ph.D. in psychology but wound up studying the music she'd once played.

In a now-famous experiment, she played Mozart's Sonata in D Major for Two Pianos to pregnant laboratory rats and their pups during gestation and immediately following birth. She found that the pups exposed to Mozart could navigate mazes faster and far more accurately than control groups of pups exposed to either white noise or the music of minimalist composer Philip Glass. Her hypothesis: the music stimulates specific neurons in brain regions controlling temporal-spatial skills, in essence making the Mozart rats smarter.

In human studies, meanwhile, Rauscher showed that college students who listened to Mozart scored higher on IQ tests than a control group who took the tests without such stimulation. Another study demonstrated enhanced language, spatial, and mathematical skills in preschool children exposed to the music of Mozart. State-supported day care centers in Colorado, Georgia, and Florida now play Mozart for children every day.

Other research has shown that classical music, particularly the slow movements of Baroque and Baroque-style compositions—with their melodic richness and predictable rhythm of 55 to 70 beats per minute—shift the brain from an overactive beta state to an alert, relaxed alpha state. Classical music stimulates the release of endorphins and reduces stress hormone levels in the blood, beneficial for mother and baby alike.

Similar findings come from Donald Shetler, a professor of music education at the University of Rochester. Though his findings are preliminary and require replication, it's worth noting his observation that children exposed to music in utero develop superior language skills. "We've seen the development of highly organized and remarkably articulate speech," he says of his experimental group of thirty. Shetler reports that infants exposed to music while in the womb "show remarkable attention behaviors, imitate accurately sounds made by adults, and structure vocalization earlier than controls."

PRENATAL UNIVERSITY?

Many researchers have, throughout the years, been tempted to go beyond the notion of emotional nurturing in utero to attempt something else: putting the unborn child through "academic" paces in an effort to increase a host of abilities, including intelligence.

Rene Van de Carr, an obstetrician from Hayward, California, for instance, has established the "Prenatal University," in which parents-to-be "teach" the fetus through a complex system of touch and words.

Van de Carr developed his system after a patient told him that each time she poked her baby through her abdomen the child seemed to kick back. When asked to try the technique, other patients reported the same result. If parents consistently stimulated the unborn child through touch, Van de Carr found, the child would consistently respond.

Based on these and other observations, Van de Carr launched his Prenatal University to teach the fetus to "pay attention" and enhance a spectrum of intellectual skills. In the first lessons, starting around the fifth month of gestation, parents are taught to respond to a baby's kicks by pushing back. The "brightest" unborn pupils, Van de Carr notes, respond with precision. If the mother pushes twice, the fetus will kick back twice; if she pushes three times, the baby kicks three times, too. At seven months' gestation, Van de Carr teaches unborn children words in twice-daily sessions lasting five minutes each. Parents use words such as "pat," "rub," and "shake" as they perform these actions on the child in the womb. Nearer term, Van de Carr introduces a secondary list of words—including "hot," "wet," and "eye"—for use right after birth.

In subsequent studies, Van de Carr says, he found that program "graduates" spoke earlier, were more alert, and were able to lift their heads at earlier ages than controls. Van de Carr says that "graduates" now in school are socially adept and consistently score higher on standardized tests than a group from the population at large. Personally, I find these studies intriguing, but I do not recommend that parents "teach" their unborn children anything except that they are loved.

BOOSTING BRAIN POWER

The newest models of neuroscience tell us that sounds, rhythms, and other forms of prenatal stimulation reaching the unborn child are not merely imprinted on the brain but literally act to shape it.

Much of the evidence, of course, comes from animal models. Working with rats, the renowned UCLA neuroscientist Marian Diamond was the first to show that pregnant rats housed in enriched and varied environments produced offspring that had larger brains and were more capable of navigating complex mazes than rats not so housed.

The findings apply to people, too.

"Though the Western world is only recently becoming aware of such a practice, Asian people for centuries have encouraged the pregnant mother to enrich her developing fetus by having pleasant thoughts and avoiding angry, disturbing behavior," Diamond notes. Indeed, just as fetal brain cells decrease in size when deprived of nourishment or exposed to alcohol, she notes, they apparently increase in size when stimulation is introduced.

Diamond suggests caution when contemplating anything more than gentle stimulation of the unborn. "We still do not know whether an enriched condition during pregnancy can prevent some of the massive nerve cell loss, as much as 50 percent to 65 percent of the total population of cells, which occurs during the development of the fetus," she notes. "It is apparent that overproduction of neurons occurs in the fetus because most neurons do not reproduce themselves after being formed: an excess number is needed as a safety factor. Therefore, those that are not involved in the early neuronal processing are 'weeded out.'

"Though enriched experimental environments have not been shown to alter the number of nerve cells," Diamond explains, "our results have indicated that variation in the experimental environment can readily alter the size of the preexisting nerve cells in the cerebral cortex, whether in the cell body or in its rich membrane extensions, the dendrites, or in synapses. The importance of stimulation for the well-being of the nerve cells has been demonstrated in many species. But of equally weighty significance is the possible detrimental effect of too much stimulation. The eternal question arises, When is enough enough or too much too much?"

The respected pediatrician T. Berry Brazelton points out that infants exposed to too much stimulation, that is, teaching, playing, noise, etc., respond either by crying, by extending their periods of sleep, by developing colic, or simply through withdrawal. Because the unborn child cannot always register her discomfort, it is all the more vital that we place limits on efforts to stimulate the baby in the womb.

"The nervous system possesses not just a morning of plasticity, but an afternoon and an evening," Diamond notes. "It is essential not to force a continuous stream of information into the developing brain but to allow for periods of consolidation and assimilation in between."

SUMMING UP

The findings of neuroscience leave no doubt: prenatal stimulation through all three communication channels is essential for the growth and efficient development of the prenatal brain. But more important, the prenatal classroom is better suited for lessons of intimacy, love, and trust than for intellectual calisthenics or IQ boosting. If nurtured in love and kindness, your child will easily acquire these other skills when the time comes.

Key Parenting Points

- You cannot truly parent without being actively involved in raising your child. This applies equally to mothers and fathers.

- Try to communicate with your child by means of all channels as much as possible. That goes for fathers, too.
- Avoid fancy electronic devices or loud music to stimulate your unborn child. He needs peace, just like you.
- Don't attempt to teach the child anything before birth. It is enough if you communicate that both of you love him and look forward to welcoming him into your family.
- Remember: manage your career, nurture your child.

5

—∿—

Birth and Personality

When Ricky Burke, age 6, walked into my office, he'd been suffering terrifying nightmares for months. Soon after he fell asleep he would thrash around violently, shrieking, yelling, and cursing at the top of his lungs. When he seemed to quiet down, he would, in fact, be uttering a mysterious series of Latin-sounding syllables. Then he resumed shouting until he awoke, trembling and bathed in sweat.

A religious Roman Catholic family from Toronto, the Burkes had a peaceful home life and other children, who experienced untroubled sleep. Besides these nocturnal torments, Ricky himself had a seemingly normal life. A long string of experts had thrown up their hands, unable to explain the problem or treat it in any way. The family was considering bringing in an exorcist.

But one day they heard a colleague of mine discussing dreams on a radio show, and the roots of Ricky's problems became apparent and the mystery was solved. Mrs. Burke's pregnancy had been fraught with complications. When she went into labor some seven weeks early, she was rushed to the hospital in the middle of the night. Exhausted and enervated by the difficult medical situation, attending physicians cursed in frustration. After hours of labor, Ricky was born barely alive, and the hospital chaplain was asked to administer last rites. Ricky's midnight mutterings were the curses and Latin phrases he heard during the first hours of his life.

Events that carry an emotional charge, especially traumatic events, are often remembered. The notion that birth can be remembered and that it can influence personality was initially proposed by the father of modern psychiatry, Sigmund Freud. "The act of birth," he wrote, "is the first experience of fear and thus the source and prototype of all future fright reactions." Bits and pieces of birth memory, Freud said, are scattered through our dreams.

Today we know that birth is not just about fear and anxiety. It is a transformative psychological event, a psychic pacemaker that unconsciously motivates our subsequent life. How we enter this world plays a crucial role in how we live in it.

THE BIRTH SCENE

No one who's witnessed births in various settings would deny the obvious: the newborn, just like the rest of us, appreciates gentleness, softness, and a caring touch. The baby responds poorly to bright lights, electrical beeps, and the cold, impersonal atmosphere so often associated with medical birth.

Chairat Panthuraamphorn, an obstetrician at the Hua Chiew General Hospital in Bangkok and an expert on birth, explains: "Inside the womb, fetuses can hear their mother's body noises at 72 decibels, feel warmth, and gain familiarity with her heartbeat and voice. At birth they hear screaming from the mother, phones ringing from the nurses' station, the bleep bleep of the fetal monitor, shouting sounds like 'Push, push!' or the loud conversation of the health team. These delivery room surroundings are noisy and inappropriate. A baby's birth under these circumstances is like bringing an individual from a rural area to the center of New York City with all its traffic and machinery."

And the disruptions go on. Dim light passing through the uterine wall accustoms the unborn child to cycles of day and night. In the delivery room, on the other hand, the newborn is bathed in bright, full-powered light from the moment her head emerges from the birth canal. In the womb, the temperature is just slightly higher than that of the mother's body, an average of 98.6 degrees Fahrenheit. Temperatures in birthing environments are typically 25 degrees lower, causing babies to chill as the thin surface layers of fat and skin lose heat. Though warm-blooded, newborns are simply unable to control their body temperatures in this environment.

In the liquid environment of the womb, a baby develops muscle tone by rotating, moving arms and legs, and turning and bending the body, head, and back. Later on, as the baby grows, the womb space is cramped. Even when the space is limited, her fluid surroundings enable the baby to easily bring fingers to mouth for suckling. But all this changes at birth with the challenge of space and gravity. Without the aid of fluid, the infant finds it especially difficult to continue suckling by bringing hand to mouth. In the hubbub of the delivery room, newborns experience rapid motion for the first time, as they are poked and prodded, lifted up and placed down. The stress is exacerbated by the depressive effect of analgesics and/or anesthetics that may have been administered to the mother during labor. And this is a picture of an uncomplicated birth. If obstetricians suspect difficulties, other interventions—fetal heart monitors, C-sections, or forceps delivery—may be employed.

It is in this alien, unfriendly environment that the newborn must negotiate the most extreme transition of all; instead of drawing oxygen from the umbilical cord and placenta, the baby must pull it from the air and process it in her lungs.

In short, modern delivery contains a series of stressful events. The challenge prospective parents face is simply this: How can we welcome the newborn with the least trauma and stress so that there will be no physical or psychological damage at birth? How can we minimize discomfort for both mothers and their newborns, so that they can joyfully bond with each other?

TOWARD A BABY-FRIENDLY BIRTH

Today, the most enlightened obstetricians counter the stress of birth by designing birth environments closely resembling the womb. The beginnings of the modern movement can be traced to the 1940s and 1950s, when Grantley Dick-Read and Fernand Lamaze advocated natural childbirth, teaching breathing techniques to lessen mothers' pain during labor. Today, in Western nations, Lamaze classes are almost as common as pregnancy itself. Including fathers as well as mothers, Lamaze techniques lay the groundwork for a birth in which parents, not technology, are in charge.

By the 1970s, experts such as the French obstetrician Michel Odent began to pioneer the so-called water birth, with laboring women—and their newborns—immersed in the warmth of a sterile bath. In 1975, French obstetrician Frederick Leboyer published the groundbreaking *Birth Without Violence,* including his method of "gentle birth." In the

Leboyer system, the delivery room is kept dim, quiet, and warm. Directly after birth the baby is placed on the mother's abdomen and breathing is induced with a massage. The umbilical cord is cut only when it has stopped pulsating, and the infant is then given a warm bath.

NEONATAL ENRICHMENT

Such practices, currently standard in many of the world's forward-thinking birth centers, are being refined by a new generation of pioneers. Chairat Panthuraamphorn of Bangkok, for instance, is known for a neonatal stimulation program designed to soothe and comfort the newborn. Six elements are key to his program:

- Low lighting and visual stimulation. Bright lights should be dimmed so that the newborn can easily explore faces, especially those of the family. Low lighting can contribute to calm, relaxed feelings and thus improve circulation. Under such circumstances, newborns appreciate eye-to-eye contact, especially with the smiling faces of mothers and fathers.
- Muted ambient noise and auditory stimulation. Sound levels of equipment are kept down so that, when close to the mother, the newborn can detect the familiar maternal heartbeat and voice.
- Soft touch. A large body of research shows that like other mammals, human babies require maternal touch at birth. One study showed that mothers rooming with infants and touching them often after birth had happier and healthier children in subsequent years. Cross-cultural studies reveal that low-touch societies have a higher incidence of aggressive behavior. To foster emotional security, mothers in the Panthuraamphorn program are encouraged to hold, stroke, and pat their babies immediately after birth.
- Warmth. Panthuraamphorn suggests that air-conditioning, intended for the comfort of those who are gowned and gloved, be switched off before the baby arrives. He also advocates the practice of Frederick Leboyer, who suggested that babies experience a warm-water bath shortly after birth.
- Supportive movement and activity. Moving from the fluid warmth of the womb to the outside world can be shocking. To ease the transition, the baby should be wrapped loosely to allow free movement of arms and legs, as in the early days of gestation, and placed

on the mother's abdomen to reconnect with the sounds inside the womb.

Breast-feeding. In utero the prenate sucks fingers and toes and ingests small amounts of amniotic fluid. Spontaneous and naturally soothing, this suckling activity in the womb needs to be continued in the form of breast-feeding. Early breast-feeding, moreover, provides immediate stimulation of the senses of taste, smell, touch, and sight.

THE NEUROHORMONES OF BIRTH

The high-tech, low-touch obstetrics of modern times alters the mix of the hormones that evolution has provided to help ease mother and child through birth. Low-impact birthing primes the laboring mother and child to produce appropriate levels of needed brain hormones, while aggressive, interventionist medical practices scramble the production of those hormones.

All the hormones released during labor originate from the primitive brain structures we share with other mammals—the hypothalamus, the pituitary gland, and so forth. Messages involved in inhibitions during the birth process, on the other hand, come from the newer part of our brain—the neocortex. During labor "there is a time when the mother behaves as though she is on another planet, doing a sort of inner trip," says Michel Odent. "This change of consciousness can be interpreted as a reduction in neocortical activity. When this is going on, any stimulation to the neocortex can interfere with the progress of labor. There are many ways for this to happen. The most common is to talk to the laboring woman. Imagine that a woman is in hard labor and already on another planet. She dares to scream out, she dares to do things she would never otherwise do, she has forgotten what she has been taught or what she has read in books. Somebody enters the room and asks her a question that requires her to think. This is risky stimulation."

While I admire Michel Odent's work greatly, I do not agree with him on this point. I believe that the presence of a loving partner outweighs the risk of overstimulating the mother-to-be's thinking brain. The greater problem is the modern, high-tech birthing center itself. Bright lights stimulate the neocortex. Loud noises stimulate the neocortex. Unwieldy machinery and continual exams stimulate the neocortex.

What women in labor require is support and security. Without a sense of security, the fight-or-flight reaction—and its chemical signal, heightened release of adrenaline—is far more likely. The noise and light of the modern medical center and the interventions of medical staff are likely to stimulate production of high levels of the stress hormone adrenaline, while effective labor requires the opposite. In the last stage of labor, sudden adrenaline release is needed for the final push, but the effect can be muted if adrenaline has been flowing all along.

If the mother produces adrenaline during these final contractions, the baby does, too. As a result, says Odent, "the baby is alert at birth, with eyes wide open and pupils dilated. Mothers, in turn, are fascinated by the gaze of their newborn. This eye-to-eye contact is an important feature of the beginning of the mother-baby relationship, which probably promotes release of the love hormone, oxytocin."

Indeed, the brain hormone oxytocin must also be sustained at optimum levels during birth to support uterine contractions. Just after the baby's birth, a peak of oxytocin is needed to deliver the placenta easily and without complication. The ideal condition for that oxytocin surge? A warm environment, with the mother holding the baby and feeling his skin. Any distraction, and the final wave of oxytocin may not arrive.

"Oxytocin is more than just a hormone responsible for uterine contractions," Odent says. "When it is injected into the brain of a mammal, even a male or virgin rat, it induces maternal behavior such as the need to take care of pups. One of the greatest peaks of oxytocin a woman can have in her life is just after childbirth, if the birth has occurred without any intervention."

Finally, both mother and baby release the morphinelike hormones called endorphins during labor and delivery. Associated with a sense of heightened joy as well as dependency, the endorphins exert their influence for at least an hour after birth. "When mother and baby haven't yet eliminated their endorphins and are close to each other," says Odent, "the beginning of a deep bond is created."

The minutes and hours after birth are truly sacred. Thanks to a precise cascade of brain hormones, says Odent, "both mother and baby achieve a complex hormonal balance that won't last long and will never happen again." It goes without saying that stressful birth and excessive intervention can impede the process.

To facilitate ease of labor, childbirth preparation classes and the attendance at birth by a midwife or a doula are extremely helpful. These childbirth professionals complement the support the pregnant woman receives from her partner. They guide a woman on how to stay relaxed and comfortable at home until labor is well established. In the hospital, they help her work with her labor and, if necessary, advocate on her behalf. They assist the parents in obtaining the type of birthing experience they desire. In that sense, I highly recommend that prospective parents seriously explore engaging a midwife or a doula in addition, of course, to a medical doctor, and that they both attend childbirth education classes.

MODE OF BIRTH AND PERSONALITY TRAITS

How do specific modes of birth, birth technologies, and interventions influence the newborn? As we all know, human beings are incredibly complex, and therefore to make any generalizations about them is fraught with danger. However, the discussion below represents a consensus of the findings of clinicians working in the field of pre- and perinatal psychology. Please also keep in mind that no one is suggesting a one-to-one, cause-and-effect relationship between mode of birth and personality. Rather, pre- and perinatal factors will create a predisposition, a kind of psychic sensitivity, similar to an allergic sensitivity in a person, which, depending on subsequent events, may be diminished and never emerge as a problem or may become exacerbated and adversely affect one's personality.

- Natural, unmedicated vaginal delivery: The basic birth has become harder and harder to obtain. Yet a child so born will have all sorts of advantages over one born through other modes of birth. She will tend to be self-confident and energetic and trust her own strength. If welcomed by a loving mother, this child will start life believing that the world is a fine place and that she is a part of it. In other words, she will feel connected to mother, society, and the planet.
- Anesthesia and analgesia: Administered in some 80 percent of all hospital births. Babies born under the influence of anesthetic have more difficulty in bonding after birth than babies whose births are anesthesia-free. This is probably because anesthetized newborns are too drugged to focus, to make eye contact, and to engage in other bonding behaviors. Babies may receive anesthesia overdoses because the drugs are administered to meet the mother's requirements, not the baby's—with lower body weight, infants receive proportionately higher anesthesia doses. Furthermore, infants retain

the anesthetic for longer periods because of higher levels of body fat. Infants whose mothers were partially or completely anesthetized are, in later life, predisposed under stress to feel confused or paralyzed.

- Birth induction and birth augmentation: Administration of the labor-inducing drugs oxytocin or pitocin to speed up or intensify contractions occurs in between 20 percent and 40 percent of all hospital births. There is a natural rhythm to the initiation and pacing of birth, much of it organized by the biology of babies. Inductions and augmentations interrupt the natural rhythms, timings, and pacings of the process. When babies' natural rhythms are altered by drugs, they initially feel shocked, confused, and frightened. They subsequently feel (in increasing order of traumatization) interrupted, interfered with, intruded upon, invaded, and/or controlled. Under stress, adults who were induced at birth tend to feel angrier and more resentful than those who experienced no such interference.

- Forceps deliveries: These involve removal of the baby from the womb with the aid of forceps. Even though most forceps-delivered babies have also been anesthetized, the pain of the forceps will override the numbing effect of anesthesia. When regressed under hypnosis to recall birth during psychotherapy, forceps-delivered patients report this kind of delivery as painful, intrusive, and violent. In the aftermath of birth, this experience interferes with bonding. In adulthood, those delivered with forceps are often defensive to the touch, with anxieties about being stroked, cuddled, or held. Under stress, they tend to suffer from headaches as well as neck and shoulder pain.

- Cesarean section: Cesarean deliveries are the number one major surgery in the United States, where the rate has gone from 2 to 3 percent in the 1970s to 25 percent in the 1990s. Today some hospitals report a cesarean rate of up to 50 percent. Many experts say that cesarean rates have increased *not* because birth complications are on the rise but rather because of false alarms raised by electronic fetal monitoring, and because of a dramatic increase in the number of lawsuits filed against obstetricians. (In legal terms, if a physician performs a cesarean, he or she can usually claim to have done everything possible to save the baby.)

C-section babies fall into two categories. The minority experience labor and progress partially down the birth canal but, for whatever reason, cannot be born vaginally. The majority are "elective" cesareans who never journey even partway down the birth canal. They are elective because the doctor or the pregnant mother decide that C-section is the best course of action under the circumstances.

The psychological profile of the "electives" consists of a triad of characteristics. First, because they missed out on the contractions-massage phase of delivery, they are predisposed to seek out physical contact—one could say they are moved by a kind of cuddle hunger. Second, they tend to get themselves into difficult situations and hope to be rescued. Third, they are prone to be hypersensitive about issues of separation and abandonment.

The C-section babies who experience some contractions are likely to demonstrate all the characteristics described above plus strong feelings of block—the sense that they are unable to complete or succeed at a task. Often, the well-known phenomenon of "writer's block" can be traced to this kind of birth experience.

- Children born with the umbilical cord tightly wound around their necks: More than others, these children live in fear of suffocation. Their necks and vocal cords often become the seat of psychosomatic illness.

- Breech babies: Constituting 5 percent of deliveries, these babies are, generally speaking, more determined, headstrong, and stubborn than their nonbreech counterparts. Their life script often reads: "I want to do it my way." (I wonder whether Frank Sinatra was a breech?) If many attempts were made to reposition them in the womb, they may also feel as if they generally are in error, doing something wrong.

I recently lectured in France, where I met a young musician named Stephanie. She told me that since childhood she had been fascinated with the fairy tale "Rumpelstiltskin." The story concludes as follows:

"Is your name Kunz?"
"No."
"Is your name Heinz?"
"No."
"Can your name be Rumpelstiltskin?"
"The devil told you! The devil told you!" the little man screamed, and he stamped so ferociously with his right foot that his leg went deep into the ground up to his waist. Then he grabbed the other foot angrily with both hands and ripped himself in two.

Stephanie worried all her life about being split in the middle without knowing why. As she continued to ponder the image of Rumpelstiltskin, she recalled being told she'd been a breech baby. Her fear of being torn apart during birth had been "forgotten" but was apparently consciously manifested through her obsession with the Rumpelstiltskin tale. Indeed, so complete was her unconscious identification with this fairy-tale image that later in life she came to fear in herself an aggressive and violent aspect that threatened to tear apart anyone who crossed her.

It follows that physiological events of birth are charged with emotional and symbolic power. The circumstances of our birth provide the material from which we create our primary life scripts, which from deep within our minds will exert a gravitational pull on all our thoughts and actions for the rest of our lives. The task of therapy or any other form of personal growth is to locate and identify self-destructive scripts that originated very early in life and then help the client exchange these in favor of new, life-affirming, constructive scripts.

BIRTH TRAUMA

From my own clinical work and the research of others, I have come to realize that a difficult birth accompanied by high levels of intervention and high levels of maternal anxiety results in birth trauma.

Babies have many symptoms that parents and physicians consider normal but which are actually symptoms of underlying birth trauma. For example, the total crying time per day for babies considered within the normal range is about two to six hours. However, it is informative to know that the average crying time per day for babies with no birth trauma is twenty minutes, and most of their crying is used to communicate their needs and discomforts.

What makes the incidence of birth trauma so high? California psychologist William Emerson points to the industrialization of society and the commensurate increases in birth-related technology. But high-tech birth technology and obstetrical interventions—surgery, forceps, and the like—are not the only causes of birth trauma. The stress of modern life, the increase in fetal alcohol and drug syndromes, unwanted pregnancy, and spousal abuse are also factors. If the mother experienced trauma during her own birth, notes Emerson, she's more likely to experience complications, and the pattern is repeated again.

BIRTH TIMING

Obstetricians agree that of all the harmful birth scenarios, the most dev-astating is prematurity. The typical period of gestation is 40 weeks, but 6 to 8 percent of babies are born at 38 weeks or less. Though medical sci-ence has made progress in recent years in increasing life expectancy for preemies, those who survive frequently suffer breathing difficulties, cerebral palsy, intellectual handicaps, and other problems.

About half of all preemies are delivered early because of premature la-bor, so physicians have naturally focused on trying to deliver babies as close to term as possible. Yet efforts at intervention have, for the most part, failed. Why? Despite their best efforts, physicians did not under-stand the causes of premature labor in the first place. What system con-trols birth timing, and which factors cause it to malfunction? Scientists just did not know.

In the last few years, however, researchers such as Roger Smith of the University of Newcastle in Australia have begun to unravel the mecha-nism of birth timing, in the process offering hope of avoiding premature labor and thus delaying delivery until the fetus is mature enough to thrive outside the womb.

Smith says, "Specifically, scientists have known for some time that throughout most of gestation the uterus is essentially a relaxed bag of disconnected smooth-muscle cells. This bag is sealed at the bottom by a tightly closed ring—the cervix, which is kept firm and inflexible by tough collagen fibers." These structural features are maintained by progesterone, which the placenta secretes into the mother's blood-stream from the earliest days of pregnancy. The placenta also secretes estrogen, which promotes contractions. At first, progesterone levels are high and estrogen levels relatively low. Parturition begins when the bal-ance shifts—when estrogen overrides progesterone and contractions can begin.

Elevated levels of estrogen cause uterine muscle cells to synthesize a protein called connexin. Connexin links the once-relaxed, independent muscle cells into a network capable of contraction. Estrogen also stimu-late muscle cells to display large numbers of receptors for oxytocin, mak-ing uterine contractions more powerful and thus inducing labor. At the same time, the unborn child's adrenal glands produce the hormone cor-tisol. Cortisol promotes the release of substances that remove water from fetal lungs, enabling them to inflate upon birth so the newborn can breathe.

But even as scientists came to understand the sequence, they remained baffled by the trigger. What stimulates production of elevated estrogen, ultimately causing the switch? Part of the answer came from studies of sheep. About midway through gestation in sheep, researchers learned, the hypothalamus of the developing fetal brain started secreting a hormone called corticotropin-releasing hormone (CRH); CRH, in turn, induced the pituitary gland, at the base of the brain, to release adrenocorticotropin (ACTH) into the fetal bloodstream. ACTH instructed the fetal adrenal glands to make cortisol, and the cortisol, in turn, activated placental enzymes that converted progesterone to estrogen.

In humans, scientists now know, a similar process is afoot, with one difference: the CRH comes not from the fetal brain but from the placenta itself. Working with graduate student Mark McClean, Roger Smith confirmed the findings in humans through detailed analysis of blood samples. But the researchers got a surprise: CRH values at 16 to 20 weeks of pregnancy—the earliest the lab tests could detect them— roughly predicted when women would give birth. Those with the highest levels were most likely to deliver prematurely, while those with lowest levels were most likely to deliver on time. McClean and Smith had uncovered a clock of sorts, set by the amount of CRH in the mother's blood.

Future benefits from this research will be profound. A CRH test early in pregnancy could identify those at risk, enabling mothers with a chance of delivering prematurely to monitor their situation closely and prepare adequately. Appropriate nutrition might also decrease the dangers for those at risk: Caroline McMillen of the University of Adelaide in Australia has noted that nutrient deprivation precipitates early delivery in sheep; an Israeli study of pregnant Jewish women fasting on the holiday of Yom Kippur found them to have higher rates of premature delivery than nonfasting bedouin women living in the same region.

I think these findings are significant on two accounts. First, they show the importance the placenta—an organ of the unborn child— plays in the preparation for and initiation of birth. And second, these studies raise the question, What causes the placenta to produce high, low, or normal levels of CRH? I suspect a combination of physical and emotional messages from the mother to the unborn child are at work here, and I look to the day this theory will be proven in the lab.

SELF-DESTRUCTIVE BEHAVIOR AND VIOLENCE

The experience of birth is so far-reaching that some studies link especially difficult or traumatic births to drug abuse, violence, and even suicide. The famed psychologist Lee Salk, for instance, attributed teenage suicide to the trauma of a difficult delivery. Comparing the birth records of 52 suicide victims born between 1957 and 1967 with those of 104 controls, he found that the suicides generally lacked early prenatal care, had mothers who were chronically ill during pregnancy, and suffered respiratory distress for more than one hour after birth.

In a related study, Bertil Jacobson of the Karolinska Institute in Stockholm found a correlation between the kind of birth trauma and the method of suicide. For example, those who asphyxiated themselves, whether by hanging, drowning, or gas poisoning, were four times more likely than controls to have suffered oxygen deficiency at birth. Jacobson also found higher rates of drug addiction among adults born to mothers who received opiates, barbiturates, or chloroform during labor.

More recent work suggests that birth complications, including trauma, result in brain damage that predisposes a child to impulsive and aggressive acts. One Danish study compared 15 violent criminals and 24 property criminals with 177 nonoffenders on the basis of pregnancy and delivery events. Delivery complications such as a ruptured uterus, umbilical cord prolapse (wrapped around the neck), and difficult labor predicted violent offending, especially in subjects whose parents were already psychiatrically disturbed.

In another study, researchers from the University of Southern California–Los Angeles and the Institute of Preventive Medicine in Copenhagen reported that when birth complications combine with early maternal rejection, an infant is at especially great risk for committing violent crime by age 18. To reach their conclusion, the researchers followed all 4,269 males born at the State University Hospital in Copenhagen between September 1959 and December 1961. The researchers rated the boys for birth complication, including forceps extraction, umbilical cord prolapse, preeclampsia (toxemia leading to convulsions), and long birth duration. They also collected demographic, family, and psychosocial information during pregnancy and at one year of age. They were particularly interested to know whether the pregnancy was wanted or unwanted, and whether the mother had ever attempted abortion.

Criminal status was determined when the boys were between 17 and

19 years old, based on a search of the Danish National Criminal Register. Offenses considered violent for purposes of the study included murder, attempted murder, assault, rape, armed robbery, illegal possession of a weapon, and threats of violence. Nonviolent crime was defined as theft, fraud, forgery, blackmail, breaking and entering, and the like. Of the original group, 145 (3.4 percent) were violent criminals, 540 (12.6 percent) were nonviolent criminals, and 3,584 (84 percent) showed no criminal behavior at all. The criminal rate of 16 percent in this sample was similar to the rate of 17 percent found in a group of English males. Amazingly, while only 4.5 percent of the subjects were found to have suffered both birth complication and early maternal rejection, this small group made up 18 percent of those committing violent crime. The researchers found no comparable association between birth complication and poor social circumstances, including poverty.

Writing in the *Archives of General Psychiatry*, the researchers suggest that birth complications may "result in brain dysfunction and associated neurological and neuropsychological deficits that in turn directly and indirectly predispose to violence." But, they emphasize, these complications do *not* predispose to violence when combined with a loving early home environment. The implication is that love and support can protect against the otherwise negative effects of birth complications. Good parental care and the opportunity to bond with a caregiver in the first year of life can reduce the risk of criminal violence, something parents should note if birth complications arise.

BIRTH ORDER

No chapter on birth and the brain would be complete without a discussion of birth order. If neither nature nor nurture can adequately explain our personalities, some experts contend, it is because we have neglected to factor birth order into the mix. According to researcher Frank Sulloway, who has spent years collecting evidence, siblings carve out unique niches for themselves in the family through a Darwinian contest for their parents' love and attention.

His research, based on thousands of historical biographies, indicates that firstborns, secure in their positions and true to parental values, wind up the most conservative. (Natural-born leaders, firstborns include all the American astronauts selected for Apollo missions to the moon.) Later-born children, who must develop diverse strategies to get attention, are often more creative, rebellious, and empathetic. The child in the middle, meanwhile, is usually lowest in confidence yet frequently takes on the negotiator's role. The youngest, often pampered and spoiled, tends to be more easygoing and popular.

I agree with many of Sulloway's observations, but there is more to birth order than meets his eye. While past studies were conducted in the framework of the social sciences, a whole spate of evidence is emerging from research into fetal life. Consider that birth weight increases with each pregnancy—the difference between first and second babies is, on average, 5 ounces, or 138 grams. First babies, therefore, have a comparatively larger placenta, which means they receive more nutrients than later babies.

Firstborns may also receive greater supplies of the long-chain omega-3 fatty acids so essential for growth of the brain. Indeed, maternal supplies of omega-3 often decrease with each subsequent birth, especially in Western societies, where dietary consumption of omega-3 is relatively low. If the mother has not supplemented her supply of this essential nutrient, each successive baby will have access to increasingly sparser stores.

Other factors affecting children are parental expectations, which differ for each child, and parental preferences, which determine who becomes the favorite among a group of siblings. Usually, firstborns are fathers' and second-born and last-born children are mothers' favorites. Middle children tend to get less attention from their parents, which explains why they are so often the least happy.

SUMMING UP

It is clear, given findings in neuroscience, that birth plays a fundamental role in shaping the infrastructure of our brain, the bedrock of our unconscious, and the elements of our personality. Birth has a lasting impact on our psyches because it is inscribed in every cell of our bodies, wiring the brain for adaptation to stress and pain, to bonding, and to love.

To encourage the flow of hormones and ease the infant's entry into the world, parents should, if possible, find a birth setting that's womblike—a warm, quiet, calm, and comfortable environment where mother and baby can relax and, ultimately, bond.

Remember, a difficult birth does not condemn a child to suffer ill consequences for the rest of his or her life. Negative prenatal and perinatal experiences can usually be overcome by loving, supportive parenting.

Key Parenting Points

- Take prenatal classes, if possible, with the father of your child.
- Avoid unnecessary medical interventions as much as possible during your pregnancy and labor, for example, an ultrasound every week just to see the baby.
- Consider engaging a midwife or doula.
- Choose only people you really like to be present at the birth.

6

—∿—

Sense and Sensibility
of the Newborn

Pediatricians' misconceptions about newborn babies go back a long time. In 1895, J. P. C. Griffith, clinical professor of diseases of children at the University of Pennsylvania, wrote, "When the baby is just born . . . it is . . . very little more intelligent than a vegetable. . . . A newborn baby cannot see except to distinguish light from darkness. . . . It seems also unable to hear . . . it is, in fact, not directly conscious of anything."

In 1946, Benjamin Spock, whose *Baby and Child Care* has been one of the best-selling books of the last hundred years, wrote on the subject of fussing: "The baby is not mad at you. He doesn't know yet that you are a person or that he is a person. He's just a bundle of organs and nerves during his first month."

But today infant laboratories around the world are discovering just the opposite: that the newborn's sensory systems are operational from birth, able to inform the baby about and help him relate to his surroundings. Because his expressive faculties, including voice, facial muscles, and movements, are also well under control, a newborn baby is far from the unresponsive, unfeeling, and unaware creature he was portrayed to be just a few decades ago.

It wasn't until the 1970s, in fact, that scientists studying newborns started taking a more careful look. Equipped with electrodes to record babies' heartbeats, pacifiers connected to an electronic apparatus to record babies' sucking patterns, eye-tracking devices, and video cameras, among other tools, researchers learned that the newborn was an active learner and communicator, keenly aware of his surroundings and capable of a surprising range of intentional behavior.

The first area to attract researchers was the newborn baby's senses. Systematic testing has shown that:

- In the delivery room a few minutes after birth, the newborn will fix intently on objects that have sharp areas of contrast, like faces.
- When the object is moved slowly, the newborn may pursue it with his eyes and head for several minutes. His face is alert as he suppresses other activities and concentrates on the stimulus.
- Newborns possess three-dimensional vision and rudimentary hand-eye coordination.
- Newborns are able to distinguish their own mother from other mothers by breast milk odors, underarm smell, and any perfume she may be wearing.
- Food-related odors classified as milky or fruity elicit facial expressions from newborns of smiling accompanied by sucking and licking movements. Fishy and rotten egg odors produced looks of disgust, often accompanied by spitting movements.
- By the age of one week, a baby can pick out her mother's voice from a group of other women's voices, and at two weeks can recognize that her mother's voice and face belong together.
- When several weeks old, infants display an entirely different attitude—more wide-eyed, playful, and bright-faced—toward their fathers than toward their mothers.
- At eight weeks, they can differentiate between shapes of objects as well as colors (generally preferring red, then blue).
- Four-month-olds discriminate between the motions of living and nonliving objects.
- Five-month-olds recognize the correspondence of lip movements to speech.

SENSORY EXPLOSION

These findings are part of the explosion of data reaching us almost daily on the skills and talents of the newborn. Indeed, over the past two decades scientists have conducted thousands of studies on the sensory capabilities of the newborn, in the process rewriting the textbook on infant psychology and behavioral pediatrics. This persuasive body of evidence has established, beyond a doubt, that newborns are not the mindless, senseless blobs of protoplasm depicted in years past.

Instead, viewed in aggregate, the research has established that normal newborns enter the world with all their sensory systems functioning and intact. While each sense is developed to a different degree, they have *all* been documented as functioning in response to stimuli. By measuring such responses as leg withdrawal, head turn, startle behavior, and eye blink, researchers have shown the extent of sensory development at each developmental stage.

Jacob E. Steiner of the Hebrew University in Jerusalem, for example, has studied the reaction of infants to taste and smell. In a series of tests he gave sweet, sour, and bitter substances to normal infants in the very first hours of life, before any type of feeding. In every instance, sweet stimulation resulted in facial relaxation and an expression of enjoyment resembling a smile. Sour stimulation led to a typical lip pursing, and bitter stimulation to mouth openings expressive of disgust. Water produced a swallow without facial expression. In another test, babies were exposed to food-related odors that had been classified as pleasant or unpleasant by a panel of adults. Fruity and milky stimulants elicited facial expressions of smiling accompanied by sucking and licking movements. Fishy and rotten egg odors produced looks of disgust, often accompanied by spitting and salivation.

When it comes to differentiating smells, babies are probably more competent than adults. This was demonstrated several years ago by Aiden MacFarlane, who asked nursing mothers to wear gauze pads inside their bras between feedings. He took the pads and placed one on each side of the subject infants' heads—the baby's own mother's pad on one side, another mother's on the other. Almost all the infants recognized their mother's pads by turning toward them.

By the age of one week a baby can pick out her mother's voice from a group of other women's voices and, at two weeks, can recognize that the mother's voice and face belong together. This was elegantly demonstrated by British researcher Genevieve Carpenter, who subjected two-week-old babies to four situations:

1. The mother speaks naturally to her infant.
2. A woman other than the mother speaks naturally to the infant.
3. The mother speaks to the infant imitating the other woman's voice.
4. A stranger tries to speak like the baby's mother.

Babies paid most attention in scenario one, when the mother spoke in her own voice, but became agitated in the last two situations. Mixing the familiar and the unfamiliar was frightening to the youngest infants, and showed sophisticated abilities to differentiate already in place.

Other experiments have shown that if you place a baby within hearing distance but out of the line of vision of a man and a woman and ask them to speak simultaneously, the newborn will invariably turn toward the woman. According to T. Berry Brazelton of the Children's Hospital Medical Center in Boston, babies pay special attention to their fathers as well. "Amazingly enough," Brazelton says, "when several weeks old an infant displays an entirely different attitude—more wide-eyed, playful, and bright-faced—toward its father than its mother." Brazelton thinks the babies perceive their fathers' high expectations as compared with their mothers' and therefore respond in more extreme ways.

EMOTIONAL RADAR

Newborns are not only able to take in and interpret light and sound, odor and taste, they can also perceive emotional nuance. Very young infants gaze at the faces of adults and respond in a way that seems tuned to the vocalizations and gestures of the adults. They smile when the adults smile and move in rhythm with them. When the infants' predictions about the other person's response are violated—when, for example, the mother reacts to her baby's cooing with a perfectly still, stony face—the baby becomes distinctly distressed.

Brazelton notes that by the time an infant is four weeks old, emotional reactions are clear. "The baby's behavior is a whole language," he says. "It tells you when they are beginning to get upset, when they are starting to get discouraged, when they're being turned off by too much stimulation, and so on. You can take most emotions that we live by and I can give you the behavior that goes with it in a newborn baby. In fact, by four to six weeks of age, we can look at a finger or toe and the way it behaves and tell you whether the baby is watching an object, or his mother, or his father, or a stranger. We can tell you which person he's watching by the way the finger or toe behaves."

SKILLED AT BIRTH

Babies are not merely sensing and feeling individuals but also active participants in their world. They emerge from the womb with a surprising array of skills.

Randi Wasserman, assistant professor of clinical pediatrics at New York University Medical Center, reports that babies are born with an "automatic grasp so strong you can pick them up and hold them" based on the strength of the grip. Wasserman says the grip may be a holdover from our evolutionary past, when the source of milk—the mother—scampered from tree to tree.

The iron grip generally disappears by the second or third month of life, but in its stead parents will find another skill: the trick of hand-eye coordination. The first step in perfecting hand-eye coordination, of course, is adequate eyesight. According to Asma Sadiq, head of developmental and behavioral pediatrics at Beth Israel Medical Center in New York, newborns can see objects within just 8 inches or so. Other doctors and psychologists think babies have an optimal visual range of 12 to 18 inches. They can see in color, but the world is a blur. Indeed, rudimentary hand-eye coordination is present even at birth, but by five months of age, as vision sharpens, babies become skilled enough to transfer objects from hand to hand. At six months of age, when visual focus is sharp, hand-eye coordination plays a large role in their interaction with the world.

Babies tune in to their parents' moods and reactions from the start, of course. But they also turn these perceptions to their advantage through their increasing skills. Arnold Shapiro, director of the Communication Disorders Center at Mount Sinai Medical Center in New York, notes that receptive language—the ability to understand what's said—develops far faster than verbal ability. And when babies do speak, it is often to communicate in areas most important to them: "baba" (bottle) and "dada" are often the first spoken words; "mama" comes later because it is more difficult to say.

Shapiro contends that spelling out words in front of even the youngest babies is a no-no. "They don't know what you're spelling," he says, "but they know it's a code and something they're not supposed to know about. I would think they'd be annoyed."

Amy Flynn, director of the Bank Street Family Center in New York, notes that toddlers interpret spoken language and the world around them in highly literal ways. One day, trying to excite a class of toddlers, she said, "I have something that will blow your socks off." Looking around, she noticed that one young boy had taken his shoes off in expectation of the sock-blowing event.

If verbal communication is often straightforward, Sadiq adds that a baby's smile may be one of the most cunning survival methods around. Infants start to smile with intent at about 2 months of age, encouraging exhausted parents to go the distance on their behalf.

But with each passing month, the baby is increasingly capable of doing things on his or her own. At 6 months of age most babies can sit up. By 9 months they are pulling themselves up on furniture. By 12 to 15 months they're taking their first steps. Says Sadiq, by 18 months of age, the average baby will be able to walk, stoop to pick up a toy, and then move on.

INFANT PAIN

One of the enduring myths of human development is that very young babies feel no pain. Despite overwhelming evidence to the contrary, some of those clinging most fervently to this erroneous notion are physicians themselves. Such attitudes, the cause of increased morbidity and mortality for vast numbers of infants, reflect an unacceptable degree of ignorance about the newborn child these practitioners are said to serve. Considering that since the early 1960s the neonate's reaction to pain has been shown to be similar to an adult's, it is hard to be sympathetic to doctors who cause infants pain on the grounds that reliable information on this subject is lacking.

It wasn't until 1987 that the medical profession finally woke up from its self-induced slumber, thanks in large part to a groundbreaking paper written by K. J. S. Anand, head of the department of anesthesia at Harvard Medical School, and published in the prestigious *New England Journal of Medicine*. His conclusion: "Numerous lines of evidence suggest that even in the human fetus, pain pathways as well as cortical and subcortical centers necessary for pain perception are well developed late in gestation, and the neurochemical systems now known to be associated with pain transmission and modulation are intact and functional. Physiologic responses to painful stimuli have been well documented in neonates of various gestational ages and are reflected in hormonal, metabolic, and cardiorespiratory changes similar to but greater than those observed in adult subjects. Other responses in newborn infants are suggestive of integrated emotional and behavioral responses to pain and are retained in memory long enough to modify subsequent behavior patterns."

Gideon Koren, head of clinical pharmacology at Toronto's Hospital for Sick Children, notes that in newborns "major surgeries are done with minimal and sometimes no analgesia at all. There's a general view that while they have pain, newborns don't remember it. But they do."

Indeed, Koren's study, published in the highly respected medical journal *The Lancet*, found clear-cut evidence of a lasting pain reflex associated with unanesthetized surgery after birth. Koren compared a group of male infants circumcised without anesthesia with a group not circumcised at all. Six months after birth, he checked the infants' lingering sensation to pain. "The circumcised infants reacted to standard inoculation with significantly more pain than the uncircumcised group," says Koren, suggesting that the trauma of unanesthetized surgery was retained.

LETTERS FROM THE EDGE

Expressing themselves in the magazine *Birth*, victimized parents described the extraordinary damage inflicted by medical professionals who insisted, despite incontrovertible evidence to the contrary, that infants cannot feel pain.

"Ten years ago our prematurely born son, Edward, was shunted for hydrocephalus while paralyzed with curare," one mother wrote. "Although he could not move, cry, or react in any way, he could see, hear, and feel as large incisions were cut in his scalp, neck, and abdomen; as a hole was drilled in his skull; as a tube was inserted into the center of his brain, then pushed down under the skin of his neck, chest, and abdomen and implanted deep in his abdominal cavity. It is a source of great anguish to me that my husband and I signed a form allowing such an operation to take place, but we were told Edward might die or become brain damaged without the operation and that the anesthesia might kill him. Besides, the doctors assured us, these babies don't really feel pain. I suspected then, and know now, that this is just not true.

"To this day, our severely retarded son will allow no one to touch his head, neck, or abdomen. Even heavily tranquilized, he reacts to the simplest medical procedures or the mere sight of the hospital with violent trembling, profuse sweating, screaming, struggling, and vomiting. I can't help feeling that on some level he still remembers the hideous pain inflicted on him during his unanesthetized surgery and throughout the course of his neonatal intensive care."

In the same issue of the magazine, another letter from a distraught mother described the treatment of her premature baby as follows: "On the morning of surgery, which had been scheduled three days in advance, Jeffrey was described by the transport team as 'a very small pink male . . . very active . . . with appropriate responses and gestures.' This was not rushed, emergency surgery but rather surgery scheduled to increase the likelihood of improvement over a length of time. In spite of this, the anesthesiologist decided the operation would proceed without delay, and she paralyzed him, using no pain relief or anesthesia of any type either before, during, or after surgery.

"For 1½ hours he had holes cut on either side of his neck, another hole cut in his right chest, a catheter inserted in his jugular vein, and these holes stitched shut. We were told by the surgeon afterward that they had trouble securing the catheter, so they repeated the procedure. Next, Jeffrey was cut open from his breastbone around to his backbone. Then his flesh was lifted aside, his ribs pried apart, his left lung retracted, and the blood vessel near his heart was tied off. Then the tissues were stitched together in layers and a final 'stab incision' made in his left side to insert a new chest tube.

"Jeffrey died five weeks after surgery.

"One of the more disturbing experiences in this process was the comment made to me by the senior neonatologist on staff at Children's Hospital. At a meeting concerning Jeffrey's treatment, he said that what happened to my son didn't matter because he was a fetus. When I asked how old someone has to be to feel pain, he placed the line of demarcation at about two years."

Edward was born in 1975, Jeffrey in 1985. Their stories are not isolated incidents. In 1987 a survey of neonatal nurses demonstrated that 79 percent thought analgesia was underused, with 33 percent of babies receiving no postoperative analgesia and 34 percent receiving no analgesia before invasive procedures. A year later, another survey found that 15 percent of pediatric anesthetists thought babies less than 1 month old could not feel pain, *none* prescribed preoperative opiates, 98 percent did not prescribe opiates for minor procedures, 30 percent did not prescribe opiates for major procedures, and 48 percent did not prescribe postoperative opiate analgesia.

J. Winberg of the Karolinska Institute in Stockholm compares the infant reaction to surgery without adequate analgesia or anesthesia to post-traumatic stress disorder, much like that experienced by Vietnam veterans, rape victims, and earthquake survivors. In other words, when newborns experience severe pain, the result is a disturbing, persistent memory, one that is provoked whenever pain occurs again.

Severe or repeated pain so early in life also assaults the brain. Fran Lang Porter of Washington University School of Medicine in St. Louis notes that brain plasticity is highest in the period following birth, "providing a critical period during early development in all species, including humans, that maximizes the influence of the environment on the brain and, therefore, on subsequent behavior." In this setting, she says, "repetitive exposure to stress or pain would be expected to have more profound and permanent effects on brain development than would similar experiences later in life."

Indeed, infliction of pain during windows of critical brain development in early infancy seems to provoke a cascade of events, including the inappropriate damage or death of nerve cells and, many researchers believe, a structural and functional reorganization of the nervous system itself. The impact as years go on, they suggest, can range from stress disorder and altered pain sensitivity to impaired social skills.

The impact of pain at the level of brain structure makes another question almost, but not quite, moot: Do infants remember the pain itself? Porter says researchers have documented conscious memory of pain in babies 6 months of age and older. In this group, exposure to pain at one juncture results in anticipatory fear when the pain stimulus is threatened again.

But Porter and others say the damage can be mitigated, and perhaps prevented altogether, with anesthesia. In a clinical trial of preterm babies, for example, researchers found that infusions of morphine and midazolam reduced the pain response and stabilized vital signs like pulse rate and blood pressure. Anesthesia also reduced the incidence of poor neurological outcomes, ranging from brain damage to death.

Managing pain is a challenge for patients of any age. But consequences are most severe for infants and babies, because in their case the pain itself can alter the structure of the nervous system, permanently affecting perceptions, coping strategies, and emotional status throughout life.

THE STRESS FACTOR

Researchers studying infant pain have suggested that a similar assault to the brain takes place under conditions of stress. Brain scientists have long known that the stress response occurs along with the production of stress hormones. A team of American and Canadian researchers studying stress now says the health of the stress response is rooted in the earliest days of life. In their studies, the researchers took newborn rat pups and subjected them to slight stress by taking them out of the nest for 15-minute periods on a number of consecutive days. The results were somewhat surprising: when subjected to stress as adults, these animals reacted with a lowered release of the stress hormone corticosterone and lower levels of anxiety than nonhandled controls. Rat pups subjected to severe stress—removal from the nest for three hours at a time—had the opposite response. As adults, they released more corticosterone and demonstrated higher levels of anxiety than nonstressed controls.

Reviewing the situation, the researchers were able to explain these confusing results. When handled pups were given back to the mother, she intensified her licking and grooming. As adults, offspring of these more tactile mothers suffered less anxiety than others. The team also found another, tantalizing side effect of "slight stress" and the extra touching it elicited: in old age, the offspring of tactile mothers exhibited memory loss much later than normal controls.

THE NEONATAL INTENSIVE CARE UNIT

Given what we know about newborn senses, the neonatal intensive care unit, or NICU, is a particularly dangerous place for babies. If pain and stress are damaging to the newborn, there are few situations where the two factors crescendo so alarmingly as in the NICU.

In an ideal world, the premature infants placed in these centers would still be in the womb. There, they would sense muted light and sound against the backdrop of their mother's heartbeat and the undulating tightening of her uterus, increasingly snug with the babies' growth. Instead, NICU preemies or sick newborns are bombarded with bright lights and the jarring sounds of electrical machines and alarms, yet left essentially untouched by caring hands in clinical bassinets. I am convinced that many preemies would be better off lying with their mothers than being placed in the noisy, aseptic milieu of the NICU, where they are constantly prodded by needles and stuffed full of tubes.

In a dramatic example of the problem, a Seattle pediatrician was treating a desperately ill baby in his hospital's neonatal intensive care unit. Hooked up to a battery of life-support machines, the baby was flooded with light and exposed to more sound than you might hear on Fifth Avenue at rush hour.

The child, who was getting insufficient oxygen, was turning blue. The doctor decided the infant was going to die anyway, so he took him off life support, shut off all the machines, and turned off the lights. Then he took the baby out of the crib and rocked him gently in his arms. Within a few minutes the baby turned pink and made a complete recovery.

This anecdote is hardly unique. In another, well-publicized story, a mother hoping to help her older son adjust to his unborn sister encouraged him to sing to the baby in the womb. His favorite lyrics: "You are my sunshine, my only sunshine."

Though the pregnancy was normal, the little girl was born with complications. In the neonatal intensive care unit (NICU) for two weeks, she hovered between life and death. As the family planned a funeral, the boy begged to sing to his sister one more time. Though children were not allowed in the NICU, the mother finally decided to take the boy to the hospital despite staff objections. If he couldn't see her now, she reasoned, he might never see her alive at all.

She dressed him in an oversized scrub suit and marched him into the NICU. He looked like a walking laundry basket, but the head nurse recognized him as a child and screamed, "Get him out of here now! No children allowed." The usually mild-mannered mother glared with steely eyes and said, "He isn't leaving until he sings to his sister."

At his sister's bedside, the boy gazed at the infant losing her battle to live. Then the three-year-old began to sing: "You are my sunshine, my only sunshine." Instantly the baby girl responded, and her pulse steadied for the first time since her birth. As her brother sang, her ragged breathing smoothed out, and as the singing continued, the little girl relaxed and even the bossy head nurse relented with tears. Plans for a funeral were abandoned, and the next day the infant was well enough to go home.

I'm hardly suggesting that we banish the NICU. Rather, we should create a better NICU. We should cut down on the light, the noise, the blood taking. We should start with the premise that the critically ill newborn needs calm and quiet just like the critically ill adult.

THE POWER OF TOUCH

Deprived of appropriate stimulation in the NICU and other environments meant to help infants at risk, premature babies may never catch up. Hundreds of studies now show that such infants suffer significantly more handicaps in physical, neurological, social, mental, and motor development and functioning than full-term infants. Part of the reason is deprivation of stimulation. In the womb, the baby receives continual tactile and kinesthetic stimulation through the movement of the mother, the amniotic fluid, and the muscular walls of the uterus and placenta. As the baby grows within the womb, the walls of the uterus close in, making tactile stimulation ever more intense.

Instead of receiving this tactile stimulation in the womb, the premature baby is isolated; while he is exposed to inappropriate levels of noise and light, touch and movement are virtually absent.

Even after he returns home, the tiny baby may be treated gingerly by parents who are afraid of injuring him and instead adopt the hospital's standard of care.

The good news today is that careful compensation in the first weeks of life can offset the disadvantages associated with prematurity, setting the smallest of infants on a trajectory for health. One of the most effective compensating techniques, a number of impressive studies show, is infant massage.

At the forefront of the research is Tiffany M. Field, director of the Touch Research Institute at the Miami School of Medicine. In one of her most revealing studies, she gave twenty preterm neonates 45 minutes of massage a day. Administered in three daily doses of 15 minutes each, the massage therapy lasted ten days. The massaged infants gained 47 percent more weight than the unmassaged controls, Field reported. Much to her surprise, the massaged infants remained awake and active a greater percentage of the time—contrary to the expectation that massage would make them sleepy. They performed better on a host of functional and neurological evaluations, and they were able to leave the hospital on average six days earlier than babies who didn't receive the extra stimulation.

Field and colleagues found the benefits extended to full-term newborns, too. Among the findings:

- Newborns placed skin-to-skin with mothers were quiet but if separated and placed in a bed began to cry. When physical contact was restored, babies quieted down.
- Infants who were massaged established more regular sleep patterns and gained more weight than a control group of babies who were rocked instead.

Although formal studies have not been done, infant massage training groups around the United States report that the technique reduces stress responses to painful procedures, including inoculations; reduces the pain associated with teething and constipation; reduces colic; and, as a bonus, makes parents feel good.

Massage has even been demonstrated to strengthen the infant-father bond. In an Australian study, fathers who massaged and bathed infants for four weeks following birth were greeted with more eye contact, smiling, vocalizing, and reaching and elicited fewer avoidance behaviors than fathers who did not bathe or massage their babies.

Massage benefits even the healthiest of babies, Field notes, in part because of its ability to reduce stress. Indeed, in a series of well-regarded studies, the Field team found that massage lowered the incidence of accepted measures of stress—including mouthing, grimacing, and clenching fists. The researchers also observed that blood levels of catecholamines—norepinephrine and epinephrine—increased throughout the stimulation period. "Although these catecholamines typically increase following stress in the adult, suggesting that an increase is undesirable," Field says, an increase during the neonatal period, following birth, is part of normal development. In short, massage therapy facilitated a normal developmental release of hormones that otherwise might have been slowed. The power of massage received support when a Swedish team reported that massaging the inside of the mouth of a newborn increased the release of hormones involved in food absorption.

Encouraged by their findings, Field and colleagues have begun massage therapy with infants suffering other problems. When massaged, cocaine-exposed and HIV-exposed infants gain more weight, exhibit less stress, and demonstrate more mature motor behavior. Massaged infants of depressed mothers, meanwhile, are more interactive, less fussy, and less prone to sleep disturbance than controls.

THE POWER OF MUSIC

Music joins massage as a powerful technique for soothing the newborn sensibility in all the right ways. A long body of research shows that music is particularly useful in promoting relaxation. Flowing, lyrical melodies, simple harmonies, and easy rhythms of 60 to 80 beats a minute (like the human heart at rest) regularly relax children and adults. Physiological measurements show that such rhythms stimulate the release of endorphins from the brain and reduce blood levels of adreno-corticotropic hormone (ACTH), which is associated with stress. Such music stimulates alpha brain waves and relaxation in muscle tone and galvanic skin response (increased electrical conductivity), among other physiological measures. It also aids the achievement of emotional equilibrium.

Our response to music most surely derives from our experience before birth. So relaxing are the rhythms of the womb that they serve to nurture the prenate from the moment it can hear, about three months before birth. From that point on, the sounds of the womb are constant and soothing. Blood rushing through the placenta can produce sound levels peaking at about 95 decibels. This rhythmic swooshing of the blood as it rushes through the placental vessels is the intrauterine lullaby we miss when we leave our mothers' bodies. Indeed, one of the most stressful changes during the baby's transition from the womb to the world is loss of the rhythm associated with maternal movements, breathing, and heartbeat.

Intuitively grasping the need to compensate, new mothers exhibit a natural preference for cradling new infants on their chests, close to their hearts. Psychologist Lee Salk thought the sound of the heart was soothing, and he hypothesized that the fetus associates rhythmic sounds with the comfort and security of the womb. Consequently he reasoned that similar sounds played right after birth would ease the transition between the outside world and the womb.

Soon scientists proved the idea correct. One team found that the rhythm of the blood rushing through the placenta had a calming effect on newborns. Another group showed that newborn infants exposed to recorded intrauterine sounds were soothed. A third team went further, showing that newborns were pacified by the music of a soap opera their mothers had watched daily while pregnant. Music was also shown to shorten labor and decrease pain in mother and baby alike.

In one impressive study, Canadian nurses June Kaminski and Wendy Hall worked with twenty newborns in a hospital nursery. They found that when they played classical music for these normal infants, the infants were far more likely to maintain their emotional equilibrium. During control periods, without the music, the infants were more likely to change back and forth between emotional states, often crying or being disoriented. When the music played, the nurses report, the babies maintained a state of relaxation—literally the opposite of the stress response.

As with touch, the therapeutic value of music is most powerful when applied to the child who is premature or otherwise compromised early on. Full-term infants, their nervous systems more fully developed, are more likely to manifest what psychologists call an organized state—they are easy to read by caregivers and spend most of their hours in quiet sleep or quiet relaxation. Preemies, on the other hand, are often too immature to maintain emotional equilibrium. Often disorganized, they spend disproportionate amounts of time in drowsy, crying, and nonalert states. Disorganized infants suffer inordinate amounts of stress and require more energy from caretakers, who cannot easily get in sync with them.

Hoping to use such stimulation to aid the preemies they work with, nurses at the Neonatal Intensive Care Unit of Georgia Baptist Medical Center in Atlanta tried an experiment of their own. The infants they chose for their trial were premature and clearly agitated, frequently exhibiting such behaviors as thrashing of extremities, excessive head movement, and facial grimacing. When babies were agitated, researchers would spend ten minutes trying to calm them and another ten playing a tape of prerecorded intrauterine sounds combined with female singing, all the while recording heart rate, oxygen saturation, and blood pressure. Preemies in the study experienced fewer episodes of oxygen deprivation and increased behavioral equilibrium while the music played, convincing the nurses that they had hit on a useful therapeutic tool.

It seems likely that music therapy not only relaxes premature infants but also rewires their brains. This is especially crucial since these infants miss out on the auditory stimulation provided by the uterine environment during the last several weeks of life in the womb. Built in response to environment, the brain of a preemie cannot, by virtue of its early entry into the world, be wired exactly as it would have been if carried to term. Intervention with womblike music may help to complete the wiring left undone, not just relaxing the baby but also equipping her with a sturdier brain for years to come.

RESISTANCE TO ACCEPTING
THE NEW KNOWLEDGE ABOUT BABIES

Although developmental psychologists and scientists are gradually revising their assumptions about the newborn's sensory and mental functioning, many professionals remain resistant.

Some psychotherapists, particularly those with a strong psychoanalytic orientation, for instance, see young children as primitive, aggressive animals motivated only by satisfaction of basic needs.

The following quote, from an otherwise very sensible and humanistic book, exemplifies this attitude:

"When she is awake and alert, the baby is always reaching out to something, though her mind is not yet aware of where she begins and ends or where everything else begins and ends. In her moments of tension and need, a helpless baby can be ruthless. She possesses and destroys the breast that feeds her. She devours the arms that hold her. She rids herself of her body products without any concern. A mother's presence in a baby's life absorbs, contains, and tolerates the baby's unruly lusts and thereby tames and humanizes them. The mother's attunement to her baby's crude and inchoate excitements transforms them into socialized human emotions and affects."

Shockingly, and in the face of overwhelming evidence to the contrary, such notions are common still. My experience is that nine out of ten medical doctors regard the newborn and, needless to say, the unborn child as essentially mindless and insensate. And, as we have already seen, most of them even doubt that babies can feel pain. Obstetricians in particular often vehemently oppose and deride the findings emerging about unborn and newborn babies from the world's leading labs. I suspect that on some level of consciousness these practitioners realize that if they truly came to regard the unborn and newborn as being endowed with human sensitivity and sensibility, they would have to change the way they treat pregnant women and newborn babies. They would have to abandon their view of women as imperfect birthing machines and of themselves as white knights riding to their rescue. It would involve a seismic shift from an interventionist, action-oriented mentality to a patient, caring, wait-and-see, baby-catching mentality.

Change is coming despite their resistance. Science has finally marshaled the research that supports what mothers have always known—that newborns have sensation, feelings, and minds and that the treatment they receive will have long-term consequences for their lives.

SUMMING UP

A persuasive body of evidence proves conclusively that normal newborns enter the world with all their sensory and intellectual systems functioning and intact. Although each sense is developed to a different degree, all healthy babies are able to see, feel, taste, touch, and hear from the moment they are born. Even more important, babies are biologically prepared to engage with their caregivers. Understanding babies' abilities will help parents relate to them right from birth on. Moreover, understanding the damage associated with stress and pain will enable parents to prevent, or at least reduce, these assaults and compensate for them should they occur.

Key Parenting Points

- Parents aware of infant sensation, emotion, and skills can use that knowledge to maximize their baby's development.
- Happy and healthy babies should eat well, sleep well, and cry only minimally.
- If your baby needs soothing, do so through eye contact, smiling, and touch. Never yell, hit, or shake.
- During the early months, an ideal place for an awake baby is on the parent's body. Do use a cloth baby carrier or a body sling.
- Look for your baby's engagement and disengagement cues and make sure you respond in kind.
- Do not allow any surgery without adequate pain relief.
- If your baby has been exposed to stress or pain, hold, cuddle, and stroke him frequently. Massage, pediatric chiropractic adjustments, and music will also help.
- Remember that the music you played during your child's gestation and birth will have a calming effect any time he or she is not feeling well.

7

—◆—

The Alchemy of Intimacy

A friend of mine was in the kitchen preparing lunch two days after the birth of her little girl when she heard her baby start to cry. "Suddenly there was this outpouring of milk from my breasts," my friend told me. "I thought, this is amazing. We are more connected than any other two people in the world."

No experience matches the power and radiant beauty of that first contact between parents and their newborn baby. To be part of that experience as a mother or father is to participate in one of life's rare miracles. The flow of love between mother, father, and infant is as palpable an emotion as one can feel; the bond formed in these first critical days and weeks will become a wellspring of love and caring for the baby and parents throughout their lives. Surprisingly, it is only during the last thirty years or so that we have come to appreciate the long-term benefits of what has been termed "bonding" or "parent-infant attachment."

Bonding is the process by which infant and parent become attached, connected, and intimate with each other. Bonding is a dialogue, a dance between child and parent that starts before birth but comes into full bloom in the first few weeks and months of life after birth.

In their now classic work, *Maternal-Infant Bonding*, published in 1976, Marshall H. Klaus and John H. Kennell put it this way: "Mother's attachment to her child is the strongest bond in the human. The power of this attachment is so great that it enables the mother or father to make the unusual sacrifices necessary for the care of their infant day after day, night after night—changing dirty diapers, attending to his cry, protecting him from danger, and giving him feedings in the middle of the night despite a desperate need for sleep.

"This original mother-infant bond is the wellspring for all the infant's subsequent attachments and is the formative relationship in the course of which the child develops a sense of himself. Close attachment can persist during long separations of time and distance, even though there may at times be no visible sign of its existence. Nonetheless, a call for help after even forty years may bring a mother to her child and evoke attachment behaviors equal in strength to those in the first year."

THE ELEMENTS OF BONDING

To enhance bonding, there must be extended periods of contact between the mother, the father, and the baby. The unconscious techniques and physical characteristics that parents may use to attract the baby to them include:

1. Touch. Skin-to-skin contact and carrying.
2. Warmth generated by holding and touching.
3. Eye-to-eye contact.
4. Odor. Through his sense of smell baby learns to identify Mother by her distinct aroma.
5. High-pitched voice. Soothing laughter and smiles.
6. Hugging and kissing. This helps transfer bacterial flora from mother to child and protects the baby from common infections.
7. Breast-feeding. Nursing at the breast builds up antibodies in the child.
8. Entrainment. The parent responds to the baby's cues through body movements, facial expressions, and speech.
9. Rhythmicity. The parents re-create the life rhythms experienced by the baby in utero, while at the same time helping the baby adapt to new rhythms.

The communication techniques and physical characteristics used by the baby to attract the parents include:

1. Eye-to-eye contact.
2. Crying.
3. Breast-feeding. Through sucking, the baby helps release the hormones associated with feelings of love and healing.

4. Odor. Especially after bath time.
5. Entrainment. Baby responds to parents by mirroring speech and other cues, including those communicated through body movement.

EARLY STUDIES

The modern era of research into the maternal-infant bond (and lately, the paternal-infant bond) started in 1945, when psychologist Rene Spitz studied two groups of children. One was made up of infants in a Foundling Home; the other, of infants born to mothers in a prison and cared for by their mothers in a nursery in the prison. In both institutions, hygienic conditions were carefully maintained. In the foundling home, the medical staff visited at least once a day. In the nursery, the physician saw a child only when called to do so.

Aside from medical care, however, infants in the foundling home received little input. With eight babies under the care of a single nurse, the foundling children were rarely stimulated and usually ignored. Nurses came in only to feed them and change their diapers, then disappeared for long periods of time. The children had no toys to play with, and so extreme was their isolation that bedsheets draped over crib railings deprived them even of visual stimulation. As if that weren't enough, they were unable even to hear the other children because glass cubicles enclosed each crib.

By contast, children in the nursery of the penal institution were exposed to the constant bustling activity of their mothers feeding, playing, and singing to their babies and talking to each other. The nursery was run by a head nurse and her three assistants, whose duties consisted mainly of teaching child care to the children's mothers. In the nursery, each child had the full-time care of his or her mother or, temporarily, the mother of another child.

On admission, the children of the foundling home had a much higher Developmental Quotient than the children of the nursery. The Developmental Index started to decline rapidly in foundling home children, however, while rising just as fast in nursery children. By the fifth month of the study, the two curves crossed, with foundling home children continuing to deteriorate while nursery children thrived.

In the end, the children of the foundling home showed all the manifestations of what Spitz called hospitalism. This was characterized by lack of social relationships as well as an extraordinarily high rate of mortality and susceptibility to infection and illness. So extreme was the deterioration that only 2 of 26 foundling home children age 18 to 30 months could speak even a couple of words. The same two were able to walk. Hardly any of the children could eat alone, and all were incontinent.

The problem in the nursery, on the other hand, was not whether children could walk or talk by age 12 months but rather how to contain their exuberance. They could all walk with support, and a number could walk without it. They vocalized freely and some of them spoke a few words.

It's obvious that the children in the foundling home suffered from severe sensory deprivation. But what proved even more damaging was the absence of maternal contact and love.

The first major studies on the impact of maternal loss were spearheaded a few years later, in the 1950s, by primate scientists Harry and Margaret Harlow of the University of Wisconsin. The Harlows and their students separated infant monkeys from their mothers at birth. I have seen films of these poor, wretched young monkeys, and it's a very disturbing experience. The juvenile monkeys are inconsolable, despondent, scrawny. They hardly eat or move. They cower in the corner of their cage or hold on for dear life to "surrogate mothers" made of either soft cloth or just wire mesh in the shape of a large monkey.

The majority of monkeys who survived early maternal deprivation were unable to mate as adults. Those that did mate—or, alternatively, were artificially inseminated and impregnated—were unable to take care of their young. In fact, more often than not, they attacked them viciously.

Such findings were synthesized in the 1950s and 1960s by John Bowlby, the English psychoanalyst famous for coining the term maternal deprivation syndrome, into what is now called attachment theory. Drawing on animal research as well as studies of juvenile delinquents, Bowlby argued that intense mother-child attachment was a requirement for psychological wholeness. Without it, he suggested, disorders of the brain and psyche would result.

Bowlby's work was extended by University of Virginia developmental psychologist Mary Ainsworth, who tried to characterize the traits of the child who was "securely attached." In her now-classic experiment, known as the Strange Situation, Ainsworth had a year-old baby and mother or father enter a stimulating, toy-filled room. During a 20-minute session, the parent left the room twice and returned twice. The first time, the baby was left with a stranger (a researcher), and the second time, the baby was left alone. Most children were upset when the parent left, Ainsworth observed, but it was the way they handled the reunions, she noted, that revealed the most about the parent-child relationship.

A baby who sought comfort from the returning parent was considered securely attached by Ainsworth. Possessing a "good enough" relationship with the primary caretaker, this child could go through life feeling confident and secure. Children who remained uncomforted by the returning parent or simply ignored him or her were said to be insecure—lacking in the basic emotional lessons of trust, interactivity, and love. Ainsworth said the latter group was "insecurely" or "incompletely" attached. Such children could function, she said, but they might be prone to insecurities, mood swings, intimacy problems, and more.

Finally, in the 1970s, Marshall Klaus and John Kennell asserted that close contact between mother and child in the hours after birth promoted a cascade of maternal hormones and the potential for healthy attachment in years to come.

THE HORMONES OF ATTACHMENT

In the last decade, scientists have come to understand that these early relationships are particularly profound because they shape—in the most literal way imaginable—the neurochemistry of emotion and the entire nervous system, including the brain. Indeed, as these systems develop in lockstep, they propel the process of attachment and write its lessons into the interstices of our bodies and minds.

We have already learned how parents communicate and bond with their unborn children. Postnatal bonding similarly occurs along three channels. The first is neurohormonal. One hormone—oxytocin—has long been recognized for its role in prompting the uterine contractions of birth and the flow of milk during lactation. Researchers now know that the hormone, especially abundant in the female brain, also enhances social and sexual responsiveness as well as the impulse to nurture the young in mothers and fathers alike.

More recently, animal and human studies have clarified the role oxytocin plays in attachment. When a baby is breast-fed, he receives oxytocin through the mother's milk. If levels of oxytocin exceed a certain amount, memory will be impaired, accounting, at least in part, for the amnesia associated with birth. But if oxytocin levels are just right, babies will be primed for physical proximity, touching, and sociability.

Production of oxytocin depends on a feedback loop established between infant and mother. When the infant suckles the nipple during breast-feeding, the mother's hypothalamus is alerted, triggering release of oxytocin from the pituitary gland into the maternal bloodstream. The oxytocin leads to the contraction of the smooth muscles of the mammary tissues, which then pump milk from the breast.

The hormone prolactin assists oxytocin in the production of breast milk. Prolactin levels increase during pregnancy and decrease rapidly postpartum. But whenever the nipple of a mother is touched, either by the infant's lips or by a finger, there is a fourfold to sixfold increase in her prolactin level and then a decrease after breast-feeding begins.

At first, physical contact may be required for the release of these hormones. But eventually, researchers have found, conditioning primes the brain so that the hormones are released merely with the *feeling* or even just the thought of love and appreciation. Prolactin levels have been found to increase when mothers simply touch their infants, whether or not breast-feeding is involved. In the case of oxytocin, they have discovered, the process builds on itself, so that the longer the feelings endure, the more hormone is released, and the more the loving feelings grow.

The mixture of love, security, and oxytocin is nirvana for the infant, quieting her sense of stress or pain and intensifying her desire to hold onto her mother. By stimulating production of endorphins, moreover, oxytocin induces a natural "high" in both mother and child. Given these findings, Michel Odent's characterization of oxytocin as the "love hormone" is on the mark.

THE BREAST-FEEDING BOND

One cannot write about attachment and its role in brain building without a consideration of the importance of breast-feeding. The scientific evidence that proves the benefits of breast-feeding for physical health is overwhelming. Here are just a few examples:

- When the infant suckles from the breast, there is an outpouring of 19 different gastrointestinal hormones in both the mother and the infant, including cholesystokinin and gastrin, which stimulate growth of the baby's and mother's intestinal villi, increasing absorption of calories.
- If the lips of the infant touch the mother's nipple in the first hour of life, the mother will decide to keep her baby 100 minutes longer in her hospital room than mothers who lack this early contact.

- Mothers who breast-feed their babies in the first hour of life can breast-feed more easily for a longer period of time.
- Mothers who breast-feed for just three months can reduce their child's risk of sudden infant death syndrome, pneumonia, ear infection, allergies, obesity, meningitis, Crohn's disease, colitis, cirrhosis, and lymphoma.
- More than a hundred studies show that breast-feeding can delay or prevent the onset of diabetes in children.
- Formula-fed infants are 6.9 times more likely to develop dehydrating diarrhea than exclusively breast-fed infants.
- Breast-fed infants have better immunity, superior vision, and higher IQ than formula-fed counterparts.
- Australian research shows that breast-fed infants are at far less risk for asthma later in life than those fed by formula.
- Having been breast-fed as a child reduces breast cancer risk in women over 40 by 25 percent.
- Mothers who breast-feed, meanwhile, are at less risk for osteoporosis, cancer, and postpartum depression than mothers who don't.
- Breast-feeding confers on mothers an earlier return to prepregnant weight, delayed resumption of ovulation, resulting in increased child spacing, and reduced risk of ovarian and premenopausal breast cancer.

But breast-feeding may be most important for the role it plays in attachment. Proximity to the mother's heartbeat acts as a major signal for the child to turn off production of stress hormones. Indeed, studies show that a recorded heartbeat played in nurseries reduces crying by 40 to 50 percent. This heart-to-heart communication initiates in the mother the production of neurohormones associated with nurturing and love.

Whether a child is fed by breast or bottle, of course, what matters most is giving the child loving, undivided attention. Only in this way will the intimacy associated with attachment occur. When the experience of feeding is consistent and pleasurable, the baby will develop a healthy sense of trust in its mother, father, or other caretakers, and eventually a healthy sense of self.

CHANNELS OF ATTUNEMENT

During the first year of life, the infant tracks the mother's (or father's) face, and most especially the eyes, with great intensity. Amplified levels of interest in the mother's face produce elevated levels of corticotropin-releasing factor (CRF), a neuropeptide that stimulates the pituitary gland to produce endorphins. It also activates the autonomic nervous system, increasing oxygen consumption and energy metabolism.

As mother and father engage with their child in attachment behavior, they enter an organized dialogue in which both partners match emotional states and adjust their social attention to each other's signals. By setting her brain to the rhythms of her mother's brain, the baby ultimately learns the art of self-regulation; in other words, these early experiences enable the child, in future years, to rejoice in as well as control her emotional self.

The notion that such interaction sets the stage for the baby's emotional health is reinforced by research showing that brain cells change and grow in response to trains of stimuli (including thoughts and interpersonal reactions) that last just a fraction of a second at a time. Harry Chugani, a neurologist at the Children's Hospital of Michigan, has been comparing PET (positron-emission tomography) scans of the brains of eight apparently healthy orphaned Romanian children adopted by Americans with scans of a control group of children reared in normal family settings. In preliminary results, all eight orphaned children show evidence of abnormal metabolism in a specific area of the brain's temporal lobes thought to be involved in social functioning. "We can hypothesize that what we saw in these scans is related to neglect," says Chugani, "to a lack of maternal-infant interaction at a critical phase." The temporal lobes are closely tied to the frontal cortex, particularly the prefrontal cortex.

Synthesizing a vast amount of research, neuroscientist Allan N. Schore of the department of psychiatry and biobehavioral sciences at the UCLA School of Medicine has shown that during the first two years of life, the maturation of the brain is controlled by interaction with the caregiver. Through this intimate relationship, both subtle in nature and precise in timing, the baby's brain is literally tuned by the caregiver's brain to produce the correct neurotransmitters and hormones in the appropriate sequence; this entrainment, or patterning, determines the baby's brain architecture in a permanent and powerful way.

The brain region most receptive to maternal entrainment is the right hemisphere of the cerebral cortex; particularly sensitive is the region known as the orbitofrontal cortex, situated above the eyes.

Maturing first, the right brain structures modulate arousal and the spectrum of primary, nonverbal emotions. Especially rich in receptors for neurohormones such as serotonin, these structures control face recognition and emotions like excitement, elation, terror, and shame. By the time a child is 1 year of age, right brain regions, especially the orbitofrontal cortex, have begun to regulate arousal and process the interpersonal signal necessary for initiation of social interaction.

Maturing afterward, in the latter part of year 2, the left brain modulates verbal social skills and emotional behaviors. A well-toned left brain controls feelings of anxiety, interest, enjoyment, and guilt.

It is the success of this process that propels babies to venture out from mother's familiar orbit to the novelty of the world. Indeed, the emotionally responsive parent creates a secure base from which the mobile toddler can explore. To accomplish this, the child uses the parent's facial expression as a guide. Is it dangerous out there? Is it okay to roam? Mother's face provides the answer. If the mood is positive, the dynamic generates high levels of energy, instilling in the infant the sense of elation necessary for play and exploration; these behaviors, in turn, lead to the creation of novel situations that promote learning and the growth of the brain.

THE SOCIAL NERVOUS SYSTEM

The orbitofrontal cortex and the "love hormone," oxytocin, both so central to emotion are, perhaps logically, connected by evolutionary design. In a powerful theory proposed by neuropsychologist Stephen Porges, the connector is a third element—"the social nervous system," the conduit between the molecules of emotion, the heart, and the mind.

Director of the Institute for Child Study at the University of Maryland, Porges says the social nervous system emerged from the ancient autonomic nervous system, used by organisms from reptiles to humans to mediate breathing, pulse, appetite, fighting or fleeing, and the like. As the body's watchdog against danger, the autonomic nervous system is complementary to the central nervous system and the immune system. Maturing from early in gestation alongside the CNS, it sends its cellular envoys to the body's vital organs on one end, and to the brain on the other. Ever vigilant, the autonomic nervous system continually monitors our vital signs and communicates them to the brain. Through this system, the brain sends instructions to our vital organs, leaving the conscious mind free for other things, like playing with the baby.

The autonomic nervous system has two modes—referred to by Susan A. Greenfield of Oxford as "war" and "peace." In the war mode, functions needed for immediate survival take over while other, less vital ones shut down. The warrior on autopilot—or the *sympathetic* division of the autonomic nervous system—is part of us all.

The peace mode is governed by the *parasympathetic* nervous system. When not in immediate danger, the brain and nervous system keep heart rate slow and steady and let digestive juices flow.

Across the range of species, war and peace modes provide a balance, toggling back and forth as needed, depending on the requirements of the surrounding world. But when it comes to mammals, evolution has added complexity. The parasympathetic nervous system, functioning as a unit in lower creatures, branches into two paths that become ever more divergent as we move up the evolutionary chain.

In reptiles, the parasympathetic system regulates stomach enzymes as well as heart rate. But in mammals this channel—formed from the tenth cranial nerve, the longest in the body, and called the vagus—is a superhighway with two lanes. One lane, the old vegetative vagus, promotes the conservation of metabolic resources (parasympathetic). The other lane, the smart vagus, fosters the development of social behaviors by controlling facial expression, head tilt, sucking, swallowing, and vocalizing.

Studies in neuroanatomy strongly support Porges's "polyvagal" theory. Scientists know that the vegetative vagus lacks myelin—the white matter insulating most nerves, speeding impulses from one part of the body to the next. The smart vagus is myelinated, like the nerves of the CNS and the brain. If neurophysiological insults from trauma to abuse delay maturation of myelinated fibers, the smart vagus would be compromised and the vegetative vagus would prevail.

As with many other parts of the brain, the development of the vagus is wired initially through the parent-child dynamic. When damaging situations like neglect interfere with the normal functioning of the smart vagus, its less evolved partner, the vegetative vagus, will become dominant.

How does oxytocin fit in? With healthy infusions of oxytocin supplied during bonding, the individual will be conditioned to produce the hormone at times of intimacy. For a person to enjoy closeness, he or she must feel safe. Perceived security plus positive early bonding experiences promote the release of oxytocin and endorphins. Then during the act of lovemaking, the instinctive old vagus lights the fire of passion while the sophisticated smart vagus lays the groundwork for intimacy and romance.

INTERACTION VERSUS STIMULATION

When a baby is born, her brain is relatively undifferentiated. She has more neurons than she needs, but few connections among them. As the child grows, the brain becomes specialized. In part directed by genes and in part by experience, nerve cells connect across the signature gaps—the synapses—that enable them to communicate through the release of neurohormones.

From birth through age 3, generating synapses by the millions is the business of the brain—in fact, synapses are produced in such quantity that they come to exist in overabundance, like the neurons themselves.

The idea, says Daniel J. Siegel, director of the Center for Human Development in Los Angeles and an expert on the neurology of attachment, is that this "genetic overproduction of synapses" provides the brain with a "built-in mechanism to create the foundation from which experience will carve out the neural connections governing basic processes such as perception and motor activity." Disuse (as in "use it or lose it") or toxic conditions such as stress and abuse can lead to the elimination of existing synapses. The point is that circuits must be at least minimally stimulated to maintain their interconnections.

The yin and yang of brain construction, these two processes—creation and destruction of synapses—work in tandem. Neural connections are maintained or lost, created or altered. In the end, the unique neural network forged in part by genetics, in part by experience—especially the experience of bonding—forms the brain we end up with. It is the essence of who we are: in short, our mind.

To Siegel, the message implicit in the two simultaneous modes of brain sculpting is absolutely clear: "There is no need to bombard infants, young children, or possibly anyone, with excessive stimulation in hopes of building better brains. This is an unfortunate misinterpretation of the neurobiological literature—that somehow more is better. Parents and other caregivers can relax and stop worrying about providing huge amounts of sensory bombardment for their children." Synaptic overproduction exists to enable the brain to develop properly within the average environment, one that supplies the necessary, minimal amount of sensory stimulation to maintain the necessary portions of the brain. "More important than sensory stimulation in the early years of development," says Siegel, "are the patterns of *interaction* between child and caregiver. Interpersonal interaction, not sensory stimulation, is the key to healthy development."

Siegel points out that development of the brain occurs over a prolonged period of time, well beyond the early years of bonding and attachment. That is guaranteed, he says, because synapses are continually created in response to experience and because, through the end of puberty (when the brain takes adult form), the pruning process continues as well. But while the brain remains plastic well into adulthood, the basic neuronal patterns—the very circuits of the self—are forged by the crucible of attachment before age 3.

Later relationships, including therapeutic ones, can alter the patterns if the person is strongly motivated to change. But it is still those first relationships that establish most thoroughly, most persuasively, the essence of who we are.

LESSONS IN INTIMACY

By 18 months of age, children have developed a sense of evocative memory—including the ability to conjure a multisensory image of the parent's face, smell, voice, and style of attunement (or lack thereof) in times of stress. "Clearly," says Siegel, "relationships that are problematic will not serve to soothe the child as well as those that are secure." Parents who recognize the importance of relationships in their lives and who can reflect on ways in which the past has influenced their development tend to raise secure children. Parents who dismiss the importance of relationships and of interpersonal, emotional communication, may raise children who are insecure, emotionally labile, or antisocial.

Intimacy, like all lessons, can be taught poorly or well. Depending on the deftness of the teacher, a child may be disposed to patterns of health or disturbance throughout life. In practice, diverse parenting styles interact with numerous social, economic, and situational factors—from siblings to unemployment to war—to produce a wide range of outcomes.

According to classic attachment theory, the primary caregiver of a "securely attached child" responds appropriately and promptly to his or her emotional expressions. The caregiver maintains the child's level of arousal within a moderate range—high enough to maintain communication but not so intense as to bombard the child with stimulation the brain cannot handle and does not need. Securely attached children grow up with the qualities of empathy and compassion. Flexible and independent, they form deep friendships and know the meaning of emotions from sadness to love.

Whether verbal or nonverbal, attuned communication is always, inevitably, disrupted. The mother must sometimes pick up the telephone, after all. She must sometimes use the bathroom, get dressed, and sleep. It is not the disruption, but rather the repair of attunement that sets the scene for health. When parent-child communication is reestablished in a timely fashion, the baby will learn a sense of well-being, and confidence in the notion that missed opportunities for communication are just the stuff of life. The lesson here is that one may separate from a loved one to venture out in the world, comfortable in the knowledge that the object of love (and the love itself) remains.

Insecurely attached infants are subject to stress because caregivers, for whatever reason, cannot really connect with them. As a result of caregiver-infant misregulation or misattunement, the child ceases to rely on the parent as a partner in management of his emotional states. If a caregiver frequently rejects or ridicules the child's requests for comfort in stressful situations, the child may develop an enduring disposition to shame, and an internal model of the parent as rejecting and of himself as unworthy of help or comfort.

Shades of Insecurity

It was Tolstoy who said that happy families are all alike, but every unhappy family is unhappy in its own way. So it is with secure and insecure children, say attachment researchers who have broken security down by type:

- The insecure-avoidant child: product of a caregiver who routinely responds with low emotional affect. This parent is hesitant in approval as well as disapproval, and his or her tendency is to withdraw. On the level of the brain, inhibitory neurotransmitters outnumber excitatory neurotransmitters, limiting emotional expression and response. The infant develops a bias toward a state of withdrawal, characterized by heart rate deceleration, low levels of activity, and feelings of helplessness. This predisposition could become permanent if the brain is consistently deprived of socializing hormones and other input allowing the parasympathetic nervous system, associated with intimacy, to expand. As adults, these people will have a limited capacity to experience intense negative or positive affect and will tend to be overcontrolled.
- The insecure-resistant child: here the caregiver is intense, emo-

tionally volatile, unreliable, and prone to overstimulate his or her charge. While successfully serving as a source of high-intensity stimulation, this parent does not reduce that stimulation and thereby interferes with the infant's attempt to disengage. Due to this parent's volatility, the infant is unsure of what to expect. Because this parent does not function as a reliable, secure base for the refueling that enables exploration, the infant shows great distress at separation and, later on, is hard to calm down. On the level of the brain, the excitatory neurotransmitters outnumber the inhibitory neurotransmitters, and impulsivity is exaggerated as control is lost. These children develop a dominant sympathetic nervous system. They are often impulsive, with poor ability to regulate anger or stress.

- The anxiously attached child: often the product of parents who have been wounded by unresolved trauma or grief. Too preoccupied with their own internal problems to react to the needs of their children, these parents are volatile and unpredictable. Their children tend to have an especially "disorganized" form of insecure attachment. They may be hostile and violent, or disassociate from reality as they enter trancelike states. As adults they may suffer major psychiatric problems.

For the most attuned parents, the findings of neuroscience and birth psychology validate experience. For others among us, they provide answers we wish we'd had when we needed them most. One mother wrote to tell me of an experience validated by the research; her tragic story is so deeply moving and illustrative, I reprint part of it here:

My second son was damaged twice in utero. The first time was two weeks before his due date, when I was punched viciously in my abdomen by his father, an alcoholic. The second time was just before he was born, when a stranger molested me, pushing and shoving very hard against my stomach and my unborn baby for over half an hour, forcing me into labor. Even though I was due, the onset of labor was definitely induced by this abuse. My son was born limp and blue after a very rapid, out-of-control labor. Subsequently he was a cranky, sickly baby, unable to nurse properly and underweight. He had constant diarrhea and was subject to frequent colds.

This baby consistently pushed me away, physically and emotionally, leaving me dejected and defeated and setting up a reciprocal response, a loop, which fed itself. This lasted for two years, but then he began to "come into his own," eventually becoming a strong, robust, healthy boy. But this was merely physical. Emotionally, he had endless problems. He was labeled a troublemaker early on. He had a short attention span and did poorly all through school—even though by now I was happily remarried and stable. Although I loved him and I know he loved me, his need to act out his pain caused a lot of heartache, and our bond with each other was seriously frayed.

When he reached his teen years, his troubles exploded and his anger and resentment, especially toward me, became unbearable. I struggled to close the gap between us, and to cope with the widening chaos his behavior engendered. He was, at first, in a series of alternative schools. By the age of 15 he was running away from home, getting into fights, and stealing, and I could not keep him in school at all.

Last July his story ended at sixteen, when he stole a car for the seventh time and crashed it at high speed, killing both himself and his 16-year-old girlfriend. The night he died, I knew it was as if the agony of his birth had manifested all over again. He was squeezed and trapped in the car from all four sides, and had died from internal bleeding by the time the firemen had arrived with the jaws of life. My son was squeezed and brutally forced out of this life in the same way he was squeezed and forced into it. His short life was one of anger and pain, and an overwhelming sense of rejection.

It is only recently that I have come to see myself as a victim, too. Sexually abused by my father from before I can remember to the age of eleven, I brought to pregnancy and motherhood the same lack of boundaries and instinct for self-protection I had learned as a child, and thus had no way of protecting myself or my baby from damage. No one I've ever tried to tell my story to has understood or even believed me, but the new findings confirm what I know in my heart to be true and, although painful, are enabling me to understand my past and finally let go.

ATTACHMENT CHALLENGES FOR WORKING PARENTS

Classic attachment theory and the new findings in neuroscience seem impossibly, outrageously exacting in the modern world. As the *Journal of*

Marriage & the Family points out, dramatic changes in family life in the latter half of the twentieth century have meant that seven in ten mothers now work in the paid labor force, the majority of two-parent families are now dual-earner families, and three in ten households are now single-parent households.

Despite these revolutions in family life and despite continuing efforts toward gender equality, the task of child-rearing remains primarily the responsibility of mothers. To wit, 88 percent of single-parent families are headed by women, and in dual-earner families, mothers are responsible for 74 percent of the total parenting hours.

Given the extraordinary demands placed on mothers in the modern era, the question remains: How can they meet prescriptions for the selfless, constant mothering required to establish secure attachment and actualize the full potential of a child's brain? The research on bonding and attachment implies that good mothers must stay home or permanently damage their children. For most of today's moms, the bar is too high.

Even Klaus and Kennell, famous for defining maternal attachment, have broadened their purview to include paternal attachment. The father's attachment will be increased if he makes facial contact with the baby in the first three hours after birth, and if he experiences the child undressed (including the change of diapers) on a regular basis during the first three months of life.

Sociologist Sharon Hays of the University of Virginia suggests that attachment theory as proposed by its founders may need a major chiropractic adjustment to survive the realities of the day. "Human children are so underdeveloped at birth," she notes, "that initially they are completely dependent upon others for their care. Yet there is a wide range of possible methods to meet these requirements. As historical, cross-cultural research demonstrates, the way any given society responds to these requirements has little to do with maternal instincts, maternal hormones, or the absolute objective truth about what is best for children or child development. What does shape the child-rearing prescriptions and practices of any given society are the economic, political, and cultural structures of that society."

In many non-Western cultures, for instance, children are not raised exclusively by their mothers but rather by a parenting team, including the mothers of other children as well as older siblings. Classic attachment theory implies that these children suffer some degree of maternal deprivation, but there's no evidence that this is the case.

In light of such findings, many researchers have, in the new millennium, broadened their outlook. The changing culture requires that some babies accommodate a hierarchy of attachment objects. And the newest studies suggest that a group of loving caretakers (as opposed to just one) will also enable them to thrive.

My observations support the notion that children can bond with more than one individual—but not with everyone who comes along. Although a child in distress may turn to a range of available adults, true bonding and intimacy occurs with mother, father, and perhaps a few select members of the inner family circle.

HANDS-ON PARENTING

The bottom line is this: During the first three years of life, the most important information for successful development of the human brain is conveyed by the social environment. This underscores the importance of hands-on parenting. It cannot happen in day care settings, where overworked caretakers are responsible for many children at once. No amount of specialized training can substitute for the emotional connection between parent and child.

The latest findings in neuroscience, in fact, fly in the face of recent assertions that parents hardly matter at all. In her 1998 book, *The Nurture Assumption: Why Children Turn Out the Way They Do*, Judith Rich Harris, for one, has asserted that personality is shaped not by early experience with adult caretakers, but by peers. Citing personal experience with her easygoing biological daughter and difficult adoptive daughter, Harris says personality and character are shaped largely by the friendships children form and by genes. Her conclusions run counter to thousands of research studies in developmental psychology and the new findings in neuroscience and prenatal psychology. Amazingly, Harris totally ignored the fact that her own daughter and the daughter she adopted spent nine months gestating in two different wombs.

It is parents, not peers, who provide the youngest children with the scaffold for emotional health and the capacity for rich inner lives. At their core, attachment relationships enable the sharing of emotional states through nonverbal cues—tone of voice, gestures, facial expression, and the like. In healthy attachment, parents will naturally amplify positive emotions like joy and elation while reducing feelings of sadness and fear.

Daniel Siegel offers a list of five elements to foster emotional health and optimum development of the brain:

1. Collaboration: Secure relationships are based on collaborative communication. The nonverbal signals of an attuned parent and child
   are directly responsive in quality and timing with each other. Each
   person should come to "feel felt" by the other.
2. Reflective dialogue: Secure relationships involve the verbal sharing
   of internal experience, including emotions, perceptions, thoughts,
   and beliefs. By directly focusing on his or her state of mind, the
   adult teaches the child that subjective experience is important and
   can be shared.
3. Repair: When communication is disrupted, it must be repaired in
   an appropriate amount of time for the child to feel a sense of security, an emotional base.
4. Coherent narratives: Construction of stories about life events
   helps the child make sense of past, present, and future as well as
   the external and internal worlds in which we all live. I would add
   here that such verbal dialogues foster a positive backdrop of memories, thoughts, feelings, perceptions, and beliefs. The joint construction of stories about lived events helps the child and the adult
   to create family myths and a sense of shared identity.
5. Emotional communication: Sharing and amplifying positive emotions like joy and excitement create the foundation for a positive
   attitude. Connection during moments of negative emotion teaches
   the child he will not be emotionally abandoned, and that his pain
   will be soothed. "Such interactive forms of emotional communication," says Siegel, "may be at the core of how interpersonal
   relationships help to shape the ongoing emotional and social development for the growing mind."

The child who has established healthy attachment to one or more loving adults has learned life's most valued lessons: how to feel feeling and
how to self-reflect. These two traits are the heart of empathic development. They are key to the capacity for compassion, joy, sadness, and
love. And there is more. The healthy child has also learned flexibility, the
capacity to take in a complex array of internal and external information,
sort through it, and make responses that are not merely reflexive and
impulsive but, instead, reasoned. Not surprisingly, say brain scientists,
the trait Siegel calls response flexibility appears to be mediated by the orbitofrontal region of the brain.

The unique relationship between parent and child blossoms during
the first three years of life. It is, after all, through constant caretaking—
the process of looking after and being looked after—that the mother-

child and father-child connections are ultimately formed. Conscious parents spend time with their children, nurture their children, protect their children, and play with their children. They develop a natural knowledge of their infants' needs and a significantly greater ability to facilitate their growth.

SUMMING UP

From the earliest moments following birth, postnatal bonding continues seamlessly the process of prenatal bonding. The emotional experience of the infant develops in tune with input from mother and father. The circuits created through this parent-child attunement will later define a person's ability to relate to others.

Modern parents are deluged with reams of conflicting information on how to raise children. But in the twenty-first century, findings from neurobiology point the way: relationships with a select group of adults, not sensory flooding, are the most important form of experience for the growing mind.

Parents aware of the research can apply these findings when bonding with their baby, positively imparting lifelong traits like empathy, independence, and the ability to love. By meeting the physical, intellectual, emotional, and moral needs of their children in predictable, empathetic, and loving ways, parents help those children actualize their full human potential. When such children grow up they will return to the world—many times over—the goodness they received.

Key Parenting Points

- In the choreography of attachment, the caregiver's expressive face, voice, and touch are all important.
- Using verbal and nonverbal cues, parents must strive to enhance feelings of joy while reducing sadness and shame.
- Take your cues from your baby.
- The more time you spend with your baby during the first two years of life, the better.
- Remind yourself of Siegel's five points weekly or, even better, put them on your fridge. When they are as natural as breathing, you'll know you have arrived as a parent.

8

—∿—

Adoption and the Search
for Identity

"I am adopted. You wouldn't know it to meet me. To all outward appearances, I am a writer, a married woman, a mother,
a theater buff, an animal fanatic—yes, I can pass. But locked
within me there is an adopted child who stirs guilty and ambivalent even as I write these words. An adopted child can
never grow up. Who ever heard of an adopted adult?"

—Betty Jean Lifton,
Twice Born: Memoirs of an Adopted Daughter

Adoptees are like everyone else, but more so. The questions they ask—
Who am I? Where do I come from? Do I belong here?—are questions
every child asks. But for adoptees, the answers often feel like a matter of
life and death.

In a recent issue of *Adoption News*, a woman described the experience
of giving birth in a small New Zealand Hospital where many of the
mothers were unmarried. "About half the babies were going home, like
mine," she recalled. "The other half were to be put up for adoption. I
shall never forget those cries. The nurse said, 'All I can think of are 'p'
words: pleading, plaintive, like they had already given up.'"

If you've read up to this point, the nurse's observation won't come as
much of a surprise. Given the intimate bond between the unborn child
and his mother, separation at birth must be traumatic. The unborn child
has, over nine months' gestation, established an intimate bond with his
mother. He has listened to her heartbeat and voice for at least the last
three months; he knows her movements, her touch, her odor, and most
important, her feelings. As a neonate, he recognizes and tunes in to his

mother after birth, even if only for moments. When, in a flash, she is gone, the newborn feels disoriented, shocked, alone.

Imagine one day going to sleep in your midtown apartment and waking up the next morning in the Kalahari Desert. Your shock would be similar to what the newly adopted child experiences as he tries to relate to his new mother—a woman with a strange new voice, rhythms, moods, and feelings. No matter how loving the new parents are, the newborn experiences sensations of confusion and, on some level, abandonment and grief.

The notion that adoptees face special problems as a circumstance of birth fits neatly with the themes of this book. Indeed, adoptees are living proof of the concepts central to *Tomorrow's Baby*—that, whether we are adopted or not, our earliest experiences have an enduring, organizing effect on personality and the brain.

In our society it is not politically correct to speak of adopted children as different from natural children in any way. Yet experts who have worked in the field—and the adopted themselves—say they are. "I'm always being asked why separation from a birth mother would affect a newborn baby," says psychologist Nancy Verrier, "and I have to admit that I had, at one time, asked the same question myself. Now, however, having had personal experience with adoption and being more acquainted with pre- and perinatal psychology, I believe the more appropriate question to be, 'Why *wouldn't* the separation from the mother to whom he/she was connected for nine months affect an infant?'"

ADOPTION STUDIES

Theories about adoptees would be easy to dismiss were they based solely on anecdote and clinical observation. But lately, more formal research has been substantiating these theories.

In one set of studies, researchers have shown that newborns from diverse cultures arrive with unique expectations from the start. T. Berry Brazelton, one of the most enlightened "baby doctors" in America, has pointed out the differences in behavior and reactivity to stimuli between Asian and African babies. A baby from a distinct culture pool is likely to arrive with characteristic rhythms and needs in terms of touch, tone of voice, food, and more.

Such findings have been bolstered by researchers at the Listening Centre in Toronto. Of 400 children who have come to the center for help, reports Paul Madaule, the director of the center, 21 percent were adopted. This is two and a half times higher than the proportion of adopted children in Ontario at large.

"The love and nurturing of the adoptive parents can in some cases go a long way to help the child heal her early scars," says Madaule. "But in numerous situations, genuine affection and love do not seem to be sufficient."

Madaule and colleagues found that adoptees at the Listening Centre shared some common traits, including:

- A sense of inner void
- A difficult social adjustment
- Difficulty relating to the adoptive mother
- A problem with authority figures
- Lack of physical and/or emotional closeness as evidenced by dislike of physical signs of affection

"The most common of these characteristics is an ambivalent mother-child relationship," says Madaule. "The child usually seeks her attention in a way that provokes negative reactions from the mother. In other words, the child asks the mother to reject him over and over again."

Madaule's therapeutic goal is to help adoptive parents understand the dynamic so they can cope.

Scores of other researchers have studied the sense of loss and rejection adoptees report well into adulthood, along with the complex of fears that often defines their relationships with adoptive parents and, by extension, the world. In her study of adopted adults, for instance, Verrier found that they consistently reported a loss of their sense of self. Most described hiding their real self while projecting a false, generally exaggerated persona loathe to express hostility or anger for fear of rejection. As one woman in the study put it, "I don't want people to know how insecure I feel. Not letting people know keeps me more in control." Verrier says her subjects feel a sense of "bodily incompleteness"—a lack of wholeness that might be compared to the pain of a phantom limb.

Moreover, whether or not the adoptee has been told of the adoption, he knows, deep down, that there is a secret surrounding his birth. There is often a sense of "not fitting in," as well as the feeling that bad behavior may lead to banishment. After all, if your own mother could unload you, a stranger might surely do the same.

Numerous studies show that adopted children and adolescents are referred to therapy far more frequently than counterparts still with their birth families. A number of teams have followed such children over time. In Sweden, researchers found that adoptees displaying behavior problems at age 11 had no such problems at 15. But the hiatus was just temporary. Investigating National Health Insurance records of 2,323 adopted Swedish adults, investigators found among them an overrepresentation of psychiatric illnesses, particularly alcohol and drug abuse and personality disorders, when compared with non-adopted controls. A Texas study compared 41 adoptees with 2,991 non-adopted children and found that adopted youngsters exceeded their non-adopted peers in frequency of conduct problems, personality problems, and delinquency. Boys experienced more maladjustment than girls. Male adoptees also suffered a higher proportion of neurosis than male non-adoptees. Most adoptees, of course, become well-adjusted adults. Nonetheless, the research indicates that in order for that to happen, adoptees need more special care and affection than non-adoptees because they were hurt more.

In a recent study, University of Ottawa researchers followed adoptees and non-adoptees referred for psychiatric care over the course of five years. The researchers discovered that adoptees seen as children suffered significantly higher rates of the most serious problems: conduct disorder, socialized aggression, attention deficit disorder, anxiety, psychosis, hyperactivity, and depression. But five years after the initial referral, adoptees and non-adoptees had both improved with therapy. What's more, the researchers found no difference between the two groups in terms of clinical diagnosis or social adaptation. Compared with controls, adoptees scored higher on a behavior scale rated by parents. Those adopted by 6 months of age were found to have higher psychosocial functioning, overall, suggesting that the earlier the attachment, the healthier the development of the brain and personality.

M. David Kirk, a noted expert on adoption and the father of four adopted children, illustrates the point with a story about his 5-year-old daughter, who had started to wet her bed and have nightmares after she received a book about Cinderella. From the beginning, the mother sensed that the story somehow undermined her own parental position, but the more she hesitated to read it, the more the little girl demanded to hear it—virtually every night. Finally, the child made the connection between the book and her nighttime problems abundantly clear. "Mommy," she said, "if I had a stepmother, what would she do to me? Would she be cruel?" The mother instantly took the question as a cue. "My dear," she said, "I too am someone like a stepmother. I was unable to bear you in my body, but I love you very, very much. Perhaps there are stepmothers who are bad, who would be mean to their children. Cinderella's stepmother was a very bad mother, but only because she did not love Cinderella." There was a pause as the little girl played with her toys. Then the child looked up and said, "Now I can have a good dream." And she did. The nightmares and the bed-wetting abruptly ceased.

Significantly, the Ottawa researchers found, adoptees tended to leave home much earlier than non-adopted counterparts. This pattern makes sense when you realize that children given up for adoption are often moved many times from foster home to foster home before they are finally adopted. Leaving home at a younger age seems unconsciously to repeat the early pattern and is probably also an expression of the adoptees' not feeling as deeply attached to their adoptive parents as other children.

The researchers note that moving out was not associated with age at adoption. The suggestion, they conclude, is that "although early adoption may have protected adoptees against serious pathology, it did not guarantee a lasting relationship between these children and their adoptive parents."

BABIES AND BIRTH MOTHERS

It is, of course, not only the separation from the mother and the subsequent feeling of abandonment that is responsible for the statistically higher incidence of problems among adoptees. It stands to reason that pregnant mothers who, for various reasons, contemplate placing their children for adoption following the birth will, generally speaking, be exposed to more stress than mothers who have no such disturbing thoughts.

The former group is largely composed of single, poor, undereducated teenagers. They may come from dysfunctional families. As a group, they are immature and insecure. The father of the child may be a casual sexual partner as poorly prepared for the responsibilities of parenthood as the mother herself.

Picture the emotional and hormonal turmoil experienced by a child in the womb of such a mother. How much time and energy will this unwed, unhappy, and distraught woman spend communicating lovingly with her unborn child? How much care will she take to rest or avoid alcohol and drugs?

Having spoken to many adoptees, I have come to the conclusion that mothers who surrender their babies fall into two categories. The first group feel overwhelmed by their pregnancy; as they decide (or are forced by parents or others to decide) to cede the baby, they emotionally withdraw from their unborn child. Children born to these mothers, I've found, rarely care to search for them as adults.

The second category is made up of birth mothers who are usually more stable, mature, and determined to succeed in the world. They love their unborn child and will go to great lengths to ensure as good a future for this child as possible. They will opt for private and open adoption wherever possible. When older and more settled, they will often search for and be searched for by their grown-up children.

ADOPTIVE PARENTS

Adoptive parents, like their adopted children, have not had an easy time of it either. After failing to conceive a child, they may suffer mutual blame and disappointment. Often one partner, usually the wife, is more interested in having a child than the other. If difficulties arise with the adopted child, the hesitant spouse may withdraw with an attitude of, "You wanted her, you look after her."

Knowledge that a biological parent was a drug addict, an alcoholic, or unwed may color the adopted parents' perception of behavior on the part of the adopted child. Even if they possess no negative information about the birth parents, adoptive parents are likely to fantasize about them. And these fantasies are rarely positive, since adoptive parents who long for a child have a hard time comprehending a woman who would willingly part from hers.

Adoptive parents are not immune to the problems their adopted children are struggling with. They worry about the child's loyalty—When she grows up will she leave us and forsake us for her "real" parents? To prevent this feared outcome, they may conceal the true origins of the child, as, for example, happened to Oedipus. And we know how tragically that story ended. Family secrets always lead to trouble, and fears we avoid dealing with will ambush us when we least expect it.

Another pitfall that adoptive parents should steer clear of is making the child feel grateful for having been "saved" from a dreadful fate. Adoptees, like biological children, resent being told how much their parents sacrificed for them. This is emotional blackmail and the child reacts by disguising his anger under a mask of dutiful compliance or becomes progressively more rebellious.

Finally, a "mixed" family that combines biological and adopted children faces similar problems to the ones encountered by "blended" families—that is, where both partners were previously married, had children, and now live with "his" and "hers" under one roof. For these arrangements to succeed requires a lot of work, patience, and honest communication by both partners.

ADOPTION AND ATTACHMENT

Despite the challenges, adoptive families aware of the problems inherent in adoption can usually thrive. In instance after instance, parents who take the time to understand their adoptive children and give them the extra time they need forge powerful bonds with them. "We have never had a biological child, so I don't know for sure whether I love him differently because he is adopted," one mother told me. "But I do know that when I look at him and tears of joy and relief start to flow, I suspect I love him more because of how he came to us. As I marvel at this little life I did not bring into the world, I whisper into his tiny ear, 'Thank you for coming into our lives. It is such a privilege to be your mother.'"

This adoptive new mother, so ready and eager to embrace her new child, may find he is emotionally unavailable at first. At Toronto's Listening Centre, therapists like Paul Madaule help adoptive parents break through. "It is not you the child tries to reach, but through you, the person by whom he has been abandoned. Therefore, there is nothing to feel bad or guilty about," Madaule tells his adoptive mothers. Then the next step: "There is something in your son that is hurting, and you are the first person in whom he can confide the pain. Because there are no words to describe such early memories, expressing the pain translates into being a pain."

When she understands the rejection-seeking behavior of her baby as his way of seeking her love, the adoptive mother assumes a new role. "The hated and rejected mother quickly becomes the healer," says Madaule, the one who is able to ease the child's pain.

Wendy McCord, a Phoenix psychotherapist specializing in early trauma and loss, advises adoptive parents to verbally acknowledge the passage from birth to adoptive parents from the start. Many adoptive parents fear such revelations, as if because a child knows she is adopted her loyalties will be divided. I really believe that these fears are misplaced. Years ago people wouldn't tell children they were adopted, so the children grow up sensing something terribly wrong with themselves. When they eventually found out the truth—because sooner or later they always do—they were shocked and felt betrayed. In the long run it helps to know who you are by knowing where you came from. By the way, I think the same goes for children conceived by in vitro fertilization (IVF), artificial insemination, and other technological aids.

The most important thing adoptive parents can do, says McCord, is empathize with their child. "Babies who have been separated from their mothers do have to mourn," she says, "and they do have to be sick. But if they have someone to understand them, they can heal."

Because adoption is complex, I summarize the challenges facing adopted children:

- They experience a stressful pregnancy.
- They may be deprived of prenatal communication and bonding.
- They may experience rejection prenatally.
- At birth or soon thereafter they feel abandoned by their mothers.
- They may spend some time with a variety of caregivers, which further adds to their feelings of rejection and confusion.
- By the time they arrive in their adoptive family, they may be in a state of withdrawal and shock.
- Their early experiences will cast a long shadow over their future, making them exquisitely sensitive to issues of rejection, abandonment, and trust.
- They may feel that their adoptive parents will keep them only if they live up to their expectations. This will predispose adoptees to develop a false, people-pleasing outer self, or an antisocial violent self, or a self-destructive self.
- Many, though not all, adoptees feel incomplete. They have a deep yearning, and ache in their souls, for union with *mother* and reconnecting with their heritage.

THE MOST CHALLENGING ADOPTIONS

Adoptees are exposed to stress and deprived of bonding in the womb and are then traumatized in the hours and days after birth by separation from the only mother they have known. These elements in themselves offer enough of a challenge, but the situation is especially damaging if the new baby experiences neglect or abuse at the hands of a birth parent or in a series of foster homes.

In the past it was not unusual for infants to be shunted from one substitute caregiver to another for several months or years before adoption. Apart from the fact that not all foster parents are ideal (just as not all birth parents are ideal), passing a child from person to person like a hot potato will produce considerable emotional damage to that child.

The consequences are sometimes gravest for families who adopt children out of institutions in Eastern Europe, specifically Romania and the former USSR. While many societies place abandoned children in orphanages, the Eastern European institutions are unique in their level of neglect. Left isolated in their cribs for eighteen or twenty hours a day, the babies who land in these warehouses receive stimulation only when intermittently changed and fed. Without interaction, let alone love, the children who pass through these gates rarely emerge emotionally intact. In fact, they are very much like the foundling home children studied by Rene Spitz.

When Americans began adopting these babies—some 20,000 in the past decade—they discovered disturbances that even large doses of love and attention could not easily overcome. Inmates of the Eastern European orphanages, bereft of any true relationships, are poster children for attachment disorder. Earmarks of the disorder may include indifference toward parents paired with indiscriminate affection for strangers; difficulty in forming friendships; inability to catch emotional cues; tendency to volatility or even violence; and, in the most extreme cases, a life of antisocial behavior and crime. Working with these children, therapists have been able to undo some of the damage, particularly with those who spent only a few months (as opposed to years) in an orphanage.

The toughest adoption cases are so problematic because of proven, early damage to the brain. James W. Prescott, former health scientist administrator of the Developmental Behavioral Biology Program at the National Institute of Child Health and Human Development, notes that Romanian institutions produce children with deep brain "spiking" (high-voltage electrical discharges); malformed brain cells in the cortex and cerebellum; and abnormal levels of serotonin, associated with depression and violence.

These abnormalities have long been associated with the loss of mother love, says Prescott. Associated with sensory deprivation, the syndrome—known as somatosensory affectional deprivation—emerges when infants are deprived of body touch and body movement. "Without this very important first physical affectional bonding with mother that is encoded and programmed in the developing brain of the infant/child, there is no brain template to support future affectional bonds." The biggest "shame and disgrace," says Prescott, is that scientific information about the disorder and associated treatments are not routinely made available to adoptive parents.

In the case of especially difficult adoptions, it has been a trend, in recent years, for some parents to give the children back. Some 2 percent of all American adoptions fail each year. For older children with special needs the numbers are far higher—10 percent for those between ages 2 and 12, and 24 percent for those between ages 12 and 17. Part of the problem has been lack of disclosure—agencies often hide the worst aspects of a child's medical history, or the fact that he or she has been "returned" by an adoptive family. Recently, U.S. courts have begun to recognize the concept of "wrongful" adoption, which holds agencies responsible if they place children without disclosing health background or history.

To prevent such outcomes, at least in part, adoption agencies are trying to do a more thorough job. In Cherry Hill, N.J., for instance, the Golden Cradle Adoption Agency asks birth mothers for a ten-page medical history detailing everything from allergies to use of drugs.

SEARCH FOR ROOTS

Rather than blame their birth parents for rejecting them, adoptees tend to blame themselves. They think, if I had been a boy, or a girl, or if I had been stronger, bigger, healthier, smarter, more attractive—my parents would have kept me. These children conclude that there was, and is, something wrong with them. This feeling, naturally, detracts from their self-esteem.

When a child is separated from his or her mother, he or she is also cut off from the trunk of the family's past history, from ancestors and heritage. Such children grow up feeling restless and rootless. They search crowds for the face of their imagined mother and wait patiently for the Prince Charming of a father to appear at their doorstep and sweep them off their feet. Usually, some major life event such as pregnancy, the death of an adoptive parent, or entering therapy will precipitate the actual search, as the following account illustrates.

"When I got engaged, I decided to visit my adoptive family to find out about my background, to try to get any bit of information that might help in my search," one adoptee relates. "My mother cried and my father got angry. They didn't understand my need to know. I told them that I felt like a piece of me was missing. They were offended and asked why they couldn't fill those needs. They weren't able to see that this wasn't something about them, it was about *my* beginning."

"It's not an accident that I became more active in my search after my adopted father passed away," says another adoptee. "I didn't want to face his hurt and anger, and I didn't want to search behind his back. I needed a lot of support and encouragement to pursue my search, and I received that from my husband. He was behind me all the way and helped me to keep going when things looked hopeless. He knew my pain. He also knew that I am a person who likes to work on a project or goal. Since I had recently passed my licensing exam, I was out of goals. Finding my birth mother seemed like a good project to take on. Plus, with a Ph.D. after my name, I felt my birth mother would find me 'presentable.'"

"My searching took many routes, and I finally ended up with my birth mother's telephone number," yet another adoptee relates. "I dialed the phone. The call was transferred. My birth mother was on the other end. In one long, rushed, tearful sentence I stated my name, my birth date, my hometown, and that I thought she was my birth mother. A moment of silence on the line, Then sobs. Yes, she was my birth mother. And how was I? Was I okay? More sobs from both of us. Yes, I was okay.

"We said we would write to each other and send pictures. We both wrote and mailed our notes to each other that day. She sent a picture of herself with her youngest son, my half brother. I studied it daily. We made plans to meet, and my brother and I spoke and met. Now the three of us continue to stay in contact. We all feel like we have known each other for longer than three years. For me, I feel like I have come home. I feel connected and centered. Much of my pain has been relieved. I know who I look like. I now have a place in the world."

According to a major study conducted in Los Angeles, the most frequent reason for relinquishing a child was that the mother was unmarried and wanted the child to be raised in a family. Fifty percent of the birth parents interviewed said that they continued to have feelings of loss, pain, and mourning over the child they gave up for adoption. "Whenever I see a girl my daughter's age I wonder whether she is my daughter," one birth mother said. Said another, "I pray that the child will not hate me."

Some 95 percent of birth parents in the study wished to update the information about themselves contained in agency birth records. They wanted their children to know that they were no longer the mixed-up teenagers of the agency files but rather respected citizens with families of their own. Most important, they wanted their children to know that they still cared about them. When asked if they would be interested in a reunion with the child they relinquished, 82 percent of those interviewed said yes, if the adoptee desired to meet them. Eighty-seven percent stated that they did not wish to hurt the adoptive parent. None expected to develop a parental relationship with their children.

A word about the birth father. Where information is available, he is often depicted as a callous, irresponsible person who was "sowing wild oats" and who cared little about his partner or the child. Yet some data show that the unmarried father demonstrates a greater concern for the woman he impregnated than had previously been recognized. You can imagine what a difference knowing that would make to his child.

THE NEW ADOPTION PARADIGM

Based on such data, I concur with experts like Suzanne Arms, author of *To Love and Let Go*, who advocates open adoptions wherever possible. "There will always be adoptions because there will always be some children whose parents cannot provide for them," Arms says. "Adoption can literally save lives, give people a second chance, and bring much joy into the world. We certainly should be able to have the kinds of adoptions that everyone can live with without remorse."

Arms points out that the standards of adoption we now take for granted arose from within a society different from today's. "Adoption in a world where unmarried women who became pregnant were considered immoral and dangerous to society, and where children of such unions were branded illegitimate, had to reflect those uncompassionate attitudes," she says. "It is no wonder that early maternity hospitals and homes for unwed mothers went to great lengths to hide the identities of the women or that names were changed on birth certificates and files kept under lock and key. Women and children deserved to be protected from stigma. They had no economic or political power, and it was nearly impossible for children born out of wedlock or their mothers to move freely in the world if their background was made known." While the stigma has vastly diminished, the tradition of secrecy is hard to change.

Yet change it must. The first step toward a more humane adoption is to make pregnancy and birth as positive as possible for both the birth mother and her newborn. The birth mother must have time alone with her new baby to consider her decision before transfer—and that transfer should be more than a cold transaction. It should be an entrustment ceremony, a ritualized handing over of the baby from his first mother and the home within her body to the welcoming arms of the adoptive family. The birth mother should explain to the child that these people will be his new parents but she will always love him.

Ideally, the new parents should emotionally adopt the mother, and the father if he is present, along with the child, as early in the pregnancy as possible. A birth mother needs to feel that she is making the right decision, and the earlier her child starts to bond prenatally to the adoptive parents, the better.

SUMMING UP

Adoption is the optimal solution for children who must be relinquished by their birth mothers. But it is a complex solution whose success can be greatly enhanced if the adoptive parents carefully examine their motives for adopting. To overcome the risks and deepen their relationship with the child, adoptive parents must empathize with the child's loss of his or her birth mother and put extra energy into the process of bonding and attachment.

Key Parenting Points

To meet these challenges, adoptive parents must:

- Be enthusiastic about adoption as a couple.
- Resolve their feelings about infertility.
- Empathize with and tune in to the adopted infant's special state of shock and bewilderment, especially when she first arrives.
- Speak to the child about what he is feeling and give him the extra care, cuddling, and patient attention he requires.
- Examine their attitudes toward the biological parents and eliminate any thoughts that they had somehow "contaminated" the adoptee.
- Tell the adoptee, at an appropriate time but definitely before the age of 5, that he or she is adopted.
- Be unconcerned about the loyalty of the adopted child. Children can have loving relationships with many people: parents, grandparents, uncles, aunts, cousins, and so on. In divorced families, they frequently acquire two sets of parents. The same will apply

should a biological mother or father step forward or be found. Adoptive parents should trust the bond they have created with their adoptive child, and the rest will take care of itself.

- Accept with equanimity an adopted child's decision, later in life, to seek his or her birth mother or father. This is not an expression of lack of love or appreciation for the adoptive parents. Rather, it is a natural function of being human.

9

Experience As Architect
of the Brain

What do babies know when they are born? How do they learn about the world, and how soon? Are they born innately good or bad? Do they know they are human from virtually the moment of birth? Do they learn to speak only from caring parents, or is this knowledge inborn, as intrinsic to the biology of humans as eyes, kidneys, or a brain?

Through the centuries, as humans tried to define infant consciousness, no one applied the scientific method to his subject until the Swiss psychologist Jean Piaget. Working with his psychologist wife, Valentine, Piaget recorded the actions of his own three children in minute detail, then analyzed the results. Based on this work, Piaget proposed four discrete stages of early development, including "sensorimotor" (birth to age 2), characterized by the ability to differentiate between the self and the environment, and "preoperational" (ages 2 to 7), defined by the ability to name objects with words. Logical thought was not possible until age 7, said Piaget, and abstraction out of reach until age 12.

Piaget revolutionized theories of child development—he was the first to suggest that we are born with plastic brains that develop through exploration of the environment. But today we know Piaget got much of it wrong. He viewed the baby·and toddler as especially egocentric, whereas new research shows babies are empathetic and other-directed. He felt infants operated by the dictum "out of sight, out of mind," while we now know that babies remember people and events outside their immediate sphere of perception. He said babies were more or less like goldfish, with little knowledge of the way the world works, yet new studies indi-

cate that as early as 3 months of age babies intuitively grasp such concepts as gravity—they realize that a poorly balanced book will fall off a
shelf. Piaget separated cognitive and emotional development into two
separate realms, yet we now know that the two work in tandem. And
though Piaget's notion of stages represented an improvement over past
concepts, its essentially linear view—with brain development progress-
ing steadily from birth to adulthood—missed the mark: the latest studies show that brain development and associated learning are decidedly
nonlinear. Instead of a consistent learning curve, humans have been
hard-wired for learning explosions, providing windows of opportunities
encompassing a different set of knowledge and skills.

ROLL THE VIDEOTAPE

Most people don't realize that the technology enabling scientists to truly
study infants, objectively measuring their abilities and state of consciousness, is something we now take for granted—videotape. Captur-
ing literally millions of details previously under the radar of scientific
observation, video revealed the infant's true nature as never before.

The revolution in knowledge started inauspiciously at the University
of Washington in 1977, when a young developmental psychologist
named Andrew Meltzoff used a video camera to test the then conven-
tional wisdom: the notion that babies couldn't really see, that they could
glean no meaning from events around them, that for the first months of
life what some parents claimed was a smile was, in actuality, gas.

His simple experiment was to see if babies had a glimmer of their humanity. To find the answer, he taped babies between 12 and 21 days of
age as they imitated adult facial expressions. Consistently, he found, infants could imitate tongue protrusion, mouth opening, and lip pursing.
He later extended the research to include newborns. Setting up a lab
next to the labor room in a local hospital, he asked the staff to call him
when a baby was about to be born. Rushing to the hospital at any hour of
the day or night, he discovered that newborns as young as 42 minutes
could imitate adults.

These findings have since been replicated in more than a dozen laboratories and studies. Moreover, several features of the studies demonstrate that these behaviors are the product of inferencelike processes
and are not merely reflexive. Very young infants gaze at the faces of
adults and vocalize and gesture in a way that seems tuned to the vocalizations and gestures of the adults. They smile when adults smile and

move in rhythm with them. When the infant's predictions about the other person's response are violated—when, for example, a mother reacts to her baby's cooing with a sad face, the baby becomes distinctly distressed.

Imitation is a particularly interesting and potent behavior because it implies recognition of the similarities between the self and the other, the imitator and the imitated. Imitation suggests an innate link between conduct and intention, and an astonishing penchant for social communication.

That communication, the studies show, is especially fluid when the adult's tone of voice is laced with loving attention, inviting the child to interact and respond. A child who hears a soft, melodious, "What did we do yesterday? What did we see?" will listen more to a parent than a child who hears a cold, bossy, "Stop that" or "Come here!"

AFFIRMATIVE ACTION

A three-year-old girl approaches her busy mother with blocks that keep toppling over. Distressed and a bit cranky, the girl demands her mother's immediate attention.

"Why are you so upset?" the mother asks the little girl, smiling and rubbing her back.

"I can't do it," the girl says.

The mother puts down her work and leans over to help. "If you put the blocks on top of the table instead of the carpet, they will stay put," she says. The little girl tries it, only to have the blocks topple again. "I'll help you as soon as I finish this," the mother says. She gets only this far when her daughter hurls the pieces to the floor. The mother looks at her, then goes over and hugs her. "Those building blocks made you mad. It's okay, we'll assemble them later. Right now, can you help me put my work away?" First reluctantly, then with more enthusiasm, the child helps her mother gather papers, and a smile covers her face.

During the course of this interaction, the little girl's mother has unknowingly been giving her lessons in empathy, understanding, cooperation, respect, and self-discipline. If these experiences are consistent over her childhood, the little girl will learn to view herself as competent, appreciated, and loved. Throughout her life this child will expect others to listen when she speaks, and she will listen in return.

Now let's play the scene again, but this time with a different mother.

A three-year-old girl approaches her busy mother with some building blocks that keep toppling over. Distressed and a bit cranky, the girl demands her mother's immediate attention.

Without looking up, the mother says, "Stop that whining—I've got enough to do without listening to you right now. Don't you see I'm busy?" The child walks away and hurls the pieces to the floor. The mother continues what she's doing. The little girl screams louder, then runs to her room and slams the door.

If such experiences occur repeatedly, this mother will, through her words and actions, teach her child that her needs are secondary, her feelings don't matter, and that when she feels bad, nobody cares. Such a child is likely to develop low self-esteem and may become either socially withdrawn or overly aggressive.

The latest findings prove that the kind of caregiving parents provide has far more impact on brain development than we ever thought possible. The new research demonstrates that language acquisition, cognition, and intelligence are mutually reinforcing and depend on the relationship between child and caregiver. What oxygen is to the brain, words spoken gently, respectfully, and lovingly are to the young mind.

BRAIN BUILDING

This makes sense in light of what we know about the brain. Even before birth, it has formed a template for personality, aptitudes, and skills. But despite all this prenatal growth and definition, the brain is far from complete. Still a work in progress, it will go through enormous change based on interaction with the external environment from birth through age 3.

The plasticity of the brain is evolution's gift to humanity. With an unfinished brain, human babies have the chance to develop those qualities and attributes they need to survive in their particular part of the world. Honed to perfection by interaction with its specific environment, the human brain is truly ecological. More complex than sheer hard-wiring by genes would ever allow, the human brain has far better odds of surviving and adapting than the brains of other species.

Brain building after birth is all about networking—the means by which brain cells interconnect and communicate with each other. Before birth, experience helps to lay down the brain's primary circuits, forming a foundation for development; after birth, the networking activity moves to increasingly higher levels of the cerebral cortex, fine-tuning sensory

perception, emotional balance, cognitive skills, and interpersonal relationships.

The process is rooted, in part, in the basic biology of cells. The neurons, or nerve cells, making up the brain communicate through electrical signals traveling down the length of the nerve cell. With the help of
neurotransmitters such as serotonin, these signals travel across the
synapse from one cell to another, strengthening the neural pathways
used most frequently.

This complex network of connections determines the fluidity of our
thought, the strength of our talents, and the happiness or anxiety with
which we take on the world. And simply, yet profoundly, experience
shapes the way the brain's circuits form. A single cell can connect with
as many as 15,000 other cells. The more synapses a person has, the
more complex and varied his neural networks and the brighter and more
creative he will be.

From birth through age 3, the brain is a synapse factory, producing
connections at a rapid pace. But nature does more than just build up the
brain. Like a master sculptor chiseling at a block of clay, experience
shapes the final product through childhood and adolescence by win-
nowing down the connections as well. From ages 3 to 10, synapses are
produced and destroyed at just about the same pace. After age 10, elimination outweighs production.

By the time he is 3, your baby's brain has formed about 1,000 trillion
synapses—about twice as many as his pediatrician has. The infant's
brain is superdense, primed not just to learn and expand but also to pare
down neurons not being used. But how does the brain know which connections to keep and which ones to slough off? When a connection is
used repeatedly, it becomes permanent. By contrast, a connection used
infrequently is abandoned. Children who are rarely spoken to, read to, or
played with in their early years will develop poor language skills and,
more important, poor social skills.

A neural circuit in your baby's brain is like a narrow footpath in the
forest. Increased traffic will widen the path, making it easier and faster
to traverse. The stronger and more established pathways will survive,
while those untraveled will eventually atrophy and disappear.

But there's more: Although Piaget was the first to suggest different
developmental stages for different learning tasks, modern-day neuroscientists have discovered a series of learning windows that literally open
and close throughout the early years of life. Views through these windows are particularly spectacular from the Michigan laboratory of neu-

roscientist Harry Chugani, who uses PET scan technology to measure the metabolism of glucose in the brain. Chugani has shown that there are specific "prime" months throughout the first three years of life when brain development is especially rapid—and during which various lessons, from cognitive to emotional, have an especially strong impact.

The Chugani scans show just when specific parts of the brain "fire up": the first systems to rev into action, he notes, are emotional. Studying newborns, he has found especially high activity in the limbic system, long considered the center of emotion. Particularly active in newborns are the amygdala and cingulate cortex, limbic structures associated with emotional control. As months pass, glucose metabolism increases in other areas of the brain, in turn. At ages 2 months and 3 months, for instance, the visual cortex and cerebellar hemispheres come into play, just in time to drive improved visual and sensorimotor skill. The frontal cortex—the last area of the brain to display an increase in glucose consumption—becomes increasingly active from month 6 on. This coincides with behaviors related to cognition—the phenomenon of stranger anxiety, improved performance on task tests, and the like. By 1 year of age, Chugani notes, the infant's pattern of glucose utilization qualitatively resembles that of the adult.

A few points get special note. Chugani has observed that healthy infant brains fire in evolutionary order, with anatomic structures of older origin (that is, the limbic system, found in mammals from rodents on) activating before newer structures (the frontal cortex, the center of complex thought). In addition, brain structures showing metabolic rates equal to or exceeding their mature levels on the scan are those that dominate behavior at any given age. For instance, when limbic structures light up, the infant is mastering emotional control. When the emphasis shifts to the brain's visual and sensorimotor areas, the infant is focusing on mastery of skills associated with hand-eye coordination. At birth the frontal cortex is about 30 percent as active as that of the young adult, but that changes fast. Between birth and age 3 or 4 years, that same brain region shows dramatic increase in activity, exceeding adult rates by some 100 percent.

Chugani has found that glucose activity measured on the PET scan corresponds not only to windows of learning but also to proliferation of synapses. The greatest proliferation, of course, occurs in the cerebral cortex from birth through age 4. Glucose metabolism *and* synaptic production plateau in middle childhood and, during adolescence, slope back down. During that period, as glucose metabolism declines and synapses are eliminated, the brain becomes less plastic and the individual less flexible—more tuned in to certain skills or talents than others, more set in his or her ways.

Chugani notes that when the process is disrupted—when the right stimulation fails to impact the growing brain at just the right time—things can go awry. Children deprived of exposure to language, for instance, can still acquire reasonably normal language skills—but only if intense speech and language therapy is introduced before age 10. In accidents where the language-dominant hemisphere of the brain is damaged, there is better recovery of language skills if the injury occurs before age 10.

Analysis of the human visual system suggests similar timing and diminished plasticity in children. A number of large studies have looked at children with a "monocular occlusion," in which a cataract or some other problem deprives them of vision in one eye. In most situations, medical correction enables children to regain sight in the obstructed eye—but only if the correction occurs before age 8 to 10.

The upshot, notes Chugani, is the presence of distinct windows of opportunity when learning is efficient and easily retained. Early intervention programs and educational curricula, he adds, would probably work best with these learning windows in mind.

SENSORY PERCEPTIONS

As parents communicate with their babies, it's essential to understand what gets through, and exactly how and when. Much of the latest information here is neatly summarized by Andrew Meltzoff and two coauthors, cognitive scientists Alison Gopnik of the University of California at Berkeley and linguist Patricia K. Kuhl, the world's leading authority on speech development and a professor at Washington University in Seattle. In their recent book, *The Scientist in the Crib*, they explain how developmental psychologists have determined infant perception, cognition, and more.

By measuring such factors as babies' eye movements and sucking action in response to pictures and sounds, researchers have determined that newborns "discriminate human faces and voices from other sights and sounds, and that they prefer them. Within a few days after they're born, they recognize familiar faces, voices, and smells, and prefer them to unfamiliar ones."

Meltzoff, Gopnik, and Kuhl note that even the limitations of newborn vision make them pay special attention to people. "It's a myth that newborn babies can't see," they write, "but babies are very nearsighted by adult standards." The gist is that objects about 12 inches away—the distance of the mother's or father's face when holding them—are in sharp focus while everything else is a blur. In essence, "babies seem designed to see the people who love them more clearly than anything else."

Eyesight improves rapidly, of course, and the window of opportunity for visual acuity extends from birth through 8 months of age. Parents need not buy high-contrast black-and-white toys to stimulate vision, but they should get babies' eyes tested as early as 2 weeks of age. If left uncorrected, a weak or unused eye will permanently lose its functional connection to the brain. Indeed, for binocular vision, in particular, the learning window closes before month 5.

THE EMOTIONAL WINDOW

As studies in vision and the other senses suggest, the emotional centers are among the first parts of the brain to fire up after birth. Research shows that emotions develop in layers, each more complex than the next, but even the youngest infants can experience such feelings as joy and sadness, envy and empathy, pride and shame. Parents attuned to this timeline will realize that only loving care can provide a baby's brain with appropriate stimulation, priming it for a life of happiness, confidence, and love. Neglect can program a child's brain for depression, while abuse sets up circuits for anxiety and violence, among other psychological ills. Even the youngest infants can tell the difference between expressions of happiness and sadness. Babies shown a picture of a happy face paired with the recording of a happy voice, or a sad face with the recording of a sad voice, researchers have found, will be significantly more attentive than those exposed to disconcerting combinations—including happy faces with sad voices, and sad faces with happy voices.

Ed Tronick of Children's Hospital in Boston has devoted himself to the study of infant emotion and the mother-child connection since the early 1980s. His studies reveal that the ability to tune in to and connect with other minds is a trait we possess right from the start.

In one study he learned that babies as young as 3 months of age can detect maternal depression. To investigate a baby's ability to pick up such moods, Tronick and colleagues had a group of mothers simulate depressed expressions during face-to-face interaction. Working with 24 infants—12 boys and 12 girls between the ages of 96 and 110 days—the researchers asked their mothers to engage in three minutes of normal interaction and three minutes of simulated depressed interaction. A control group engaged in two to three minutes of normal maternal-infant interaction. Interactions were videotaped and infant behavior described in five-second intervals in the order of occurrence. During normal interactions, the infants tended to engage in positive, upbeat interactions with their caregivers. During depressed interactions, however, they became negative, protesting and exhibiting wariness. The negativity continued briefly even after the mothers switched to normal modes of interaction.

In general, Tronick's studies reveal that infant facial expressions are appropriate to the occasion and reflect the meaning communicated to them by caretakers. In children as young as 6 months of age, their voice, gesture, and posture accurately communicate their emotional states, internal feelings, and outward goals in the world.

TRANSMITTING MATERNAL MOOD

Working with psychologist Andrew F. Gianino, Jr., director of a National Science Foundation project on the infant's capacity to cope with stress, Tronick has explained why offspring of happy mothers generally communicate a sense of joy while infants of depressed mothers often seem sad and withdrawn. The answer, the team contends, lies in the researchers' "mutual regulation model"—a system in which infant and caretaker form a feedback loop to facilitate balanced internal emotion and healthy engagement with the world. These two functions are inextricably linked because internal emotion affects an infant's motivation to interact with the environment. A distressed infant, for instance, will be unable to maintain engagement with a person or object because of the distraction of his inner pain. An angry baby will lack motivation to play cooperatively or seek positive reinforcement. A happy baby, on the other hand, is most motivated to do so.

How can babies regulate their own emotional state given the immaturity of the nervous system and environmental brickbats, from hunger to sudden noise to too much heat or cold? Normally, they learn to do so with the help of a parent. The mother or father will focus on the baby and read his behavior as communicating a specific need, be it to eat or relax or sleep. By helping to meet these needs, the parent makes it easier for the baby to regulate his or her internal moods. Much of the time the parent's job is simply reduction of stimulation, enabling the infant to better control disruptive overstimulation from the environment. Other times, the parent facilitates a goal. For instance, the infant may want to reach for an object but lacks the ability. The observant parent will note the child's gaze and gesture and bring the object closer to the child, eliminating feelings of distress and facilitating engagement with the world.

IN TUNE

In an ongoing study, Tronick and Gianino learned that parents are in sync with babies only a fraction of the time. In the ideal interaction, the parent responds appropriately to the infant's signal, and the infant responds in kind. But even the most attuned of parents make interactive errors most of the time. For instance, when the infant signals "Let's play" by smiling, the mother may fail to respond. Alternatively, the mother may try to initiate play, but the infant may turn away or become glassy-eyed, communicating the message, "No, I need to stay quiet." We sometimes forget that just as adults require some time to themselves, children also need to be left to their own devices. Children need to experience companionship as well as solitude to properly develop.

Using the tools of their trade, including videotape, the psychologists have found that for infants at 3, 6, and 9 months of age, the interaction is coordinated just 3 percent of the time. The key to healthy development is in the repair process. Indeed, the researchers found, 34 percent of the interactive errors were repaired in the next step of the interaction. The normal interaction moves from poorly regulated to well-regulated states and back again on a frequent basis. Whenever the parent tunes in, the infant's emotional state improves.

Most developmental psychologists now agree that repairing an interaction gone awry is a linchpin of healthy infant development. Consistently going from a poorly regulated to a well-regulated state teaches infants to regulate themselves and to recover from disruptive or disconcerting experiences. The child comes to understand that a breakdown in his or her primary relationship can be corrected, and thus feels secure. That security creates a core of positive feeling and establishes clear boundaries between the self and others. The infant can use this model to establish future intimate relationships, carrying a sense of confidence and power as he or she moves out into the world.

Indeed, knowledge that breakdowns in communication will generally be repaired fosters a sense of independence that frees the child to leave the side of the primary caretaker to explore. After all, leaving the mother or father for a foray into the great unknown is far less intimidating if the child can be sure that, upon return, the relationship can be reestablished and the intimacy resumed.

If healthy development is tied to the experience of coordinated interaction, unhealthy development is associated with sustained periods of negative emotion and interactive failure. This explains why infants of depressed mothers so often become sad and withdrawn. Because of her own emotional state, the depressed mother fails to respond to her infant's signals and thus fails to provide the infant with appropriate regulatory help. For a time, the infant may keep trying to repair the relationship, but with each failure, the child turns more and more inward to cope. Eventually, accumulated experience with the depressed parent adversely affects the psyche and the structure of the infant's brain. The child learns to avoid social engagement, and increasingly relies on strategies that reduce his sensitivity to the inappropriate emotional feedback provided by the parent.

The child will develop a sense of self as ineffective and a sense of the parent as unreliable. Once this pattern is established, it will guide the child's interaction with the world. The chances are that he or she will grow up overly self-reliant, expecting to receive scant emotional support from others.

What does all this mean for mothers and fathers? What does it tell us about the way we should interact with the youngest infants to maximize emotional health? The message is clear: we must pay attention to our babies and respond to their wants and needs. We must engage them in emotional interplay that is joyful, animated, positive, and respectful.

Contrary to popular opinion, the findings do not call for intense levels of stimulation or constant interaction. Instead they demand consistent, loving care and a sense of playfulness as well as periods of engagement and disengagement so that infants can master personhood on their own.

VENTURING OUT: THE SOCIALIZATION WINDOW

As babies move from early to late infancy, they undertake ever more complex tasks. A 6-month-old will typically play with an object and a person at the same time. At 1 year of age it's typical for babies to play with adults they don't know that well, or with peers. These tasks place more demands on the baby's developing brain: to negotiate these challenges, the baby must be attentive to detail, organized in intent, and focused on the situation at hand.

When the infant becomes a toddler, the healthy emotional relationship
with mother and father—and the nature of brain building—changes.
During the first year, 90 percent of parental behavior consists of affectionate play and caregiving. In sharp contrast, the parent of a 13- to 17-
month-old toddler becomes more of a socialization agent, expressing a
prohibition about once every nine minutes. In year 2, parents must persuade children to inhibit unrestricted exploration, tantrums, bowel
movements, and a host of activities that they enjoy. Without the element
of inhibition as a check on gratification, the child would lack self-control
and could not, ultimately, function in the world.

UCLA psychiatrist Allen N. Schore notes that if parents have done
their job well during year 1, the toddler who ventures out in year 2 will
be propelled by high levels of excitement and elation (accompanied, of
course, by such feel-good brain hormones as endorphins). Instead of
working to enhance this scenario, as they did during the first twelve
months of their baby's life, it is now the parents' job to constrain it. Parents most effectively inhibit the emotions of pleasure, Schore notes, by
instilling a sense of shame. Making its appearance in the firmament of
human emotion by age 14 to 16 months, shame uniquely reduces self-
exposure and exploration by lowering levels of the feel-good brain hormones and inhibiting interest, excitement, and joy.

The introduction of shame as a basic emotion alters the parent-child
relationship for good. Face-to-face encounters that once engendered
only joy between the healthy parent-and-child pair now also elicit stress.
The primary context for the shame experience, these encounters result
in severe misattunement. If the child has ventured out beyond the
boundaries of safety, a disgusted parental facial expression induces
in that child a sense of shock and deflation. Positive emotion within
the child quickly turns negative—and this rapid transition from positive to negative emotion is the feeling we have come to call shame.

Many experts believe that small doses of shame are healthy, the cau-
tionary tool parents wield to socialize their babies and keep them safe.
Here I disagree. I believe that children should *never* be shamed. Whether
it is dished out in small or large doses, shame is always toxic.

The parent who is attuned to his child does not need to reign in the
child's behavior in a critical, painful way. If a certain action on the part of
a child is undesirable, all that a parent needs to do is to indicate so
through words, tone of voice, facial expression, and gesture: "Please
don't do that" or "That hurts, please stop it." If a child persists in throwing food off the table, take away the food and say, "I guess you are not

hungry." After such an interaction parents can quickly help the child make the transition back to a state of alert relaxation and calm.

Parents who have inhibited a toddler gone astray will notice a negative facial expression, postural collapse, gaze aversion, and blushing as nonverbal signals of internal distress. A caregiver who is sensitive and responsive will soon reinitiate and reenter a state of mutual connectedness, repairing the recent break. She will "stay with" the baby from initial encounter through the reprimand experience she has triggered until she repairs the connection, easing the stress and helping the child experience positive feelings again. Children skillfully brought in and out of the different emotional states at appropriate moments develop brains for vigorous living.

THE LANGUAGE WINDOW

As discussed in the early chapters of this book, the newborn has learned to recognize the sound and melody of its mother's voice in the womb. From the seventh month of gestation through about 6 years of age, the human brain is wired to learn the meaning, sound, and context of words. Linguists now say that the window for speech recognition itself starts to close down after 10 months of age, though the circuitry for picking up syntax stays open until age 5 or 6. Once these basic skills are established, the circuits for acquiring vocabulary will never close.

For parents, the lesson here is simple: Talk, talk, talk. By talking to children a lot, parents will help them to develop their linguistic abilities to their full potential.

Psychologists Betty Hart and Todd Ridley recently studied a group of 42 children born to professional, working-class, and welfare parents. During the first two and a half years of the children's lives, the researchers spent an hour a month recording every spoken word and every parent-child exchange in the home. Collating 1,300 hours of interaction involving millions of ordinary utterances from birth, Hart and Ridley finally gave the children standard IQ tests at age 3.

They found that children of professional parents scored highest. But analysis showed that the key variable was language. A child of professional parents heard, on average, 2,100 words an hour during the recording sessions. Children of working-class parents heard 1,200 words. And those with parents on welfare heard only about 600 words.

By the time the children were age 2, all the parents in the study started talking more to their children. But by this time, the divergence among the children was so great that those left behind could never catch up. The divergence in academic achievement remained in each group through primary school.

As a pacemaker for cognitive skills, the brain's brief language window is pivotal. A recent study of day care by Hart and Ridley found that children who were talked to at very young ages were better at problem solving later on, research that again underlines the critical importance of the spoken word to the mental development of children.

But talking is not enough. What is even more important than the amount of talk is the emotional charge the words carry. Hart and Ridley found that language was a key emotional energizer as well. Children of professional parents gathered positive feedback thirty times an hour— twice as often as the children of working-class parents and five times as often as the children of welfare parents.

The way we talk to our children can set the stage for a lifetime of failure or success. One set of studies shows that the high-pitched, singsong speech style known as parentese helps babies connect objects with words. Other studies prove that talk delivered with feeling boosts brain power far more effectively than talk devoid of emotion. Gentleness wins over anger, and patience over irritability, every time.

STYLE AND SUBSTANCE

Experience is so influential that loving parents from different cultures impart different styles of thought. A culture's cognitive signature may stay constant for generations, and through the course of each child's life.

University of Michigan social psychologist Richard Nisbett devised a series of experiments in which students from Japan and the United States were shown an animated aquatic scene with a large fish swimming among smaller ones. In describing the animation later on, Japanese students tended to pay attention to the background, describing the color and ambience of the lake, the texture of the lake bottom, the seaweed, and so on. American students, on the other hand, zeroed in on the big fish first, then described the smaller fish in relation to it, especially if they were doing something notable like swimming fast. In all, Japanese students commented on the background environment 70 percent more than American students, who tended, instead, to focus on the foreground. When Japanese students were shown the same fish in a different setting they had difficulty identifying them, while the Americans did not.

Particularly notable was a study of American and Chinese students on the approach to contradictory arguments and the tendency to see things in black-and-white or shades of gray. The students were asked to take a stand on an issue—in this case, funding a project on adoption. When presented with weaker arguments contrary to their own, Americans redoubled their defense of their position, decimating opponents in debate. Asians, on the other hand, softened their opinion to accommodate critics. When asked to comment on a dispute between a mother and daughter, the Americans sided with either one or the other. Chinese, on the other hand, equivocated, commenting that mother and daughter must work harder to have a meeting of the minds.

In a nutshell, the scientists found, Easterners think more holistically, paying greater attention to context and more easily accepting contradictions—the yin and yang of an issue. Americans, on the other hand, think more analytically—separating an object from its context, and applying formal logic to drill down and arrive at a version of truth.

Despite the transmission of thought style through the generations, studies show that attitudes are clearly rooted in experience, not in genes. Asian Americans born and raised in the United States share a cognitive style with European Americans, not with their relatives in China, Korea, or Japan.

The Michigan findings challenge a basic tenet of psychology—that no matter what the cultural milieu, all humans share the same basic thought processes deep down. Nisbett and colleagues have learned instead that thought processes vary from culture to culture, revealing our brains as products of experience, prone to vast differences depending on the environment in which one has been reared.

SUMMING UP

The kind of caregiving parents provide permanently affects brain development. Language acquisition, cognition, and intelligence are mutually reinforcing and depend on the interactive, affectionate relationship between child and parent. What oxygen is to the brain, words spoken respectfully, and hugs given lovingly are to the young mind.

Key Parenting Points

- Parents who want to stimulate their child's brain will do so most effectively through a warm, caring relationship with the child.

- Infants need both stimulation and reduction of stimulation.
- Parents support a child's goal-directed behavior by helping him or her achieve it, thus eliminating feelings of distress and facilitating engagement with the world.
- When the intuitive mental connection between parent and child is temporarily disrupted, parents should quickly reestablish the connection to set the situation right. Repairing a relationship gone awry is a linchpin of infant development.
- Introduce a sense of playfulness in your interactions with your child as often as possible.
- Infants must learn to entertain themselves and to be content on their own. Allow them to move away from you in a safe environment.
- The best way to teach language is to talk to children with appropriate emotion, and to read them books aloud.

10

—◦—

The Mystery and Power
of Early Memory

In May of 1983 I received the following letter in the mail.

Dear Dr. Verny,

For your files, I wish to report my own recollections of my life in the womb:

1. My first discovery was: "I exist."
2. I found that I could move.
3. I began to exercise. I would stop and rest when I decided I had enough.
4. I do not remember hearing heartbeats or music. I was very comfortable.
5. After a very long period of time passed, I began to feel periodic pressure. Finally an opening appeared and I began to move toward it. For the first time I felt apprehension and perhaps fear.
6. There came a time when events happened very quickly. I lost touch with the details of events. I found myself in the hands of much larger creatures, and I was exposed to very bright lights.
7. I located a source of food and a way of getting it into my body.
8. From time to time I felt hunger. It became VERY IMPORTANT that I find my way back to the source of food and comfort: my mother.

I was born on May 23, 1912, to John and Emily Fields of Greensboro, North Carolina.*

For the first three years of my life, these were simply memories of an earlier life, where things were much simpler and problems did not exist. When I learned that babies lived for nine months inside the body of their mothers, I suddenly understood that this earlier existence was my time in the womb.

I have always hoped that someone would undertake to interview children from five to seven years of age and record how many have had prenatal memories of their own.

*Names have been changed to protect privacy.

THE MEMORY SWITCH

Since 1983, when I first read this note, researchers have made enormous strides in uncovering our earliest memories. The results might startle you. For years it was thought that human memory—the continuum of consciousness seamlessly connecting the moments of our lives—starts somewhere around age 3. But an abundance of evidence now shows that this is not the case.

If we push our memory back as far as possible, we eventually hit a wall. Some people can go back further than others, but the continuum of consciousness we think of as personal history generally comes to a halt at age 3 or 4. Many have patches of memory from before that time, but these isolated images are not part of the unending stream we recall as our lives. Freudians use the term infant amnesia to describe the phenomenon. One of the pioneers of prenatal psychology, Frances J. Mott, called it the last great forgetting of the human being.

Many people think of memory as something mysteriously switched on at the age of 3 or 4. But that is simply not true. We are thinking, feeling, and learning long before age 3. However, our memories become clouded and buried under an avalanche of subsequent experiences, making retrieval difficult though not impossible.

"We all carry with us, deep in our feelings, the record of an almost antediluvian period which we lived through between birth and 3," Mott proposes, from his study of dreams. "Birth is still an earlier cataclysm. And much as we tend to believe that there is no memory of life before birth, dreams reveal that this is quite untrue. Indeed, prior to birth there was the most vivid awareness of still another stage of life. And there probably exist layer upon layer of memory associated with the building of the body. . . . Memory wells up from the fertilized egg, and continues to develop as we develop. In the end it wells up into our conscious minds. But underneath our conscious minds there are layer upon layer of forgetfulness."

THE ORIGINS OF MEMORY

What is memory, and when does it begin? In the most basic sense, memory is the process by which we retain what we experience and learn. By its very nature, experience alters as we grow. The unborn child does not experience the same thing or experience it in the same fashion as the toddler, just as the toddler does not experience the same thing as the adult. The vast chasms between these states of being do not mean that one realm of existence is wiped out as we enter the next.

The great brain scientists of the past century have taught us the errors of reductionism: the brain is made of neurons and synapses, neurotransmitters and their receptors, but the *mind* is more than the sum of these parts. Working together, the elements of the brain form a network that results in the complex consciousness we call the mind.

Yet in the very beginning, before we had brains or even bodies, we consisted of nothing more than a cell. First an egg and a sperm that merged to form a single cell, and then a collection of cells dividing again and again. The biochemical "experience" of those early cells forms the first precursors of memory—not memory as we think of it in our present-day lives, but an ancient, cellular memory from a time when, chrysalis-like, we had a different form.

During the last thirty years, exploring the frontiers of prenatal psychology, I have seen ample evidence that the physiological events of conception and its immediate aftermath—including the journey of the multicellular organism called the zygote down the oviduct and the implantation of this zygote into the uterine wall—give rise to the initial layers of memory and profoundly impact the mind.

At first this notion may strike you as far-fetched. Yet consider the critical moment of development when the zygote is implanted in the womb. Most embryologists now believe that 50 percent of fertilized ova are aborted between the time of conception and the first few days after implantation. The reason is that half the proteins in the very early fetus—at this stage called the blastula—come from the father's sperm.

Recognized as foreign by the mother's immune system, the blastula comes under attack by its maternal environment; depending on the outcome of the struggle, the blastula either dies or succeeds in implanting in the uterine wall.

These physiological events—the first "experienced" by the new embryo—serve as the earliest template for a host of sensations associated with aggression, fear, and depression. According to cellular biologist Bruce H. Lipton, this follows from a long-standing tenet of traditional cell biology: cells read their environment, assess the information, and then select appropriate responses to maintain their survival.

How many people, retracing the cellular struggle waged in the earliest days of being, strive for acceptance by a country club, a university, a fraternity, or a group of friends? How many dream of quicksand, swamps, storms, shipwrecks, and wild, buffeting winds? Some explore new environments with confidence, others with trepidation—yet others suffer fatigue or an inexplicable lack of willpower in the face of life's demands. While such characteristics can often be understood in light of influences after birth, sometimes they cannot. In these instances, we might look for a clue to the very first struggle we have ever faced—implantation in the wall of the uterus.

These influences constitute the first memories, long since fossilized beneath more recent layers of experience. Indeed, those of us working in the field of prenatal psychology have begun to gather clinical evidence for the notion that ancient cellular memory may help determine who we are. Working with a variety of techniques, such as hypnosis, drugs, and regressive psychotherapies, patients have reported on their earliest impressions, some going back—amazingly—to conception. I remember one man, who, while recalling an incident with his mother, went into an altered state of consciousness and started to talk as if he were in his father's head. The father was drunk and angry. He wanted to have sex with his wife. The next moment my patient identified with his mother. He could feel her revulsion and rage as his father proceeded to violate her. All his life, this man has felt torn between feminine and masculine impulses, between aggressiveness and passivity. He was one of the most ambivalent people I had ever known.

I do not mean to suggest that this man literally witnessed the scene as he would today, with the full range of visual and aural perceptions we experience as human adults. Rather, he experienced the event as only a cell can—when the biochemistry of violence and abuse, well documented in the lab and covered later in this book, impinged on his conception and initiated predispositions to certain character traits. Reliving his conception—impressed on his cells—in a supportive, therapeutic environment has started him on the road to recovery and health.

A CELL NEVER FORGETS

If you doubt the potential for cells to remember, you need look no further than the human immune system. Our immune defenses operate through cells that recognize and *remember* infectious invaders, all the better to attack them when they return to infect us again. It is the immune response that enables vaccines to work. If you expose someone to a weakened or dead form of a germ (the vaccine), the body will produce attacker cells capable of recognizing that germ should it ever appear again, even many years later.

In fact, neurobiologist Candace Pert of the National Institutes of Health notes that viruses and neurohormones share the same receptors for cell entry. Depending on how much of a particular neurohormone is present at any given time, there will be only a certain number of receptors left over to transmit the virus into the cell. This explains the long-observed connection between mood and disease and suggests a mechanism through which one person may get sick from the same loading dose of an infection that barely affects another.

"Could an elevated mood, one of happy expectation and hope for an exciting possibility or adventure, protect against certain viruses?" Pert asks. One suggested pathway involves rheovirus, shown to be a cause of the viral cold. Rheovirus enters a cell by attaching to the receptor for the neurohormone norepinephrine, associated with positive states of mind. Presumably, when you are happy rheovirus can't enter the cell because the norepinephrine blocks all the potential receptors.

Scientists have noted the connection between emotion and disease since the days of Aristotle. "Soul and body, I suggest, react sympathetically upon each other," the philosopher is credited with saying. But it wasn't until the beginning of the twentieth century that researchers had the tools to discern the links and to demonstrate that one of those links, the immune system, was trainable.

Past studies have shown that the immune system could be conditioned at the subconscious, or autonomic, level. But it wasn't until 1990 that Howard Hall of Case Western Reserve University in Ohio showed that the immune system could also be consciously controlled. First he trained his human subjects in such self-regulatory practices as alert relaxation and guided imagery, self-hypnosis, and biofeedback. Using several control groups, Hall showed that his trainees could use these techniques to consciously increase the stickiness of their white blood cells as measured by saliva and blood tests.

Communication between the brain and the immune system is virtually constant, a busy two-way street. Stress generated in the brain, for instance, dampens the immune response—probably because immunity is a long-term strategy for survival while an organism under outside threat must focus its energy on the short-term defense or escape.

In recent years, scientists such as Candace Pert and Ed Blalock of the University of Texas have found that the same peptides produced by the immune system are present in the brain and the lining of the stomach. "The nervous, endocrine, and immune systems are functionally integrated in what looks like a psychoimmunoendocrine network," Pert notes. It's long been known that emotional resonance with memories stored in our minds influences the strength of the immune response. But now we know the opposite to be true as well. Memories recorded in the cells of immunity influence the operation of the brain, regulating mood and emotion, and changing the way we behave.

BODYWIDE MEMORY

Today this notion has been pushed further still. It isn't just the brain and the immune system that experience and remember and communicate, scientists have learned; the phenomenon reaches to every region of the body and multiple types of cells. The idea was articulated by Francis Schmitt of the Massachusetts Institute of Technology in 1984, when he proposed the existence of a second, parallel system of "information substances." Schmitt used the term information substances to describe the collection of transmitters, peptides, hormones, and factors surging through the body and brain. Known in aggregate as ligands, these substances bind to specific cell receptors, much as a particular key fits a specific lock. The immune system is a participant in this phenomenon of whole-body information exchange and memory storage, but it is hardly alone.

"Though a key fitting into a lock is the standard image, a more dynamic description of this process might be two voices—ligand and receptor—striking the same note and producing a vibration that rings a doorbell to open the doorway to the cell," Pert explains. "A chain reaction of biochemical events is initiated as tiny machines roar into action and, directed by the message of the ligand, begin any number of activities— manufacturing new proteins, making decisions about cell division, opening or closing ion channels, adding or subtracting energetic chemical groups like the phosphates. In short, the activity of the cell at any moment is determined by which receptors are occupied by ligands and which are not. On a more global scale, these minute physiological phenomena at the cellular level can translate to large changes in behavior, physical activity, even mood."

This system of ligand flow through the body is indisputably more ancient and far more basic to the organism than the nervous system. The new paradigm, now widely accepted by neuroscientists, involves a vast array of cells in every region of the body, from the gut to the spleen to the heart. Though the cells are of multiple type, they all have one thing in common: they produce a flow of ligands that travels the river of extracellular fluid to communicate feeling, mood, and memory to far-flung regions of the body and the emotional centers of the brain.

How do these molecular crosscurrents, launched by our body's cells, translate into actual emotion—happiness or sadness, anxiety or calm, or something in between? Seeking the answer, Candace Pert and her team charted the destination of the ligands within the brain. They found that the receptors for the communicating chemicals and a range of mind-altering drugs—heroin, opium, PCP, lithium, and Valium—were densest in the limbic system, long associated with the emotional self. Perhaps more striking, receptors for these substances were spread throughout the body as well.

In short, the last revolution in neuroscience suggests that true intelligence and memory—the very essence of self—are located not just in the brain but throughout the body. This discovery rings in a new age of body-brain-mind unity. They constitute a single, interactive network. They are one.

What are the implications of these discoveries for early human development?

The youngest of our children, including the unborn, do not need fully developed central nervous systems or brains to receive, store, and process information. Information substances from the mother, be they stress-related cortisol or feel-good endorphins, enter the baby's blood system, affecting receptors at every stage of development, no matter how early in life. Before our children have even rudimentary brains, they are gathering within the cells of their bodies their first memories. Our earliest memories are not conscious, nor even unconscious in the standard sense. Before the last great forgetfulness of Mott, before the event of birth, before we have even had a glimmer of sight or sound in the womb, we record the experience and history of our lives in our cells.

I firmly believe that one day scientists will be able to identify millions of memory fragments in each body cell. Formed throughout the days of our lives, these fragments, when called for, will be found to coalesce and form complete memories in the higher centers of the brain.

FROM OCEANIC BLANKNESS
TO A SENSE OF SELF

When does memory become conscious, something we can access with effort or even at will? Psychologists specializing in the study of memory note two forms: conscious memory, also called explicit memory, and unconscious memory, referred to as implicit.

Explicit memory includes the recall of facts, events, and lists. Working memory, in which we store visual or verbal information in a mental buffer zone until it's needed, is also explicit; so, too, is the memory of your ninth birthday party or the furniture in your childhood room.

Other memories are implicit. Though not available for conscious recall, they instruct us nonetheless. A seemingly irrational fear response in particular situations may come from implicit memory; so can skills like touch typing, riding a bicycle, or building a castle in the sand.

It is in the womb, during our journey to consciousness, that memory, first implicit and then explicit, develops. It's safe to assume that early embryos made up of just a few cells most often experience oceanic blankness. As a matter of course, that "normal" state is soon disrupted by interactions with the uterine environment and by surging maternal hormones. Each hormonal jolt—precipitated by maternal upset, joy, or some other mood—creates a primitive memory in our cells. Since we lack brains and even bodies, our cells alone record these impressions as the first implicit memories we will ever have.

As these traces of memory accumulate over time, the prenate understands, in her implicit way, the separation between herself and the surrounding womb. By the sixth or seventh month of gestation, when the unborn child has a brain and even a cerebral cortex, she not only perceives emotion coming from her mother but discriminates among different types of hormonal changes. Through her senses she perceives and remembers motion, light, taste, and sound. She starts to recognize voices. She makes sense out of the input and, based on memory, creates an appropriate response—whether excess movement to express agitation, or sucking her thumb to help her calm down.

Every so often, we have learned through years of clinical study, an individual will recall a patch of memory from the womb. One mother told me she was shocked to find her two-year-old daughter sitting on the living-room floor chanting, "Breathe in, breathe out, breathe in, breathe out." The words were part of a Lamaze exercise the woman had practiced during the last weeks of her pregnancy. She had not uttered those words since.

Another mother wrote me that one day, sitting around the dining-room table, she'd joked about the pajamas she'd frequently worn while pregnant with her little girl. "Do you remember those pajamas?" the three-year-old girl was facetiously asked. The child's answer floored the group: "I couldn't see what you were wearing; I could only hear what you were saying."

"What was it like?" the mother asked.

"It was dark and crowded like a big bowl of water," the child said.

"What was your favorite food?" asked the mother.

"I didn't get any food," replied the daughter.

"What did you think when you were born?"

"It wasn't crowded anymore," said the girl. "I could finally stretch."

"The amazing thing," the mother wrote, "is that my daughter described the entire experience without ever saying she had seen anything. She related only what she had heard and felt. She never slipped or answered a question wrong."

In a recent report, psychologist Alice M. Givens says her research reveals unborn children may literally absorb the mother's experience and carry it within them throughout life, as if it were their own.

In one such case, she was able to verify a patient's report with the mother. "A couple of years ago Rose came in to therapy for several months," she related. "One day when she was directed back to the prenatal period, she started saying, 'I'm cold. I'm cold and I'm so tired of digging I'm ready to drop.'

"After a few minutes we established that the mother was outside shoveling snow, and Rose had recorded all of it as if it was her own experience. I told her to say the next words that came to mind.

"'I'm tired and my back hurts, but if I just keep shoveling snow, I'll get rid of this baby. The worse the pain is, the more likely I am to lose it. Just keep going; shovel, shovel. I can't take anymore.'

"This incident in Rose's therapy was forgotten when her file was stored away. Almost two years later her mother called to ask for a few sessions. We talked about her life in detail, and when we got to the subject of Rose's birth, she said, 'When I first got pregnant, I hated it. There was no way that I could have that baby. I was afraid to take anything, and I didn't even know anything to take. I thought of falling downstairs but was afraid of a serious injury. Finally, I decided to exhaust myself. There was deep snow outside, so I went out and started digging. I just kept shoveling snow over and over until I was utterly exhausted.'

"Suddenly I remembered that day in her daughter's therapy, and I asked her, 'Did you ever tell Rose about that?'

"'Oh no, I've never told a living soul, I'd be too ashamed,' she told me.

"I went to the inactive file where I could quickly find Rose's records, and there I found almost the exact words about shoveling snow and getting rid of the baby."

Indeed, numerous studies show babies remember mothers' upset, at least implicitly, and react to that memory throughout life. For instance, Australian researchers showed pregnant women a disturbing twenty-minute segment of a Hollywood movie. When briefly reexposed to this film up to three months after birth, the babies showed recognition of the earlier experience. Studies of a thousand babies whose mothers had experienced various degrees of depression during pregnancy themselves displayed depression at birth and in proportion to the depression scores of their mothers.

BIRTH MEMORY

Although memories of the womb are not generally spontaneous, thousands of people say they've accessed bona fide prenatal memories through psychotherapy, dreams, and hypnosis. Perhaps most compelling, and best documented in the literature, are powerful memories of birth. Though it is always wise to exercise caution when examining memories elicited by hypnosis or psychotherapy, lest they be induced by the process, the body of evidence from divergent sources is persuasive.

One of the first people to study the birth memory phenomenon was California obstetrician David B. Cheek. In one of his most impressive studies, Cheek showed that people retain a muscle memory of the way their heads, shoulders, and arms moved as they entered the world. "As an obstetrician," Cheek explains, "I knew that when a baby comes out the birth canal, it automatically rotates its head in a particular fashion. I also noticed that whenever I asked my patients about birth, they spontaneously turned their head in a similar way. So I got the idea that maybe they were remembering the same physiological mechanism they'd experienced while being born."

To investigate this theory, Cheek recruited some patients he had delivered decades before. He asked them under hypnosis to recall their births, and after checking his records, he found that "a hundred percent remembered the way their head rotated as it came out of the birth canal. Almost everyone remembered which arm came out first as well."

San Diego psychologist David B. Chamberlain, one of the leaders in the field of prenatal and perinatal psychology, has spent years collecting birth memories. He says he was fascinated by the phenomenon the first time he heard a patient describe being born. "I was sitting opposite her," he says. "There was a big, beautiful asparagus fern and a huge picture window behind us, and the sun was shining in. Across the room was a baby grand. All of a sudden, my client, a fiftyish woman named Lee, described a vision of her birth. 'The doctor is holding me up, laughing,' she said. "'I told you it would be a girl,'" he said to Mother. Now Mother is turning her face away.'"

Determined to explore this further, Chamberlain conducted a study of ten mother-offspring pairs. He reports that while under hypnosis, mothers and offspring alike recalled startlingly similar details of the offspring's birth. One daughter, for instance, correctly described her mother's hairstyle at the time. Another correctly recalled her mother smelling her, then expressing concern over the normality of her toes.

Why are such memories relatively rare? It is probably because of a combination of factors. For one, it may have to do with increased flow of the peptide oxytocin prior to birth and for as long thereafter as the mother breast-feeds. Oxytocin facilitates lactation and uterine muscle contraction and also, studies show, in high concentration extinguishes memory. Perhaps one reason we have no memory of our prenatal and perinatal lives is the flood of maternal oxytocin bathing us during that period. An anesthetic for the mind, oxytocin brings on the first great forgetting and protects us from remembering the agonies of birth. Rats who have learned pole-jumping behavior, for instance, lose their knowledge of the skill when given injections of oxytocin. Memory loss is most extreme when rats are dehydrated, a frequent condition of the woman in labor as well. Another factor is the stress hormone cortisol, which also acts to extinguish recall of traumatic memories.

The lesson for parents is that unborn children remember the experience of gestation, implicitly, in the deepest part of themselves—the cells that give rise to their bodies and brains. They absorb joy and sadness, calm and anxiety, through a multitude of channels—cellular, sensory, and cognitive—in an array of centers from single cells to the limbic lobe to the cerebral cortex itself. Though these memories rarely rise spontaneously to adult consciousness, they become the substrate for feelings and behaviors throughout life.

THE TIME BETWEEN: INFANT AND TODDLER MEMORY

Even though we don't remember much from our first three years, it's clear from observing babies that their memories are intact. Carolyn Rovee-Collier and a research team at Rutgers University in New Jersey had infants from 2 to 5 months of age learn to move a mobile attached to one of their legs by string. When the infants kicked, the mobile moved and the babies showed enjoyment. When the same babies came back to the lab a couple of days later, they kicked frequently and spontaneously, apparently remembering the mobile and anticipating its reappearance. The older the baby, the longer the memory of the mobile was retained. Two-month-olds retained the memory for a couple of days, 3-month-olds for a week, and 6-month-olds for two weeks.

The impression was so strong, in fact, that infants shown different mobiles on two subsequent days failed to react, while those shown identical mobiles did. Amazingly, the team learned, infant memory is specific: when a cloth liner behind the mobile is decorated with squares one day and circles the next, 6-month-old babies stare at the mobile but do not kick with recognition. They kick frequently during the second visit only if both the liner and the mobile are the same.

Context, says Rovee-Collier, is the key. "Infants don't recognize a mobile out of context, much as you and I might not recognize our dental assistant in a movie theater line."

And University of Massachusetts experimental psychologist Eve Perris has found that 6-month-old infants retain impressions of events for years. The 24 6½-month-old infants in her study had to reach for a rattle under two different conditions—when the room was lit, and when the lights were suddenly turned off. Two and a half years later these children were presented with the same task alongside a group of controls. The experienced children reached and grasped far more frequently than controls without the earlier exposure, and were four times better able to withstand the slightly scary experience of being plunged from light into dark.

As babies get older, as their brains mature, their powers of explicit recall increase. Psychologist Andrew Meltzoff has shown that 9-month-old babies can recall events after the passage of a week. In one experiment, Meltzoff had researchers bang the top of a plastic box with their foreheads in view of infant subjects. When the babies returned a week later and were given the boxes, they banged the boxes with their heads. A control group of babies had seen the box but not the behavior; when they returned, they almost never banged the box with their heads.

Other studies show that 13-month-old babies can remember how to assemble a gong from several props after watching a researcher do it first. The powers of explicit recall continue to develop with language, of course, and it is our use of language that helps weave the narrative history we recall as adults.

WHAT WE REMEMBER AND WHY

How much of our early lives can we recapture in memory—even with help from hypnosis, psychotherapy, and the like? Is it really possible, as Marcel Proust suggested, to trigger a memory with your personal version of a madeleine and be transported back?

Not all memories are created equal. Short, intermediate, and long-term memories are formed through different molecular processes in the brain. And when it comes to the duration of explicit memory, intensity is the key. Short-term memories are created when proteins in nerve cells are modified. When the need for the particular memory has passed, the cells revert back and the memory fades. Indeed, if the memory is of no further consequence, why waste space in the brain? In intermediate memory, the brain produces more of those modified proteins. But in long-term memory, new genes turn on, creating entirely new proteins and new connections among nerve cells. Short-term memories change the molecular structure of brain cells, often just temporarily. Long-term memories rewire the neural circuits of the brain.

To shed light on the filing system, Matthew Wilson of the Massachusetts Institute of Technology and Bruce McNaughton of the University of Arizona studied mice. They found that when a mouse entered a new environment, groups of nerve cells in its hippocampus fired off electrical signals, the patterns varying with the environment itself. Then, during the night, as the mouse slept, the whole process was repeated, with exactly the same nerve cells firing in just the same way. It is through this process, Wilson and McNaughton explain, that experiences stored in the hippocampus during the day are permanently archived in the cortex at night. Listening to the hippocampus, the cortex takes it in and fires in a corresponding pattern.

Which memories make it into the archives, and which are relegated to the brain's trash bin, never to be seen again? Yale scientists studying serotonin say one criterion is repetition.

Another standard for retention is the intensity and drama of the event. After President Kennedy's assassination, for example, psychologists observed the phenomenon of "flashbulb memories," so called because most people retained an enhanced memory of where they were and what they were doing on receiving the news. Flashbulb memories were observed during the attempt to assassinate President Ronald Reagan and the explosion of the space shuttle *Challenger* as well.

Intense, long-term memories are also forged by fear and reawakened through life by stress. Studies of mice at New York University are instructive: when exposed to a ringing bell followed by electric shock, mice remember and fear the sound of the bell. If, in subsequent trials, the bell rings but the shock is withheld, the fear response—and the memory that triggered it—seems to fade. But once shocked, the mice are forever predisposed to fear. The terror returns with a vengeance if previously shocked mice are exposed to stress in other situations—even if those mice have not been shocked for months.

Such memories are not only more vivid but also more accurate and less prone to change as time goes on, even when subjected to misleading suggestions. In a study of children, researchers found that the stressful event of inoculation was associated with relative enhancement of memory for the central details when compared with the less stressful situation of meeting with a friendly stranger in the doctor's office.

Because love is gentle while fear is generally intense, the neurocircuits of fear may be more difficult to erase. NYU neuroscientist Joseph LeDoux suggests that this may be why phobias are so difficult to cure. Even after seemingly successful treatment, memories of the feared experience remain embedded deep in the brain. They might remain dormant for years yet become reactivated and cause havoc under stress.

FALSE MEMORY OR TOTAL RECALL?

At age 2½ to 3, most children retain and later retrieve some type of verbal memory of a traumatic event. But University of California child psychiatrist Lenore Terr has found that children who lack verbal memory—

those under age 2—suffer greater consequences. Traumatized children from this group showed detailed behavioral memory of their traumas, reenacting in play or other behaviors at least part of the traumatic experience. For instance, a child who had been sexually abused in day care from birth to 6 months of age was able to reenact the exact details of her abuse (as verified in photographs confiscated from the day care center by police) at age 2 years 11 months.

While frightening and dramatic events are more likely than dull events to be consciously recalled, the worst forms of trauma and abuse are often forgotten. As many as 38 percent of trauma victims who experienced abuse severe enough to have to go to the hospital have no explicit memory of the event twenty or more years later. Even though unavailable to the conscious mind, memories of traumatic events may be deeply, implicitly entrenched determinants of behavior throughout our lives.

In many instances, behavioral reenactment of early trauma continues even if the context has changed. Take the case of "Monica," born with congenital closure of the esophagus and followed by scientists for thirty years. For the first two years of life, Monica "ate" by lying flat on her back with a feeding tube inserted in her stomach. She was never held while feeding, as healthy infants are. As a child, Monica fed her dolls in this same lying flat/no contact fashion. As a mother, she fed her three infant daughters in this way—and they, in turn, used the technique to feed their dolls.

What of the controversy involving "false memory syndrome," in which recollection of abuse is allegedly induced by therapists looking for problems where none exists? Although that may occasionally occur, a team of psychiatrists from Yale points to overwhelming evidence that the brain reserves special powers of repression—but not erasure—for traumatic events. When traumas are repressed, psychiatric conditions from post-traumatic stress disorder to amnesia and dissociative (multiple personality) disorder evolve to help the individual survive. Numerous studies now show that neuromodulators released during stress have both strengthening and diminishing effects, depending on the concentration and particular type of neuromodulator. One result is change in the structure of the hippocampus and amygdala, brain regions involved in memory. The changes suggest that memories of abuse are different from normal memories, and research bears that out. Locked away in the recesses of our brain so we are shielded from their intensity, these memories are more difficult to retrieve than other memories, but also more difficult to alter and erase. Because these unconscious, implicit memories are so powerful, they influence behavior throughout life.

If memory of trauma exists somewhere in the brain, it's possible to draw it out, epecially if we re-create the conditions under which the memory was made. This is called "state-dependent learning." If extreme fear or sadness predominated at the time of the trauma, plunging into that mind-set in therapy or through some life event might trigger sudden recall after many years.

ON FAMILY TIME

As parents, it is especially important that we examine our own memories, explicit and implicit, conscious and unconscious. If memory is unwittingly influencing us, it may adversely affect the way we relate to and raise our young.

Unwitting ties to our parents and our past make life complex. Whether we carry memory implicitly, in the cells of our immune system; explicitly, in the cerebral cortex; or historically, through the cycle of family patterns, we'll function best if our connection to the past is understood. As parents, we are not only wiring our babies' brains but providing them with memories, implicit and explicit, that will guide them the rest of their lives. Toward that end, it behooves us to become fully aware of our family histories before we have children. The more we understand ourselves, the more likely we are to see our children for who they really are instead of mistaking them for ghosts from our past. The more we recall, the less likely we are to confuse our babies' needs and communications with our unmet needs.

SUMMING UP

What is memory, and when does it begin? In the most basic sense, memory is the process by which we retain what we experience and learn. By its very nature, experience alters as we grow. The unborn child does not experience the same thing as the toddler, just as the toddler does not experience the same thing as the adult. The vast chasms between these states of being do not mean one realm of existence is wiped out as we enter the next. Rather, from the moment of conception, the stories of our lives become encoded in the cells of our bodies and the neural circuits of our brains. Parents who understand how these memories are formed will be better equipped to create happy and positive memories for their children.

Key Parenting Points

- Enhance good memories, which emerge from repeated nurturing and positive interaction between parent and child. Play with your child, sing to your child, talk to your child, hold and touch your child every day, and those loving memories will endure.
- Protect your children from painful events. A single stressful experience will fade, and may not even be permanently encoded in the brain. But the same traumatic experience, repeated again and again, will become a pervasive, unconscious template for psychological disturbances throughout life.
- Put your own memory banks in order as soon as you can, preferably before you embark on parenthood. If you are inexplicably sad or depressed, or suspect early abuse, do all you can to uncover your early memories so you can defuse them. Otherwise you are at risk for passing psychological problems on to your children.

11

—∾—

Depending on the Kindness
of Strangers

Lana still remembers how she worked up to the moment she went into labor; that way, she reasoned, she could devote as much time to her baby as possible before going back to work. Though she wished she could have spent the next year or so at home just caring for her new son, it was an impossible dream. With both her and her husband working, they earned just enough to make ends meet in modest circumstances—and her salary was, by far, the bigger one.

As the time to return to work drew close, she tackled her search for a caregiver as she tackled all her other projects, with determination and focus. But the task was more difficult than she had expected. One person showed up riding an adult-sized tricycle of the sort once used to deliver groceries; the woman's demeanor was lovely, but with advanced multiple sclerosis and slowed reflexes, hardly the ideal candidate to chase the active toddler Lana's infant would become. Another person came but refused to give Lana references; a third began snapping at Lana's simple questions, coming off as hostile and overly rigid. Lana finally settled on a grandmotherly woman named Angelica and, full of trepidation, returned to work.

There was no question that Angelica kept the little boy safe, but her major interest turned out to be the daytime soap operas. She rocked the little boy, Sammy, back and forth in his carriage until he fell asleep while she sat watching *One Life to Live, The Young and the Restless,* and more.

Aware of the situation, Lana tolerated it because it meant Sammy had far more waking hours with her at the end of the day. She was often up playing with him well beyond midnight, and though she generally went through the workday exhausted, she felt glad that she'd had more hours with her son than he'd had with the nanny. In the years that followed, Sammy was Lana's son all the way—even down to the unfortunate habit of staying up past midnight through the early grades of school.

This exhausting scenario—not one I recommend—is just one of myriad child-care solutions parents have found in recent years. The complexities of modern life, including the dissolution of the nuclear family and the extended family and the frequent need for both parents to work, have brought a new agenda to the fore. Not only must parents now pay attention to their own child-care skills, they have the added task of orchestrating a nurturing experience for their child in their absence.

In the United States alone there are 22 million youngsters age 6 and under who must be watched, for at least part of the day, by people other than mothers and fathers. By the early 1990s, according to the National Institute of Child Health and Human Development (NICHD), a branch of the National Institutes of Health, more than half of the mothers of infants 1 year of age or less were in the labor force. In fact, the institute found, the majority of infants now spend time in nonmaternal child care, typically beginning in the early months of life.

We've long recognized the role of predictable, responsive, and sensitive care in supporting the development of our youngest children. But the latest discoveries—that young brains are literally wired by relationships with the brains of primary caretakers—cast a new light on modern trends. Given the latest in brain science, how can parents of the youngest children delegate their most vital responsibility? How can they determine which qualities are beneficial in caregivers, and which are harmful? How can they decide how much nonparental care is appropriate, and what impact it might have?

Part of the answer comes from the study published by the Early Child Care Research Network of the NICHD in 1997. The group's goal was to compare maternal sensitivity and infant-mother engagement based on nonmaternal child care arrangements—including father care, grandparent care, care by a nonrelative in the child's home, child-care homes, and center-based care.

The NICHD team first reviewed its studies going back decades. Results of the previous work, in aggregate, show that nonmaternal child care was positive in some situations and negative in others. For families about to break under the burden of poverty, illness, or psychiatric problems, high-quality nonmaternal child care was often a plus. In these circumstances, the advice, support, and education offered by child-care professionals was often a godsend. For children from dysfunctional families, it makes sense that day care centers can in many instances be more organized and nurturing than the home. On the other hand, the research revealed, nonmaternal care could push things the other way. The NICHD researchers found that just twenty hours of day care a week before age 1 increased negative interactions between parents and infants 15 to 21 months of age, particularly if other risk factors, such as maternal depression, were already in play.

The NICHD team was the first to examine the effects of child care in the context of other factors shaping children's development and their relationships with their mothers—from economic status to the mother's psychological well-being and intelligence to the child's sex and temperament. In short, the design of the study made it likely that effects discerned were truly due to child care and not a function of other influences.

Following subjects from birth through grade one, the study asked essential questions about nonmaternal child care and its impact on young children and their families. Conducted by scientists at fourteen universities nationwide, the study was spurred by many questions from parents, developmental psychologists, and policy makers about the effects of early child care on children's development. The team followed an exacting procedure: features of child-care use were tracked every three months. The quality of the care and of mother-child interactions were assessed at four major data-collection ages—6 months, 15 months, 24 months, 36 months—across the first three years of life.

Among the investigators' core interests were how these child-care experiences affected children's cognitive and language development and the way in which parents and children related. These were important focal points because early language skills predict future school achievement, while patterns of mother-child interaction predict social, emotional, and cognitive development.

The results confirmed what neuroscientists have theorized in their studies of the brain: the more hours a child spends in nonmaternal child care, the less sensitive the mother seems to be to that baby's feelings and moods.

The study team also placed value on quality care—defined as a high degree of positive interaction between caregivers and children. Of particular importance was language stimulation, which the investigators assessed by measuring how often caregivers spoke to children, asked them questions, and responded to their vocalizations. Children receiving this quality care demonstrated superior verbal and socialization skills, and consistently tested higher on standardized tests. What's more, mothers whose children received the better care became more sensitive to them. The NICHD concluded that working mothers looked to superior caretakers as role models, and were more likely to respond positively to children with better verbal and social skills.

"The most striking aspect of the results is that children are not being placed at a disadvantage in terms of cognitive development if they have high-quality day care in their first three years," said NICHD's director, Duane Alexander. Adds study coordinator and investigator Sarah Friedman: "The amount of language that is directed at the child in child care is an important component of quality provider-child interaction. This language input is predictive of children's acquisition of cognitive and language skills, which are the bedrock of school readiness."

THE DAY CARE CENTER DILEMMA

While NICHD scientists have shown that nonmaternal day care may often be adequate, other studies reveal that this is not always the case. When it comes to day care centers, the overriding problem—the tip-off to potential disaster—is straightforward lack of quality.

Some of the most disturbing findings come from "Quality 2000," a definitive six-year study of day care centers and family child care facilities across the United States. The researchers found that a mere 12 to 14 percent of the children they studied were in situations promoting growth and learning, while 12 to 21 percent were in facilities that jeopardized their development and even their safety. When it came to infants and toddlers, the findings of "Quality 2000" were even more alarming: some 35 to 40 percent of day care children under 3 had been relegated to settings detrimental to their health, safety, and development.

Though the numbers are appalling, people who have read the news or toured such facilities themselves in search of an appropriate place for a child of their own would not be surprised. Rusty, broken-down equipment, hallways smelling of urine, and teachers with harsh, inappropriate behavior are all too common. University of Pennsylvania psychologist and day care expert Jay Belsky estimates that 20 percent of day care is poor, 60 percent fair, 15 percent good, and 5 percent very good.

Next, research is demonstrating that the child's personality and family circumstances influence her day care experience. An insecure, anxious child will probably become more so in a strange environment. This in turn will further imperil his or her relationships both with peers and with caregivers. The relaxed, cheerful, and outgoing child will of course make friends and have a much easier time. The consensus, say experts, is that family factors combine with positive and negative day care features to determine the outcome of the experience as a whole. While no one questions that high-quality care can compensate for risk factors like parental drug use or extreme poverty, children fared better or worse in any situation based on factors such as family income and maternal vocabulary. Most experts agree that the less advantaged a child is, the more he or she may be influenced in either a positive or a negative direction.

Problems are compounded when day care centers accept the youngest infants. Sadly, the majority of U.S. states allow infants to enter day care any time after birth. I spoke recently to a young woman who had worked in a Texas day care center for six months. She was given thirteen toddlers, all of them under the age of 2, to take care of. They were all in diapers and the parents expected her to toilet train these children while also providing them with a richly stimulating program, feeding them, and keeping them from harming each other. When she asked for more help, the owner replied that by law she did not need to provide more than one child-care worker per thirteen children!

The practice of placing a child (especially a newborn) in the care of untrained, unmotivated, and underpaid strangers is deeply disturbing. Perhaps the implicit assumption is that little knowledge or experience is necessary to care for young children and that as long as their basic needs are ministered to they will be okay. Clearly, the new findings in brain science prove this assumption wrong. Unfortunately, except for the lucky few who attend the top bracket of day care centers, emotional, intellectual, and social needs will not be met.

Other research shows that child-care centers are a major source of infection. Children in day care centers have higher rates of diarrhea, hepatitis, meningitis, and ear infections than do children who are not in day care. According to a recent Norwegian study, toddlers who attend day care or nursery school are twice as likely to develop asthma. "One possible reason for the increased asthma prevalence in children attending day care is the indoor environment they are exposed to. This may include indoor allergens such as pet dander and exposure due to building characteristics," according to Wenche Nystad, head of the research team. Researchers from the University of Montreal found that day care can even damage hearing. Most facilities the team inspected were not acoustically designed for the decibel level a group of exuberant toddlers were bound to generate, and impairment of hearing across the group as a whole was a frequent result.

NICHD results notwithstanding, the latest research shows that this sense of chaos takes its toll on the developing brain. A new study, conducted by Andrea Dettling, Megan Gunnar, and Bonny Donzella of the University of Minnesota's Institute of Child Development, questioned whether physiological measurements might reveal internal stresses that straightforward observation of mother-child interaction could not.

Common sense suggests that "group care may be challenging for young children," the researchers say. "The length of the day, the need to sustain interactions with many other children, and the need to organize and reorganize security-seeking behaviors around multiple adults are examples of challenges facing young children in these settings. While these challenges may stimulate development of social skills, they may also tax emotional resources and coping competencies and result in intermittent stimulation of stress-sensitive physiological systems."

The physiological system the Minnesota scientists targeted was the HPA (hypothalamic-pituitary-adrenocortical) axis of the brain. Mediator for the autonomic nervous system, the HPA controls such functions as heart rate and breathing. The HPA is the generator of stress hormones such as adrenaline and cortisol and source of the fight-or-flight reaction—it was designed by evolution to respond when predators attack, in times of famine or flood, in the wake of extraordinary stress. Closely linked to the amygdala and the hippocampus, structures of the limbic brain involved in emotion and memory, the HPA reacts whether stress is derived from physical or psychological events.

If the HPA axis showed unusual activity during the day care experience, the researchers reasoned, they could detect it by measuring production of HPA hormones—specifically, the amount of cortisol in free-flowing saliva. Already well documented in children and adults is the fact that cortisol levels are normally at their highest in the morning and taper off thereafter. The Minnesota researchers found that for children in full-time day care, the opposite occurs. Morning cortisol for this group is somewhat lower than in the population at large and continues to rise throughout the day. The higher cortisol levels in the day care population were associated with anxiety, inattention, and lack of self control. Spikes of cortisol coincided with aggression in the day care group.

The University of Minnesota scientists say that immature social skills combined with the need to sustain interactions with other children and

adults over many hours may help explain these findings. Difficulty nap-
ping restfully in the day care environment may make the problem
worse. Because the Minnesota study was conducted in a model facility
used for teacher training, the elevations noted represent a best-case scenario for young children in full-day group care. Other studies suggest
that as quality of care decreases, the rise in cortisol is more pronounced.

What does the rise in cortisol—indicative of stress—mean for the
emotional and cognitive development of the children themselves? How
can researchers make sense of the often-contradictory reports regarding
the impact of day care on the very young? Hoping to find an answer,
Claudio Violato and Clare Russell analyzed eighty-eight published reports involving 22,072 children. Despite the shortfalls of many individual studies, including lack of long-term scope, "meta-analysis" of the
literature puts things in perspective to a degree. As the NICHD team
learned, nonmaternal care has little negative impact on the cognitive
skills of the child, providing the care is of high quality. But across-the-
board review of the studies showed that emotional, social, and behavioral measurements were significantly higher for children in maternal
care. Indeed, analysis revealed, the type of nonmaternal care was virtually meaningless—whether babies were cared for by day care centers,
baby-sitters, or older siblings, those in nonmaternal day care (even high-
quality day care) scored lower on behavioral and emotional scales than
those being cared for by their mother.

One surprising result of the analysis was the finding that males fared
more poorly than females in every domain. Visiting a local day care center as part of his own investigation, researcher Henry Brandtjen of St.
Mary's University in Minneapolis had an 8-month-old boy crawl into his
arms and fall asleep shortly after his arrival. The child spent much of his
free time with Brandtjen for the next couple of days, as did other boys in
the group.

Quick gravitation to a stranger on the part of the children, Brandtjen
believes, reflects inadequate or insecure attachment to parents. Children
in the centers he visited were exposed to biological parents only a few
hours a day, he reports, and were often passed from staff member to
staff member instead of being assigned to just one. Each caretaker had
unique expectations and reactions, leaving their charges confused. "Most
of the children appeared detached, spaced-out, or resigned," he says. "In
one typical center, two of the boys were overly aggressive, and only three
of nine toddlers ran to greet their parents at the end of the day."

Full-day child care, it seems, places the youngest charges at risk for
problems with attachment, signaled by withdrawal on the one hand and

indiscriminate sociability on the other. It takes a mind to build a mind, and children exposed to too many caretakers are likelier to end up uncertain of their place in the world and emotionally insecure.

The parent conscious of the brain's requirements can, of course, compensate. By taking as much time off as possible before returning to work, and by securing flexible work arrangements thereafter, full-time working parents can create enduring bonds with their babies—especially if two parents coordinate the effort in the spirit of a team. By spending many hours with a child, and by being truly sensitive and responsive to the child's moods and feelings, working parents can forge a secure attachment with their baby, day care center or not.

MANAGING THE DAY CARE CENTER EXPERIENCE

Louise Bates Ames, associate director of the famous Gesell Institute on Human Development, stated recently: "I would say that if a parent can wait until the child is 2 or 3 years of age before going to a day care center or nursery school, that would be the best thing. It would be very hard for me to put a baby in a day care center."

I could not agree more. Even the best of these facilities can be detrimental to infants a year old or less. However, parents may find themselves in a bind. A professionally trained nanny may be too expensive, or a trusted sitter may take ill or decide to move. If parents must work, and if organized group day care is the only available solution, they should put considerable effort into finding the very best day care they can afford.

High-caliber day care centers may be recognized by the following features:

- Caregivers are trained professionals with degrees or diplomas in psychology, early childhood education, nursing, and the like.
- Caregivers are responsible for no more than five children. (Group size is crucial. The smaller the better.)
- The facility is tidy, safe, properly lit, and well stocked with toys, books, and art materials.
- There is an outdoor, fenced-in playground adjacent to the facility.
- Sleeping arrangements are clean, safe, and comfortable.
- Meals are healthy, hygienically prepared, and properly served.
- The children's artwork appears on the walls throughout the center.
- There is no routine TV watching. Instead, children are played with, told or read stories, and otherwise intellectually stimulated.

- The staff progresses with the children from year to year: difficult to find but ideal.

It is not enough to check these qualities off a list and, requirements met, go your way. Parents must be ever vigilant—even when things seem perfect. Already guilt-ridden by leaving young children in day care, parents will view the facility through rose-colored glasses, reluctant to acknowledge problems that might exist. This is human nature. One mother rhapsodized to a reporter about her son's day care: "He's having such a great time that he doesn't want to come home when I go to pick him up. There are parent meetings, but to tell you the truth, I've never been to one. I don't have anything to complain about."

It turned out that the center in question was run by an untrained supervisor, in direct violation of Ontario law. Few licensed teachers were in evidence, and the ratio of children to staff was appallingly high. In the playground, one little boy ate sand unhindered. The son of the woman who recommended the place sat alone on a swing, seemingly oblivious to everything around him.

Another mother tuned out her child when he sobbed at having to return to school. Overwhelmed by her job, and unable to entertain the notion of taking time off to find another solution, she forced him to return again and again. Eventually the child had a true nervous breakdown. The mother subsequently discovered, through one of the parents, that a day care worker had repeatedly verbally abused her child as well as other children. Though complaints had been submitted by many parents, the director of the school refused to place the child-care worker under review.

To stay on top of such issues, it is essential that parents talk to their children about their daily experiences at the day care center. They must get to know the staff and the facility. They can do so by volunteering to help at the center on a regular basis, attending meetings with the caregivers, and entering the premises during the day unannounced. More than anything else, involved parents keep the day care center honest. And it's a two-way street—the manager and staff need and appreciate the support of an enthusiastic and energetic parent body.

THE NANNY-GO-ROUND

When women are pregnant, it's common wisdom that others refrain from discussion of difficulties in labor. Who needs to know about the fourteen hours of closely spaced contractions, the emergency C-section,

or the baby born with jaundice and shortness of breath? But another often verboten topic, and one that should probably be aired with greater
frequency, is the difficulty of finding adequate child care in the form of
a nanny or baby-sitter for infants just a few months old.

Next to regulated and unregulated day care centers, baby-sitters, au
pairs, and nannies are the most frequent minders of children, particularly for more affluent families.

Au pairs are young women, usually from abroad, who wish to see the
world and/or learn a language and support themselves by looking after
young children. In the United States they cost about $125 a week, plus
board, in contrast to about $800 to $1,000 a week for a trained nanny.
Typically, the only experience that "prepared" them for this job was baby-
sitting their younger siblings. Although au pairs may be perfect assistants
for parents who stay at home but need some help, they are inappropriate
as the sole caretaker of a newborn, young infant, or toddler. If working
parents cannot afford a mature baby-sitter or nanny, I recommend a quality day care center over an au pair.

I've heard high praise for nannies and baby-sitters, and horror stories,
too. One couple had the same live-in baby-sitter watch all three children
from the time the oldest was 6 months old until the youngest turned 14.
This trusted family member was a supportive, nurturing presence; she
truly loved the children she was paid to watch and helped the parents
provide a sense of stability and security while they worked outside the
home. When her charges became too old to require her services, she returned each week to visit anyway because she had grown to love the family and the children she helped raise.

Another woman, a single mother bringing up her little girl alone, recalled how, when the child was just a year old, neighbors in her apartment
building reported the sound of endless crying jags coming from behind
her door almost every day, from late in the morning until late in the afternoon. Leaving work early one day to investigate, this mother found that
the baby-sitter she'd hired had simply left her baby alone. The baby-sitter
returned to the apartment about a half hour before the mother would normally have been due home and confessed: she had been taking off for
much of the day to attend to business of her own. This mother fired the
baby-sitter on the spot, but the following month she learned, through a
friend, that the woman had secured an identical position in a neighbor-
ing town.

Such stories can frighten parents about to hire a full-time nanny, but
they need to be told. If your baby-sitter is depressed, anxious, or self-

centered, if she dislikes playing with children or speaks English poorly, she can impede the mental and emotional development of your child. If she is cruel, impulsive, or deeply troubled, the child is in danger. I am reminded of one woman who, after five years of psychotherapy, had finally gotten her life together. She married, she had great success in her career, and eventually she had a little girl. After firing her second baby-sitter, the woman confessed, "If my therapist [since deceased] could see these events, he would turn over in his grave. After all the work he did with me, I'm giving these dysfunctional people a role in raising my little girl." Admittedly, there are a few bad apples in every barrel, and for every au. pair or nanny gone wrong there are dozens of warm, caring, highly skilled, and competent ones who do a wonderful job.

Nonetheless, parents must stay on guard. With appropriate diligence, you should be able to feel secure that your child is in good hands. However—and this is the key—diligence is a must.

When hiring a nanny, calling references on the phone is simply not enough. I suggest that you interview the prospective candidate two or even three times. Under the repeated stress of the interview process, it is much more likely for someone with emotional problems to slip up. Whether the issue is depression, religious fanaticism, a desire for control, or misrepresentation of experience, I have found it likely that with enough talking problems will emerge. If possible, arrange to do the final interview at the sitter's home. By visiting the person who will watch your child on her home turf, you can learn a lot about her. You might not want to hire the woman who has painted her walls black, or the one who has no furniture and sleeps on a mattress on the floor.

Finally, though references are not enough, they are essential. Those who have something to hide will decline to give references and may even act offended if you request them. "What, you don't trust me?" No, you do not. If the person cannot offer professional and personal references, you should not give her a job.

Once you have hired a sitter, do not simply leave her with your baby on day 1 and rush back to work. I would strongly urge that parents take time off and spend at least a couple of weeks at home with the new nanny, breaking her in and easing the transition for their baby.

If you have followed these steps, you should have some level of comfort. But you must maintain a watchful stance. The need to have someone tend to one's children can produce a certain blindness in a parent, an unwillingness or inability to read danger signals. You tell yourself that it's okay: you're being overly suspicious. After all, the sitter came recommended by a top agency. You don't want to make false accusations or hurt her feelings, and you push your misgivings out of your mind. It's called wishful thinking or denial.

Please don't. If anything makes you uncomfortable—even if it's just a feeling—do everything in your power to check it out. You are not para-noid. You are not overreacting. You are being a parent, doing what a parent should. Your child's welfare must take precedence over all other considerations. If you have nothing more tangible to go on than a gnawing doubt, trust the feeling. You need nothing more than the sense that something is awry to let a baby-sitter go, though I caution you to heed the danger in too much change. A series of sitters can be damaging to young children, so weigh your actions carefully and, most important, try to learn from your experience so that you do not make the same mistake twice.

Even if you feel confident that things are going well, I recommend that you arrive home unexpectedly every so often, and that you observe the sitter (without her knowledge) in a variety of situations in and out of the house. If you can afford it, I also recommend a hidden camera that will broadcast audio and video to your office over the Internet. It is your right and responsibility to protect your child any way you can. This is not invasion of privacy.

CHILD CARE AND TV

No discussion of early formative influences could be complete without an examination of the profound effect television has on young minds. Television is a ubiquitous presence in the homes of virtually all children in developing countries. On average, 6-month-old infants watch TV for an hour and a half a day. By the time they are 5 they have seen 6,000 hours of TV. On completion of high school, a "normal" adolescent has been exposed to 18,000 TV murders and 800 suicides. Indeed, each year a typical American child observes 12,000 acts of TV violence, 14,000 references to sex, and 1,000 rapes. By the time they reach age 70, today's children will have spent seven years of their lives watching television.

Excessive time in front of the TV damages children in numerous ways—by displacing their other activities, by exposing them to violent and dysfunctional content, by suppressing their creative imagination, and by raising the level of stimulation required for everyday comfort while shortening the attention span.

In his marvelous book *Evolution's End*, Joseph Chilton Pearce notes that TV has replaced family conversation and storytelling in the majority of modern homes. Children often eat breakfast in front of the television—and dinner as well. Indeed, it's not unusual for spouses who keep different hours to have meals with the TV for company. When this happens, parents and children don't have a formal, ritualized way of interacting. Parents don't learn as much about the children's day. Children don't learn about the real world, about their parents' jobs and pursuits; they don't learn about family history, including the struggles of grandparents or the exploits of Uncle Bob; and most important, the family does not interact as a unit day to day.

Recall Konrad Lorenz's goslings and ducklings, which after hatching, would follow their mothers or, if the mother was removed, any moving object, whether a person or a mechanical toy. In a way, TV seems to produce a similar kind of imprint. If exposed to television too early and too much, children can become attached to it instead of their parents. This process of detachment from people and attachment to television is exacerbated by lack of close contact with parents. Parents or caregivers who park an infant in front of the TV set instead of taking the time to interact are depriving them of intimacy, attention, and love.

Television also cuts down on the time children spend flexing their imaginative skills. When parents read fairy tales or other stories to little children, when they show them picture books, when they tell them nursery rhymes or poems, the imagination is given free rein to fill in the missing details. Television does not permit that. With sound tracks and laugh tricks, viewers are told how to react and what to feel.

Television also has a restricted vocabulary when compared with children's stories. If an adult uses a word that the child does not understand, the child can ask for an explanation. In this way a child's vocabulary expands. No such interaction can occur with the TV set. So children who watch TV for extended periods of time do not develop their language skills as well as children who interact more with their parents and caretakers.

The fact that it is easier and more exciting for a young child to watch TV than to read further diminishes the acquisition of language and information. One reason TV quashes the imagination is lack of metaphor. It is what it is, and is not open to interpretation like a picture book, a sandbox, or a few blocks.

Children who watch too much TV are therefore at greater risk of growing up inarticulate, illiterate, and habituated to violence. Accustomed to the high-decibel bombardment of constantly changing images, they may become restless and ill at ease without novel stimulation. That's where gangs, violence, and substance abuse can enter the scene. Research shows that convicted violent criminals have a markedly restricted capacity for fantasy and were raised on TV.

A great deal has been written about the connection between television violence and violent behavior in children and adolescents. Considering the statistics, how could it be otherwise? On TV life is shown to be expendable and cheap. Any noble stirrings are systematically suppressed in favor of glorifying power, selfishness, greed, and materialism. And as one team of researchers stated: "We cannot rule out the possibility that some message other than violence (for example, depiction of material wealth, which might lead to feelings of relative deprivation) is responsible for the 'increased violence.'" In other words, even "good" children's shows may be harmful in large doses.

Other research suggests that television exposure (note, I am not saying television violence) has a domino effect on those who are vulnerable, leading them from playground bullying to petty delinquency to violent crime. Finally, the research shows, children exposed to excess television are at greater risk for becoming violent young offenders if they have also experienced violence in their homes.

What we have here is synergy. When TV reflects the ordeals of the child's everyday life, then it has a greater and more corrupting impact. With mounting economic pressures and today's job-related stresses, many parents are deeply concerned about the lack of time they spend with their children. Unfortunately, asking the TV set to entertain and inform children in the parents' absence is not the answer. And blaming the television industry for all the ills of the world is just shirking responsibility.

As a conscious parent, you must regain and reclaim your children from the Pied Piper of television. The TV should not rule the household, dictating when and where the family eats, works, and sleeps. Even in the face of loud protests from your kids, which no doubt will occur, you must regulate both the quantity and the quality of the television that is being watched by all members of the family (that means you, too).

When the TV is on, watch it along with your children as often as possible so you can judge, interpret, and explain the programs to them. When the TV is off, it's your opportunity to engage with your children in genuine interaction such as playing, talking, storytelling, bathing, doing homework, and other joint activities. Remember, parenting is not a popularity contest. Your kids may kick and scream now, but eventually they will thank you for raising them to be intellectually alive and emotionally stable adults with a social conscience and a system of values that goes beyond consumerism.

WORK AND LIFE: PUTTING IT ALL TOGETHER

In the light of these findings, what are the parents of young children to do? If they can manage it, one of the parents should stay at home with the child for as long as possible. To be on the safe side, I recommend that families who are financially and emotionally able to do so have a parent home for the first three years. At an absolute minimum, I suggest three to six months of parental care in the period after birth. This is the mandatory period anyone needs to develop parenting skills, to bond with the baby, and to influence the infant brain as only a parent can. Furthermore, if the mother is nursing her baby, the longer she can stay at home, the more her baby will benefit from this experience.

I am not suggesting that children in nonparental care need be damaged. If the parents of such children remain aware of their children's emotional and neurological requirements, if they consistently and lovingly compensate in the evenings, on weekends, or whenever they can, things should be fine. After all, an infant should sleep about two hours in the course of an eight-hour day; if the day care facility or nanny is gentle and nurturing, six or seven hours without the attunement of the mother or father will be okay. The attentive parent who focuses on the baby during the remaining hours should have plenty of time to prime its brain for positive attributes—especially if the parent spent time with the baby before returning to work.

One caveat: New research reveals that the so-called quality time working parents set aside for their children can do more harm than good. In a study involving more than 1,000 working couples over ten years, researchers found that when parents tried to cram a day's worth of interaction into a couple of hours, children became overanxious and had trouble forming relationships later on. The time you spend with your children should be natural. A couple of hours of intense stimulation can be damaging, but more natural rhythms—including the process of engagement, disengagement, and reengagement—set a more normal pattern that will enhance the parent-child relationship and correctly wire the brain.

SUMMING UP

The complexities of modern life—including the dissolution of the nuclear family and the extended family, and the frequent need for both parents to work—have brought a new agenda to the fore: how to provide our children with child care that is emotionally nurturing and intellectually challenging. The newest studies from Yale show that day care situations promote growth and learning in a mere 12 to 14 percent of children. When it comes to infants and toddlers, the findings are even more alarming: some 35 to 40 percent of day care children under 3 are relegated to settings detrimental to their health, safety, and development.

This information is not meant to frighten parents who are considering engaging a mother's helper or placing their children in day care. But we have to face facts. The pajamas your baby wears, the crib your baby sleeps in, the paint in your house—they all have to pass stringent safety standards. But no such standards apply to the person in whose care you entrust your baby eight to ten hours a day.

Across the board, review of the studies shows that emotional, social, and behavioral measurements are significantly better for children in maternal care. Indeed, analysis reveals that children in day care (even high-quality day care) score lower on behavioral and emotional scales than those being cared for by their mothers or fathers.

One other thing to keep in mind: boys fare more poorly than girls in day care.

Key Parenting Points

- Full-day group care for children younger than 2 is very taxing on the child and should be avoided if at all possible.
- Full-day child care places the youngest children at risk for problems with attachment, signaled by withdrawal on the one hand and indiscriminate sociability on the other. It takes a mind to build a mind, and children exposed to too many caretakers are likelier to end up uncertain of their place in the world, and emotionally insecure.
- If you wish to employ a nanny, check her references, interview her more than once, and arrange to spend some time at home with her.
- No matter what kind of child care you obtain, be sure to talk to your children about the details of their day.
- Excessive time in front of the TV damages children by displacing

other activities, exposing them to violent and dysfunctional content, suppressing creative imagination, and raising the level of stimulus required for everyday living while shortening attention span.

- The so-called quality time that working parents set aside for their children can do more harm than good.

12

—∿—

When Things Go Wrong:
Sad Children, Angry Children

Some years ago I attended a meeting of the American Psychiatric Association in Toronto. A lecture by a University of Massachusetts pediatric psychiatrist shocked the audience. Perihan Rosenthal was reporting on eight suicidal children between the ages of 2½ and 4 that she had treated during the previous five years. She related the story of Benji, 2½, who stopped eating for two weeks, threatened to jump in front of cars, and bit himself severely. She presented the following brief excerpt from a therapy session.

Therapist: Why is the little boy hurting himself?
Benji: He is a bad boy. Nobody loves him.
Therapist: Why?
Benji: Because mommy and daddy [foster parents] went away.
Therapist: Why did they go away?
Benji: Because Benji is bad. Now he has to get hurt.

Though suicidal behavior among children is generally considered rare, Rosenthal believes this is because parents and psychiatrists have turned a blind eye to the evidence. They simply cannot accept the concept that children are capable of feeling severely depressed.

Rosenthal's evidence shows otherwise. One of her studies compared 16 suicidal preschoolers age 2½ to 5 with another group of 16 behaviorally disordered, but not suicidal, preschoolers matched by age, sex, race, and parental, marital, and socioeconomic status. She found that 13 of the 16 suicidal children were unwanted by their parents and were physically abused or neglected by them. The remaining three had very disturbed relationships with their caregivers.

Recently, at a conference at New Children's Hospital in Sydney, Australia, Louise Newman, clinical director of the government health service in South Western Sydney, reported on infant depression as well. She told of babies as young as 2 weeks old showing signs of depression, stress, and anxiety. "All these things mean the infant is not soothed, not contained, not held in the right way. Their symptoms reflect the problems of their parents," she told the audience. "People never used to think about babies and infants having feelings, let alone something like depression. But the picture we are building up of babies is that they are not the passive, totally dependent creatures we thought they were. They are complex, socially active little beings." As such, feelings of sadness are in their grasp.

Ian Goodyear, of the Child and Adolescent Psychiatry Department at Cambridge University, estimates that between 2 and 5 percent of school-age children suffer a serious depressive disorder. A new survey in America shows that up to 10 percent of children succumb to depression.

In this age of the HMO and managed care, it is easier for doctors to prescribe psychiatric drugs than to provide time and space for children and their parents to talk about what's really bothering them. Increasingly, the trend has been to treat behavioral problems with stimulants, tranquilizers, and antidepressants, warranted or not. In 1997, U.S. physicians prescribed Prozac and other antidepressants for 600,000 children between ages 13 and 18, a 46 percent increase from the previous year.

Large segments of the public, under the direction of leading opinion makers, have come to believe in the medical model of mental illness— that is, that all psychological problems are brain problems. The argument runs like this: depression is an illness like diabetes or pneumonia, and like these diseases it will respond to the right drug. The magic bullet of the moment, the lord of prescription pads, is Prozac.

William, age 9, takes a combination of a stimulant and an antianxiety drug. His doctor has suggested adding Prozac. His mother is enthusiastic about the medication. "There are enormous pressures on children, and William had difficulty coping when he was younger," she said. "He had low self-esteem, was struggling in schoolwork, and found it difficult to make friends. Since taking the medication, he has been much happier and calmer."

For a child like William, medicine can certainly help. Whether his problems have been caused by genetic predisposition, ineffectual tuning of the brain early in life, or a family crisis like divorce, if he is too hyper-active or depressed to participate in activities, appropriate drug treat-ment can help him focus in psychotherapy and in school. An ability to control his impulses will help William feel better about himself; as a re-sult, his teachers will stop regarding him as "a troublemaker" and other children will want to become his friend.

But for real progress with problems of self-esteem, William will need more than a pill and positive feedback from others. All the research on adults and children shows that they do better if they receive a combina-tion of psychotherapy and drugs. By viewing depression, panic attacks, alcoholism, bulimia, and the like as merely "genetic" or due to "a chem-ical imbalance," we absolve from any responsibility not only the afflicted individual but also the family of origin and society at large. Instead of confronting and resolving past hurts and traumas, acknowledging their own shortcomings, and working to improve family life and social condi-tions, people pop more pills, develop more depressive illnesses, and com-mit more crimes.

A study of UCLA's Neuropsychiatric Institute showed that 5 percent of the 662 preadolescent children treated there over a four-year period were seriously self-destructive or suicidal. Morris Paulson, the clinical psychologist who conducted the study, found a common denominator among these disturbed youngsters. "Every one of them had a home that wasn't providing the understanding and caring that the child needed." Such children tend to feel unloved, unwanted, inferior, inadequate, and alienated. They perceive themselves as unworthy individuals and, like Benji, often blame themselves for their own neglect, rejection, or abuse.

Girls usually hide their feelings of depression behind psychosomatic symptoms: headaches, stomach upsets, and eating disorders. Boys tend to act out aggressively—engaging in bullying, vandalism, or other petty crimes. Both sexes are likely to exhibit dramatic changes in their grades, interests, and sleeping habits and a markedly increased incidence of se-rious accidents.

In nearly every study reviewed, a high incidence of broken homes be-cause of death, separation, or divorce was reported and identified as an important cause of childhood disturbance. One group showed that the quality of home life subsequent to early parental loss is critically related to the development of later psychopathology. The evidence leaves little doubt that inadequate parenting, irrespective of early loss, is associated with a higher incidence of depression. In cases of parental loss, the like-lihood of deficient parenting increases since the parent in whose care the child remains is himself or herself struggling to cope with grief, anxiety, or anger. These feelings obviously compromise the parent's ability to attend to the child's needs.

Each child's response depends not only on the surviving parent's feelings and behavior but also on the kind of relationship the child had with the lost parent. This is a very complex matter because even a mean and abusive mother may become idealized by a child who needs to cling to the fantasy of a good parent, while a wonderful and nurturing father can be demonized by a child who is angry with him for abandoning him or her. With that caveat, generally speaking, a positive relationship with a lost parent will lead in the short term to more grief but in the long term to greater emotional health.

We have already seen the effect that anxious, stressed, and depressed mothers can have on their babies, both before and shortly after birth. Later on, children who are themselves depressed will find that their mood further aggravates an already compromised neurobiological system. There is strong evidence associating depression with a modest but statistically significant increase in the activity of the autonomic nervous system, especially the sympathetic nervous system and the area along the hypothalamic-pituitary-adrenal axis. As a result, blood levels of the stress hormones cortisone and beta-endorphin rise while immune function is impaired. If this child also finds himself alienated from his parents and his community, then he may become the victim of something far more dangerous than depression—aggression, violence, and crime.

AGGRESSIVE CHILDREN

When a child grows up in a dysfunctional family within a larger, disintegrating social milieu, the chances that he will turn his anger against others rather than himself rise considerably. Studies indicate with some consistency that abused children, starting with toddlers and infants, manifest significantly more antisocial and conduct disorders than nonabused, nonneglected children. Abused and neglected children have a higher likelihood of arrests for delinquency, adult criminality, and violent criminal behavior than matched controls. Males have higher rates of delinquency, adult criminality, and violent criminal behavior than females.

Unfortunately, violent crime among children as young as 10 has soared in recent years. Virtually every day we read shocking accounts of a phenomenon that knows no national bounds. The crime that stopped Britain in its tracks in February 1993 was the sadistic "killing for kicks" of a 2-year-old child who had been abducted from a shopping center in Liverpool. When his body was later discovered, the little boy had suffered such appalling injuries that policemen wept in shock. But the security cameras in the shopping center had captured his abductors on videotape, and they were later arrested. They were two 10-year-old boys who, it was alleged, had previously limited their torture to neighborhood animals.

In Orlando, Florida, a 9-year-old boy was charged with aggravated battery and domestic violence after he threatened to kill his mother and three other children if he did not get the toy he wanted at Burger King. The hamburger chain had been distributing small toys based on characters in a Walt Disney movie, *The Hunchback of Notre Dame*, in its children's meals. When his mother headed home instead of going to the fast-food restaurant, the boy grabbed her hair and pulled her head to the floor of the van until she persuaded him to let go. He later produced a pocketknife, held it to her throat, and said he would kill her and the other children unless she returned to the restaurant for a Kid's Club meal.

In Tokyo, meanwhile, police arrested a 14-year-old boy they said confessed to killing a younger boy and dumping his severed head in a school yard. The boy, whose name was not released, lived in a neighborhood where the mutilated head of a 1-year-old victim had been found. The infant's eyes had been gouged out and the mouth split open from ear to ear. In a note stuck on the victim's mouth, the killer called the police "fools" and declared that this was "the beginning of the game . . . It's great fun for me to kill people. I desperately want to see people die."

In recent years we've seen an explosive increase in the number of children who commit violent, psychopathic crimes. It's been popular, in decades past, to attribute such tendencies to genes. And of course, genes play a role. But the latest studies show that risk of disturbance and pathology may be dramatically increased by damaging conditions during gestation and the first few years after birth. A depressed caretaker can wire her offspring's brain for disappointment and despair. An infant who is ignored or continually insulted can retreat into various forms of disorder—anxiety, depression, and psychopathology. Carried to extremes, stress and abuse can shift the brain's emotional thermostat to antisocial behavior, explosive anger, and violent crime. If the input is abusive enough, even the healthiest of brains may be damaged.

By the same token, children genetically predisposed toward psychopathology or traumatized before or during birth can be rescued from an unhappy future life by loving, responsive parenting.

THE ORIGINS OF VIOLENCE

The flexibility of the human brain has been key to our species' success. Only a brain built by its environment could respond to such diverse conditions as the expanse of the African savanna and the onslaught of an Ice Age, the rigors of farming and the precision of toolmaking, and the diversity of language, from Chinese or English on the one hand to signing on the other. Because so much of our early history required a talent for handling danger, traits now expressed through violence were high on the list of evolutionary needs.

In our effort to understand violence and its impact on the young, the long view is instructive. Some 250,000 years ago a few thousand *Homo sapiens*—our ancestors—migrated out of Africa to begin the multigenerational process of inhabiting and finally transforming the globe. Success came in large measure from the flexibility of the brain: it could accommodate a wide range of environments, pass information from generation to generation, and evolve in the cultural (as opposed to biological) realm. Without such a brain, we could not have prevailed—for most of our history, life was unpredictable and dangerous. From natural disasters and extremes in climate to attacks by wild animals and the relentless aggression of other humans, our forbears inhabited a capricious, brutal, unforgiving world. It takes experience to build a brain—and for our ancestors, that experience was violent.

Bruce D. Perry, director of the Child Trauma Programs at Baylor College of Medicine and Texas Children's Hospital, notes that brains honed on violence will reflect that in the cultures they spawn. "The evolution of complex cultures and 'civilization' has not protected millions from the brutality which characterized the 'ascent' of humankind," Perry says. "While 'civilization' has decreased our vulnerability to nonhuman predators, it has done little to decrease intraspecies violence." Indeed, institutionalized violence, from slavery to the Inquisition to systematic genocide, has followed us into modern times.

But this legacy of violence no longer serves our survival. In fact, nuclear and biological weapons, the latest tools of violence, could destroy us all. Despite the cooperative requirements of modern life, our psyches have preserved the culture of violence from ancient times. When unable to channel that instinct to the cause of survival, we filter it through the fabric of our daily lives. Domestic violence, physical, sexual, and emotional abuse, rape, criminal assaults, racial violence, the blatant aggression of armies and terrorist attacks, the oppression of governments, and the brutal imagery reaching us through the media—all this creates a mood of violence in the most vulnerable, especially the very young.

THE CYCLE OF VIOLENCE

For today's children, the culture of violence may feel pervasive. How many American children witnessed the tragic destruction of the World Trade Center towers, at least on television? How many now anticipate terror attacks from the skies, their mail, even neighbors they do not know or trust? The ambience of violence, a backdrop to our evolution, is with us still.

The experience of violence often takes place within a community context of risk. Thirty percent of children living in high-crime neighborhoods of cities such as Chicago have witnessed a homicide by the time they are 15 years old, and more than 70 percent have witnessed a serious assault. Appallingly, these figures are reminiscent of experiences during times of war. A National Institute of Mental Health study showed that 43 percent of fifth and sixth graders had witnessed a mugging in a "moderately violent" neighborhood in Washington, D.C. In the American combat zone, guns have become an accepted fact of daily life for children as well as adults. Children in such communities are often poor and at greater risk for neglect and abuse. They are more likely to live in families in which the father is absent, to contend with parental incapacity due to depression or substance abuse, and to be raised by caregivers with little education or prospects for employment.

Despite the prevalence of violence on television and in the community itself, most violence in America takes place in the home. And it is early experience within the family that most often explains the behavior of teenagers and adults who later engage in predatory crime. The most severely exposed of our children are literally "incubated in terror," a process that permanently alters the brain. These damaged children enter the cycle of violence that passes from one generation to the next.

When it comes to violence, in fact, a multitude of studies puts the nature-versus-nurture question to rest. It's been popular, in recent years, for the press and some psychologists to tout the so-called neurobiology of violence. The most violent criminals, the theory goes, will commonly show some biochemical marker. The search for this marker in blood, spinal fluid, and DNA has been thorough but fruitless. While some violent criminals do suffer some abnormalities, scientists have never been able to detect a consistent difference in the genes.

Instead, the only reliable marker for violence in adulthood has turned out to be early exposure to violence and neglect. Abused children often become abusers, and young victims of violence are at risk of becoming violent offenders themselves. In aggregate, data from hundreds of studies now solidly document the intergenerational transmission of violence and abuse.

New York University psychiatrist Dorothy Otnow Lewis has studied violent youth for years. In one study she compared homicidally aggressive children with a group of controls. Across the board, she found homicidal children were more likely than others to come from violent homes. In 62 percent of families with homicidal children, fathers had been physically violent to mothers, compared with only 13 percent of control families. Alcoholism was significantly more common for fathers of homicidal children—52 percent versus 10 percent for fathers of the control children. Some 29 percent of the homicidally aggressive children had been abused by their fathers, versus 7 percent for control children. The homicidal children often had a history of psychiatric illness in the immediate family as well—43 percent of their mothers had a history of psychiatric hospitalization, versus 7 percent for mothers of controls.

In a later study, Otnow Lewis followed a group of nine boys exhibiting extreme violence for six years, between the ages of 12 and 18. One of these boys had burned his bed at age 4, raped a young boy at age 14, and was charged with felony murder at age 19. Another boy choked a girl at age 2, threw a dog out a window at age 4, broke a sibling's arm during middle childhood, assaulted and raped a girl at 16, and finally, raped and stabbed a woman thirteen times at age 18. As her study illustrates, aggression, like intelligence, tends to remain stable over the life span.

That notion finds support in a twenty-year study of 875 primary school children in rural New York. The researchers found that those judged most aggressive by peers at age 8 were also rated most aggressive by themselves and their spouses at age 30. Among the findings:

- Boys are consistently more aggressive than girls, but if a girl is aggressive at 10, she will continue along that path just like the boys.
- Early aggressiveness displayed at school has the potential to escalate into major antisocial acts in young adulthood.
- The most aggressive children become the most aggressive adults.
- Those considered violent when young have a greater likelihood of perpetrating criminal behavior, as well as physical, spousal, and child abuse, as adults.

• Aggressiveness is transmitted within families, from one generation to the next.

The natural history of one such youth, related by a pediatrician,
brings the point home:

"I first met Buddie when he was 13 years old. He was in grade 8 in a
good high school in Vancouver's east side. The family physician who referred him had known Buddie's mother since she was a child and had
cared for her, and later Buddie, since then. He said there had been many
prior referrals for behavioral assessment and treatment during elemen-
tary school. He told me that despite living in chronic poverty and chaos,
Buddie's mother had tried her best.

"I requested the school and family doctor's files and promised to review
them before seeing Buddie. But before I knew it, he was brought in as an
emergency referral by his mother and stepfather, at the insistence of a
school counselor. Buddie had just been suspended from school for fighting in the halls. What's more, he had pulled a knife on his opponent."

Though Buddie had some symptoms consistent with those of fetal alcohol syndrome, his neurological exam was normal and he could read
well enough from the age-appropriate books on hand. "Buddie and his
mother confirmed that he'd had difficulties since kindergarten," the pediatrician noted. "His approach to schoolwork had always shown ability,
but lack of application. He was a regular visitor to the principal's office,
frequently skipped classes, would bully others into doing his homework,
and always seemed to be in the vicinity when items went missing."

The case was complex: Buddie's history included setting fires, destructive rampages, shoplifting, glue sniffing, and complaints of sexually suggestive behavior. His mother and stepfather had been investigated by
social services for neglect and abuse; both had a history of alcoholism and
multiple drug use.

"I was amazed that Buddie was coping as well as he was and made the
mistake of telling his mother so," the pediatrician explains. "She was
irate and stormed out of the office. Buddie just gave me a sly smile as he
followed her out.

"What followed was a string of minor misdemeanors but no charges.
Meanwhile, Buddie was beginning to use drugs and gradually got caught
in the local crack-using culture. School was long since forgotten and his
mother rarely saw him. But for some strange reason he would still turn
up at the office for appointments—well, for about every second one."

Eventually the doctor discovered why: Buddie had been stealing prescription pads and writing fake prescriptions for Ritalin. "I felt that the

only thing to do to get help for Buddie was to enroll him in a court-ordered forensic psychiatry program and get him out of circulation. He went into a detention facility and while there sent me some rather vile and threatening notes."

The pediatrician never saw Buddie again but was able to follow his progress. "Until he was 18, I could keep track of what was going on because one agency or another would write me to request copies of his medical records," the doctor explains. These requests were punctuated by a string of reports in the local press: an armed robbery, a suspected rape, several impaired-driving charges, and finally, the vicious beating of a local store clerk. The victim almost died and would remain permanently disabled.

"I wish I could have done a better job with Buddie," the doctor told me. "I probably share that feeling with the hundred or so other professionals who have interacted with him and his mother over the years."

VIOLENCE AND THE BRAIN

The path from terrorized infant to terrorizing adolescent must pass through the arbiter of behavior, the brain. It is the brain, after all, that allows the child victim to adapt to conditions of violent trauma, and the same brain that, years later, spawns the violent behavior of the victimizer the child has become. How do adaptations meant to help the child survive violence evolve, as the child grows, into acts of aggressive violence?

Searching for an answer, Bruce Perry has synthesized a wide range of studies, including his own, to suggest a theory of how violence germinates in the brain. "The amazing capacity of the human brain to develop in a 'use dependent' fashion—growing, organizing, and functioning in response to developmental experience—means that the major modifier of all human behavior is experience," Perry states. "As the brain develops in a sequential and hierarchical fashion, the more complex areas of the cortex and limbic system begin to modulate, moderate, and 'control' the more primitive and 'reactive' lower portions of the brain. These various brain areas develop, organize, and become fully functional at different stages during childhood. At birth, for example, the brain-stem areas responsible for regulating cardiovascular and respiratory function are intact, while the cortical areas responsible for abstract cognition will not become fully functional for years.

"A frustrated 3-year-old with a relatively unorganized cortex," says

Perry, "will have a difficult time modulating the reactive, brain-stem-mediated state of arousal—he will scream, kick, bite, throw, and hit. The older child when frustrated may feel like kicking, biting, and spitting but has 'built in' the capacity to modulate and inhibit those urges."

The process of brain development is always sequential. As the child grows, more evolved regions of the brain, especially the cortex, become increasingly competent at inhibiting urges from more primitive, less mature, regions. If the cortex is impaired, if it loses function through injury or illness—for example, stroke—the ability to inhibit the primitive brain and its urges will be impaired. But impairment will also result if the cortex has been deprived of the experience required for its development. In that case, the urges of the primitive brain will prevail, predisposing an individual to overreact.

Violent individuals take this phenomenon much further. If, during early childhood, the lower brain has been overstimulated through exposure to continual traumatic stress, while the upper brain has received scant amounts of nurturing, the scales will be tipped strongly in favor of violence.

The concept here is simple: flooding the brain through the doorways of perception, traumatic experience organizes billions of brain cells and trillions of synaptic connections into diseased neural networks. Recent research at Rockefeller University in New York shows that such trauma literally functions like a genetic switch, causing the protein-building apparatus to stop and start at inappropriate times; abnormal brain cell networks are the result.

One characteristic of such diseased networks is overproduction of the stress hormones cortisol and adrenaline. Stressful environments lead to overexpression of genes responsible for survival under life-threatening situations; when these genes are too productive, an increase in aggressive and violent behavior under a wide range of circumstances is the common result.

Why is trauma early on more destructive than similar insults later in childhood? Developmental neuroscience makes it clear. Because of the sequential development of the brain, disruptions during prenatal and perinatal periods alter the structure of the brain stem and midbrain. Such malformation will, necessarily, alter development of the limbic brain and cortex, since these advanced regions depend on signals from lower regions for normal organization.

The neurophysiological chain of development is immutable. As a result, a 12-year-old child could survive two weeks in isolation, experiencing neither touch nor the spoken word, but for a 2-month-old infant, such isolation might be devastating, causing permanent damage to the brain.

THE PHYSIOLOGY OF TRAUMA, ABUSE, AND NEGLECT

Developed in use-dependent fashion, the brains of children exposed to continual violence or trauma must, by necessity, adapt. They do so by sustaining a state of hypervigilance. Bathed in constant fear, they achieve a perpetual state of fight-or-flight readiness. If the brain detects danger, after all, it is the body that must run, cringe, or fade into the background and hide.

It's clear why children subjected to frequent, unpredictable bouts of violence must be hypervigilant and hypersensitive, perpetually ready to field the trouble or escape. But the qualities that protect them from abusive parents become liabilities later on. Organized by experience, the adult brain of that once-abused child has a distorted view of the world. Reacting to everything through the same low-level state of fear so adaptive in childhood, these individuals tend to misinterpret benign language and behavior as acts of aggression and to react to the perceived insults impulsively, often violently, in line with the structure of their brains and the memories they have stored there.

One of the most damaging assaults on the developing brain comes from parental neglect. One 15-year-old boy described by Perry saw a pair of fancy sneakers on the feet of another child and pulled them off at gunpoint. Still not satisfied, the 15-year-old put the gun to the child's head, smiled, and pulled the trigger. Asked later whether, if he could turn back the clock, he would do anything differently, he replied: "I would have cleaned my shoes." His bloody shoes had led to his arrest. While regretting his capture and arrest, the boy felt no empathy with the pain of his victim and no remorse over the act itself.

What happened to make this boy so unremittingly vicious by age 15? Neglected and humiliated by his primary caretakers when he was young, Perry says, he was rendered emotionally retarded. Lack of critical experience prevented development of the part of his brain that would have allowed him to feel connected to other human beings. Just as the cognitively retarded child lacks the capacity to understand abstract concepts, this young murderer lacked the capacity to relate to other human beings in a healthy way.

Reporting on the chronically traumatized children under his care,

Perry describes a consistent physiological profile: increased muscle tone, low-grade increase in temperature, increased startle response, profound sleep disturbance, difficulty in controlling their tempers, and significant anxiety. Boys tend to externalize these symptoms with predatory, aggressive behaviors and even show decreased heart rate—indicating greater calm—when asked to discuss specific violent events. Girls, on the other hand, may internalize the symptoms, resulting in self-destructive behaviors, including eating disorders and self-mutilation.

Is it any surprise we've seen an explosion in the incidence of eating disorders in the United States? According to the House of Representatives Select Committee on Children, Youth, and Families, anorexia and bulimia affect as many as 10 to 15 percent of adolescent girls and young women. The incidence of anorexia nervosa has nearly doubled over the past two decades. And estimates of bulimia among college women range as high as 19 percent.

Not long ago a young woman patient of mine said, "I overeat, overdose, and oversex. If I did not do these things, I would break everything and everybody in the house." In two sentences she had elucidated a tangled web of competing scientific diagnoses, theories, and treatments. Growing up with a sense of anxiety, helplessness, dejection, anger, and rejection, she could survive her psychic pain in either of two ways: she could internalize it through a range of self-destructive behaviors, from addictions and depressions to suicide attempts, or she could externalize it in the form of violent and aggressive acts against others.

THE VIOLENCE COCKTAIL

Most emotionally neglected or traumatized children do not turn into violent criminals or sociopaths. Usually, if these children have had some positive relationships—for example with a grandparent or cherished teacher—they will manage to function, even prosper. However, those not so lucky will most likely suffer a sense of emptiness and loneliness, because they are unable to connect with others. Others connect, but only through relationships that are destructive or disturbed. Because to various degrees they lack empathy and trust, they are much more likely than others to behave in an antisocial fashion—to lie, cheat, or steal.

Research has shown that the most violent among us emerge not *just* from early abuse but rather from a mix of factors, including genetic predisposition, birth trauma, lack of nurturing, and lack of cognitive stimulation.

Let us consider for a moment the histories of two notorious killers. David Edwin Mason and Robert Alton Harris spent their final years on death row before they were gassed by the State of California in 1991 and 1993, respectively, for heinous crimes of violence. The dossier on Mason reveals him to have been a sad and lonely child whose mother tried to induce a miscarriage to avoid having him in the first place, and who was never allowed to forget that he was unwanted. Older sisters describe a household where hugging or laughter were prohibited, and in which young David was beaten almost daily with his father's belt or his mother's switch.

When only 5, the child attempted suicide by swallowing a bottle of pills and setting his clothing on fire. At 8, he was taking out his hostility by setting fires at church and at school. His parents started to lock him away in a room they called the dungeon—a bedroom with the windows nailed shut. When he wet his bed or soiled his clothes, David was forced to walk around with the soiled clothes wrapped around his head.

At age 23, Mason went on a nine-month killing spree in the neighborhood where he had grown up, strangling four elderly men and women. He later confessed that it was "something I have always wanted to do."

Harris's beginnings were strikingly similar. He was born three months premature after his mother was kicked so brutally in the abdomen by an angry husband that she began hemorrhaging. As in the Mason family, both parents inflicted frequent beatings—the father with his fists, causing a broken jaw when Robert was not yet 2. While sitting at the table, if Robert reached out for something without his father's permission, he would end up with a fork in the back of his hand.

For sport, the father would load his gun and tell the children they had thirty minutes to hide outside the house, after which he would hunt them like animals, threatening to shoot anyone he found. The senior Harris was jailed for sexually molesting his daughters, while the mother smoked and drank herself to death.

Like Mason, young Harris soon began showing anger toward animals and people. At 25, he shot two San Diego teenagers to death. Prosecutors told the jury that Harris taunted the victims before they died, laughed at them after he pulled the trigger, then calmly ate the hamburgers they had bought for lunch.

Discussing the psychiatric, neurological, and family characteristics of murderers, Dorothy Otnow Lewis emphasizes that the combination of violent behavior by parents, severe abuse, psychiatric illness of a close relative, neurological impairment, and psychotic symptomatology most strongly distinguishes murderers from other criminals. Although exposure to violence puts children at greater risk for violence in adulthood, it is the combination of all these factors that most often characterizes the truly vicious criminals.

Social and cultural decay in some communities make the problem worse. For children who grow up in poverty or in single-parent families, with mothers who are teenagers or drug abusers, and without good schools to offset the damage, a violent upbringing may tip the balance, making criminal violence the result.

Moreover, studying children in his center, Bruce Perry has found that sometimes the straw that breaks the camel's back is a system of belief. "Racism, sexism, misogyny, children as property, idealization of violent 'heroes,' cultural tolerance of child maltreatment, tribalism, jingoism, nationalism—all unleash, facilitate, encourage, and nurture violent individuals," Perry says. Until we understand and address the relationship between cultural belief systems, child-rearing practices, and the prenatal and perinatal influences as described in these pages, we will be unable to prevent the violence in our midst.

EMOTIONAL BATTERING

Some parents may not lift a hand to hit children but may batter them emotionally until the damage is just as bad. Constant screaming, criticizing, belittling, and shaming thrust children into the same fight-or-flight mode they might experience had their parents smacked them.

If this verbal abuse is accompanied by physical abuse, the damage can be more devastating still.

One recent study looked at the worst of these abusers—called cyclically/emotionally volatile batterers by psychologists. These abusive parents, the researchers found, hit and shamed their children just like the parents of Mason and Harris. Moreover, boyhood shaming, primarily by fathers, was found to be the most powerful factor contributing to wife abuse when the child grew up. When physical abuse in childhood was factored out, shaming experiences were still strongly related to adult rage and abusiveness. But the opposite did not hold: physical abuse by the father did not, on its own, turn the son into a batterer. Instead, the lethal combination of physical abuse and shaming was required for the child to become a cyclically/emotionally volatile batterer. Unfortunately, the researchers found, the combination of physical and verbal abuse was far more common than physical or verbal abuse alone.

COGNITIVE DEPRIVATION AND VIOLENCE

Depriving children of cognitive stimulation may predispose them to violence as well. It is the cerebral cortex, the seat of thought, after all, that plays a major role in inhibiting the violent impulses of our primitive brain. The richer the resources of the cortex, the more likely it is to effectively regulate signals rising from below. An infant brain deprived of sensorimotor experience, including environments rich in colors, sights, sounds, and smells, the give and take of language, and an attuned caretaker or guide, is bound to be underdeveloped in the cognitive realm. For example, when he examined the brain scans of twelve severely neglected children Bruce Perry found seven with underdeveloped regions of the cortex. These areas had been present at one point, he contends, but had atrophied from disuse.

THE ROOTS OF PSYCHOPATHOLOGY

Abuse and neglect don't make most children violent, of course, but depending on frequency and severity, they do induce a spectrum of psychiatric ills.

- Suicide: In her study of violent youth, Dorothy Otnow Lewis found that 57 percent of children who were so aggressive they were literally homicidal had also tried to commit suicide. What's more, 80 percent of those children had entertained suicidal thoughts.
- Dissociative disorder (multiple personality disorder): Children surviving especially brutal physical or sexual abuse are at higher risk for developing multiple personality disorder. "The abuse in multiple personality is usually severe, prolonged, and perpetrated by family members who are bound to the child in a love-hate relationship," notes psychiatrist Philip M. Coons, an expert on multiple personality disorder from Indiana University School of Medicine. For example, in one study of twenty patients, abuse occurred over periods ranging from one to sixteen years and in only one instance was the abuser not a family member. The abuses included incest, sexual molestation, beating, neglect, burning, and verbal abuse.
- Depression: Children who were abused suffer far higher rates of depression as adults. In fact, those who were emotionally abused are at greater risk for depression than those who suffered physical

abuse. Not surprisingly, other studies show that victims of child abuse have lower self-esteem.

- Anxiety disorders: Sexually and physically abused children suffer far more social phobia, panic disorder, and anxiety disorder. One study shows that victims of physical abuse have increased lifetime diagnoses of obsessive-compulsive disorder, while victims of sexual abuse have increased lifetime diagnoses of simple phobia.
- Post-traumatic stress disorder: Those who have been sexually abused are often diagnosed with post-traumatic stress disorder as adults. Nightmares are far more frequent than in control groups of nonabused individuals. Some researchers have found that sexually abused people have much in common with traumatized veterans of the Vietnam War. In fact, physical abuse during childhood turned out to be a strong determinant of whether or not the veterans developed post-traumatic stress disorder; the only factor that played a larger role was exposure to combat.

   Traumatized survivors of child abuse who appear psychotic are often misdiagnosed as schizophrenic, but the auditory and visual hallucinations they report are far more likely to result from post-traumatic stress disorder than actual psychosis. Likewise, adults who were abused as children often suffer manic episodes reminiscent of bipolar disorder—increased verbalizations, distractibility, racing thoughts, and psychomotor agitation. This, too, probably reflects trauma and not bipolar disorder itself.
- Substance abuse: Numerous studies show that children exposed to verbal, physical, and sexual abuse are far more likely to be substance abusers in adulthood. One important finding is that abuse seems to contribute to the development of alcohol-related problems even more than a family history of substance abuse, suggesting that the influence of environment in some cases outweighs genetic factors.
- Sexual dysfunction: Victims of sexual abuse are more likely than others to report sexual dysfunction, including distrust of partners, dependency, avoidance, decreased sex drive, sexual anxiety and guilt, inability to enjoy sexual activity, and a history of multiple brief sexual relationships.
- Personality disorder: Studies indicate that between 67 percent and 75 percent of patients with borderline personality disorder (repetitive pattern of disorganization and instability in self-image, mood, behavior, and close personal relationships) report a history of early

abuse. Males who were abused as children are far more likely than the general population to be diagnosed with antisocial personality disorder, characterized by a pervasive pattern of disregard for and violation of the rights of others.

- Severe mental illnesses: Research shows that maltreatment in childhood may be a risk factor for severe mental illnesses such as schizophrenia and bipolar disorder. One group found that psychiatric outpatient women with a history of sexual abuse scored significantly higher on the schizophrenia scale than women without a history of sexual abuse or related trauma. Another study showed that among a group of chronically psychotic patients, childhood abuse survivors had an earlier age of onset of psychiatric symptoms, more dissociative symptoms, and relapsed more frequently than the nonabused subjects. The consensus is that child abuse cannot *cause* schizophrenia and bipolar disorder, but it can significantly increase the risk for those who are already vulnerable.

PREVENTION AND INTERVENTION

Once criminal activity has begun in childhood or adolescence, it frequently continues into adulthood as well. This finding points to the importance of early intervention or, even better, prevention. The newest findings in neuroscience give powerful support to those who have long advocated for early intervention when children are at risk.

The human service professionals and educators who are supposed to protect these children are unfortunately hampered in their work by having themselves become traumatized by exposure to violence. They are generally overworked, underpaid, and disheartened. They have become victims of "compassion fatigue." Thus it is sometimes difficult for them to recognize all but the most blatant high-risk situations. If we want them to succeed at their tasks, we will have to train and pay them better, and treat them with more respect.

The need for early intervention may often be signaled by the parents themselves. High-risk mothers and fathers may have trouble providing appropriate care and feeding for their infant. When that's the case, society must step in with a helping hand.

The high-risk parent is likely to be characterized by the following:

- Single, separated, or divorced.
- Income is inadequate—if married, both unemployed.

- No permanent address.
- No telephone
- Less than twelve years of education.
- No immediate family members available for support.
- A history of substance abuse.
- Late or no prenatal care.
- Has had an abortion in the last twelve months, or has had two or more during her lifetime.
- Has sought an abortion for the present pregnancy.
- Was previously or is currently involved with child protective services.
- Has received or is currently receiving psychiatric care.
- Suffers from depression or has in the past.
- Considered giving up the baby for adoption.
- Demonstrates unrealistic expectations of infant behavior.
- Shows a low tolerance to babies crying and no understanding of the needs of a toddler.
- Has a tendency to scream at, shake, or hit the child.

To circumvent the cycle of violence, we must persuade our governments to act in more constructive ways. We need to institute early prevention programs along the lines of Healthy Start on the island of Oahu, Hawaii, a federally funded pilot project in early intervention launched in 1985. Since then, Healthy Start has spread across all seven of Hawaii's main islands, achieving an almost unbelievable success rate of 99 percent in preventing child abuse and neglect. The program has also been confirmed as vastly improving parent-child relationships and spotting children's medical and emotional problems early on.

Increased federal funding for such programs would be meaningful, indeed. Government programs to reduce poverty and income inequalities would have a significant impact on rates of violence in children and young people. Eliminating video games and television programs featuring gratuitous violence would be beneficial. Reducing the sexual and economic exploitation of children should be a high priority on any government's legislative agenda.

But in the end, this task will fail if we leave it up to governments or other bureaucracies remote from our personal lives. If we really want change, it will have to come from us. The latest research shows that we are creating so many violent children so rapidly that we will never be able to treat or rehabilitate them all. And the alarming statistics of infanticide, delinquency, and criminality are just the tip of the iceberg. Underneath the water are the invisible scars on each child's soul, subtle changes that will, depending on the presence or absence of certain protective factors, lead to a life assailed by anxiety, depression, failed relationships, lack of motivation, addiction, or suicide. To solve problems passed from one generation to the next, we must revolutionize the culture of child-rearing itself.

Our children represent the future of our planet and our species—whether they are our own offspring or not. We must wake up to the fact that children at every socioeconomic level and in every region of the world are being neglected, abused, humiliated, and harmed in myriad ways. If we can lavish billions of dollars on space probes to other planets, we should be able to spend a fraction of that money on programs that would emotionally and intellectually nurture our very young.

SUMMING UP

Life's most devastating problems are often the psychological ones—depression, anxiety, and disturbances so great they cause individuals to sabotage relationships or commit crimes. According to recent research, such problems, ranging all the way up to violent behavior, are often related to abuse, neglect, or trauma in the earliest stages of life. Early stress produces neurophysiological deficits that render children excessively impulsive and irritable. Their condition is further aggravated by a chain of linked factors consisting of poor language skills, poor abstract reasoning, inability to concentrate, and lack of interest in reading. In concert, these factors inevitably lead to academic failure and early dropping out from school, which in turn often lead to a life of addiction and crime.

Although many aggressive children do not grow up to be violent adults, very few violent adults have failed to show signs of aggressive behavior in childhood or adolescence. Sad children can grow into "bad" children quickly and inexorably in an environment of continued violence and social disorganization.

Pregnant parents and other caring people must learn to appreciate the essential humanity of unborn and young children and the value of communicating to them that they are loved and wanted. The future of the world may well depend on how successful we are at promulgating this simple but vital message: As you do unto your own children, they will do unto the world.

Abuse and neglect cause invisible scars on each child's soul that will, depending on the presence or absence of certain protective factors, lead either to relatively good mental and physical health or to a life assailed by failed relationships, a variety of psychiatric problems, and a high risk for developing diabetes and cardiovascular disease.

Key Parenting Points

- Continual fighting between spouses will predispose a child to violent behavior, even if that child is merely a witness to and not a participant in the fights.
- Verbal abuse and emotional neglect can cause more psychiatric difficulty than physical battering.
- Exposure to gratuitous violence on television will increase the chance that your child may become violent himself.
- Even watching too much "good" television has negative effects on your child's creativity and intellectual development.
- Do not minimize signs of aggression in your child with a comforting bromide such as "Boys will be boys." If your child hits, bites, or otherwise causes pain to animals or people, this is a problem that needs attending to.

13

—∿—

Cultivating Basic Goodness:
How to Enhance Empathy,
Compassion, and Altruism

THE NATURE OF ALTRUISM

The word *altruism* is rooted in the Latin *alter*, which simply means "other." The term itself is credited to Auguste Comte, who conceived of altruism as selfless devotion to the welfare of others. Since Comte coined the word 150 years ago, the original meaning has been expanded to denote behavior that is voluntary and intended to benefit others, whether animals or humans, even at the risk of damaging oneself. A fundamental motivating force of altruism is empathy for the suffering of another.

Indeed, humans possess a broad spectrum of helping behavior, generally categorized in the literature as "pro-social." These unselfish acts include: patriotism, martyrdom, heroism, good Samaritanism, philanthropy, and just plain good deeds like helping an old lady cross the street. The difference between all of the above and altruism is that altruistic persons extend themselves toward others out of genuine kindness and decency without regard to their personal safety or expectation of external reward.

In a sense, the distance between pro-social behavior and altruism illustrates the difference between the brain and the mind. I think we can all agree that without a functioning brain there can be no mental activity. Is a functioning brain a necessary condition of the mind? I believe so. But is it sufficient? Probably not.

THE TRIUNE BRAIN

The structure of the brain—and the leap from that brain to the human mind—reveals much about violence and love. Brain researchers have established that in the course of evolution each of us has developed a "tripartite" brain consisting of a hindbrain, a midbrain, and a forebrain. The most primitive brain lies at the base of the skull and is part of the brain stem. Phylogenetically, this is the oldest part of the brain, its core or chassis, roughly corresponding to the basic structures of the reptilian brain. This brain, the archaeocortex, is primarily concerned with survival: eat or be eaten. It has no feelings. It acts and reacts in strictly genetically programmed ways.

The second oldest brain, built on top of the reptilian brain, is called the mammalian brain, or mesocortex. It is made up of the diencephalon, the seat of sleep and appetite, and the limbic lobe, responsible for sexual behavior and instinctual emotions. If you think of the reptilian brain as the brain of a shark, and the mammalian brain as the brain of a horse, you will get a sense of their difference.

In late mammalian times a third brain, known as the new mammalian brain, or neocortex, started to evolve. It is the function of the cortex, and especially the gray matter located beneath the forehead, called the frontal lobes, to modify the raw impulses that flood the brain from the lower parts, and formulate actions based on past experience and social connections. It is the dominance of the cerebral cortex that is responsible for making us human. It is by virtue of our neocortex that our brain becomes the seat of the mind.

The American poet Robert Bly has made the interesting observation that just as the reptilian brain is associated with cold and the mammalian brain with warmth, so the human brain is associated with light. This may explain why the Buddha's head and the heads of saints and sages of all religions have always been depicted as surrounded by a golden aura. It's probably why kings took to wearing golden crowns. If you can't emanate, imitate.

Our forebrain, or neocortex, five times bigger than its two lower cousins combined, provides not only the matrix for rational thought but also the neurological substrate for empathy, compassion, love, and altruism. The triune brain is an integrated, hierarchical system. Depending on perceived need, the lower intelligences are subordinated to the highest, or vice versa.

Animal experiments in which the neocortex was surgically disconnected from the mesocortex have been used to study this phenomenon. Interestingly, personality remains intact for a cat without a cortex unless that cat is threatened: without the neocortical controls, the cat becomes emotionally explosive and ferocious. Similarly, removal of the amygdala (a neurological center in the midbrain, which is involved in attacking behavior and is also a storehouse of emotionally charged memories) permanently tamed a predatory and vicious lynx.

From these and many other related experiments it is evident that certain localized centers in the midbrain and hindbrain, if appropriately stimulated, will lead the animal to act aggressively. However, and more significantly, an emotionally healthy higher mammal, including man, will carefully evaluate a situation with his neocortex and then choose how to react based on all the information at his disposal. For example, you have prepared dinner and your husband does not show up at the usual time. After thirty minutes have elapsed and there is no sign of him, your aggression centers are hopping mad. They scream: "I'll make mincemeat out of him. Where is that bum?" But then your neocortex, with its memory banks, kicks in and informs you that today is Tuesday and he's got a baseball game with the neighborhood team. You immediately calm down, and your neocortex orders those steroid-swilling little devils in the amygdala to chill out. With the ability to retrieve and assess information and select responses based on such information, the cortex can override or moderate the violent or aggressive urges of the lower systems.

The dramatic shift from shark mentality to Mother Teresa mentality over the millennia of human evolution is reflected in the development of the neurohormones of emotion; present in abundance, these hormones predispose us to socialization, empathy, and love. This chemical soup, at elevated levels in humans compared with other species, includes such feel-good neurohormones as prolactin, oxytocin (the nursing hormone), and vasopressin, synthesized in the hypothalamus (part of the mammalian brain) and released by the pituitary. Receptors for these hormones are found throughout the brain but are especially prominent in the forebrain.

Scientists studying nonhuman primates have shown that oxytocin injected into the brain promotes tranquility, friendliness, and maternal behavior. Increased levels of prolactin enhance caretaking behavior, while vasopressin brings out the paternal impulse in males. All three neurohormones, moreover, have been associated with increased levels of endorphins—the body's natural opiates, associated with a sense of well-being and reduction of pain.

These hormones are at work in humans from their earliest days in the womb. One particularly fascinating story comes from Italian pediatrician and psychoanalyst Alessandra Piontelli, known for her ultrasound studies of twins. While examining one pregnant mother of twins with ultrasound, Piontelli found that the little boy (Luke) was far more active than the little girl (Alicia). "Luke kept turning and kicking and changing positions and stretching his legs against the uterine wall," Piontelli says. But from time to time he would interrupt his motor activities and turn his attention toward his sister. "He reached out with his hands and through the dividing membrane he touched her face softly, and when she responded by turning her face toward him, he engaged her for a while in a gentle, stroking, cheek-to-cheek motion." From that point on, Piontelli and her team nicknamed the two the kind twins. Alicia initiated contact less frequently than Luke, Piontelli says. "Most of the time she seemed asleep, or else moved her head and her hands slowly, almost imperceptibly, but each time responded to her brother's tender stimulation."

When Piontelli went to visit the twins in the hospital following their birth, she found them true to form. Luke was lively and alert while Alicia was peaceful and calm. Even more interesting, a full year later, the empathic nature of their relationship was still intact. "Their favorite game had become hiding behind a curtain and using it a bit like a dividing membrane. Luke would put his hand through the curtain and Alicia would press her head against his hand and their mutual stroking, accompanied by gurgles and smiles, would begin."

EMPATHIC FROM THE START

The eminent and brilliant University of Washington psychologist Andrew Meltzoff believes that infants at birth already know that they are like other people. That is why they can differentiate between inanimate objects and people, nonsense words and meaningful words, and their mothers in person and on video. "From the beginning," says Meltzoff, "the human infant feels a deep connectedness to other beings." We start out by fully identifying with our fellow human beings and only later learn to feel the pain of separation and conflict.

Everyone who has studied newborns agrees that they cry in response to the crying of another infant while ignoring noises of similar intensity. In addition, researchers found, the infants' cries were not just simple, imitative vocal responses lacking emotion but rather vigorous, intense, and indistinguishable from the spontaneous cries of children in distress. This reactive cry is the mark of empathy, born fully formed with the infant itself.

FROM EMPATHY TO ALTRUISM

Marian Radke-Yarrow, chief of the Laboratory of Developmental Psychology at the National Institute of Mental Health, has pioneered the study of early manifestations of altruistic and aggressive behavior. The research strategy she adopted was to train mothers to provide her with a running record on audiotape of incidents in the home and outside it that elicited altruism and aggression.

For nine months the mothers, who had answered ads in local newspapers, observed and faithfully recorded their observations. "It was a revelation for some of the mothers to see how sensitive their babies were to everything that went on around them," Radke-Yarrow states.

Working with these children, ranging from 10 to 20 months old, the researchers collected a gold mine of 1,500 incidents. Even they were not prepared for the warmth and attentiveness very young children repeatedly demonstrated. When one of the mothers went to the doctor with a sore throat, for instance, she made a choking sound when the doctor swabbed her tonsils. At once, her 12-month-old son tried to knock the swab out of the doctor's hand. Another woman in the study was visibly upset by a phone call from her sick father. Noticing her reaction, 20-month-old Billy rushed over, put his arms around her, and said, "I love you." Then he gave her a kiss. Such stories, the Radke-Yarrow group found, were not the exception but the rule. Moreover, they learned that children who demonstrated empathy and altruism early on continued to do so as they got older.

In another interesting experiment at the University of California at Berkeley, psychologists presented a group of 18-month-old infants with a plate of goldfish crackers and a plate of broccoli. The experimenter indicated her preference for one food over the other by producing facial expressions of pleasure or disgust. She then reached her hands out to the infant and asked for some food. In a control trial, the experimenter reversed her preferences. Even when the preference of the researcher differed from the infant's, 18-month-old children gave the experimenter the food for which she had expressed a preference; the children did not hesitate to serve up broccoli to those who desired it despite their own, unalterable preference for the crackers. Obviously, these children understood the psychologists' feelings and were able to act accordingly. Such actions demonstrate an incredibly high level of social sophistication.

Many studies show that to enhance empathy and altruism, parents must provide reasoned, rational explanations of why specific behaviors are desirable or not. The explanations must be delivered forcefully, with emotional emphasis. Stating in a flat tone, "Heather is hurt," for instance, or, "You should not take that boy's toy," will have little impact. However, messages delivered in a feeling fashion are persuasive. "Don't you ever do that again!" and "It makes me so happy and proud when I see you sharing your toys" will reverberate in a lasting, meaningful way if they carry an emotional charge.

Radke-Yarrow has found that the most empathic children are those who are treated with concern. If parents respond attentively to a child's cuts and bruises, his likes and dislikes, the child will reflect that helping behavior and natural empathy back to the world.

It has been established for some time now that attachment, or bonding—development of affectional ties to a significant person, usually the mother, shortly after birth—represents a prototype of later relationships. Recent research shows that children who form secure attachments will later manifest more effective and positive peer relations. A secure first relationship (prenatal and postnatal) that is marked by parental responsiveness to the child's needs is likely to be an important starting point for the development of altruism and might lessen the probability of aggression.

If a child is held gently, if she is treated kindly, if she gazes into her parents' eyes and reads *love* in them, if every contact with them tells her that she is adorable, bright, and good, she will feel secure and will become self-confident and willing to treat others the way she was treated. Of course, once the child moves out of the protective warmth of the parental home, she will be exposed to other experiences and interactions, which may either support or repress her empathic character.

THE MORAL CHILD

Children learn from the specific types of behaviors that are encouraged or discouraged, rewarded or punished. They learn from what their parents say and do. The latter is referred to as modeling. Seeing parents

helping others in need and showing concern for the weak and the desti-
tute leads to the adoption or internalization of these values.

Samuel and Pearl Oliver, in their splendid book *The Altruistic Personality*, examine the personality traits of rescuers of Jews in Nazi Europe.
They write: "For most rescuers, helping Jews was an expression of ethical principles that extended to all of humanity and, while often reflecting
concern with equity and justice, was predominantly rooted in care. The
rescuers' commitment to actively protect or enhance the well-being of
others did not emerge suddenly under the threat of Nazi brutality. Instead, those who acted as rescuers integrated such values into their lives
well before the war began—and remained committed to them long after
it ended."

Rescuers described their early family relationships in general, and
their relationships with their mothers in particular, as more affectionate
than did nonrescuers. Rescuers also felt significantly closer to their fathers than did bystanders. Taught by the example of family relationship,
rescuers placed more importance on responsibility, caring, and depend-
ability.

Children learn moral behavior by engaging in moral conduct. The
more they are encouraged to practice moral behavior in everyday life, the
more they will internalize these values.

Parents take note: moral values are not only desirable for their own
sake but also essential tools for self-protection in this complex, often
dangerous world. Without an internal moral compass, our children can
be corrupted by the bravado of unattached, unbonded sociopaths, who
will befriend them and victimize them in relationships, in the work-
place, and in a host of unethical or illegal ventures.

One way to start our children on the road to realizing their full human
potential would be to adopt, in some form, a prenatal bonding custom
practiced by a tribe in East Africa. In this tribe the birth date of a child is
not the day of his or her physical birth nor even the day of conception, as
in other village cultures, but rather the first time the child appears as a
thought in the mother's mind.

Aware of her intention to conceive a child with a particular father, the
mother goes off to sit alone under a tree. There she sits and listens until
she can hear the song of the child that she hopes to conceive. Once she
has heard it, she returns to her village and teaches it to the future father
so that they can sing it together as they make love, inviting the child to
join them.

After the child is conceived, the mother sings this song to the baby in
her womb. Then she teaches it to the old women and midwives of the vil-

lage, so that throughout the labor and at the miraculous moment of birth itself, the child is greeted with his very own song. After the birth, all the villagers learn the song of their new member and sing it to the child when he falls ill or is hurt. It is sung in times of triumph, and during rituals and initiations. The song becomes a part of the marriage ceremony when the child is grown, and at the end of life, his loved ones will gather around the deathbed and sing this song for the last time.

Children conceived in love, nurtured on love, and born and raised with love grow up in a state of grace and return to the world many times what they received. If we yearn for goodness to prevail over evil, we must eventually learn to subordinate materialism to maternalism, despair to hope, and love of technology to love of children.

SUMMING UP

Our brains contain primitive structures capable of influencing our behavior toward the aggressive satisfaction of our basic survival needs, such as food, sex, and personal safety. However, with the evolution of a superior neocortex that considers its options from a much broader perspective, we have developed a powerful apparatus not only for modulating and inhibiting these aggressive lower impulses but also for substituting new social impulses directed toward other living beings around us.

In the process of moving along the evolutionary path from the hindbrain through the midbrain to the forebrain, we have also evolved from self-centeredness to selflessness, or, as Martin Buber said, from an I-It to an I-Thou attitude that entails treating others not as objects but as people like us. If we were all hard-wired by evolutionary design to become violent and aggressive, would we really have the neurochemical makeup for a love hormone? Would we be flown into the world on the wings of a loving mother and father only to be dropped later to scurry in the gutter among rats? I don't think so.

Key Parenting Points

- Rational, reasoned explanations of why certain behaviors are or are not desirable should be delivered in a forceful, feeling way. The parent's message has to carry an emotional charge to have a lasting effect.

- Children learn from the specific types of behaviors that are encouraged or discouraged, rewarded or punished.
- The importance of parental values and example cannot be overemphasized. If you scream and hit your children, they will scream and hit back. If you treat your children with concern and compassion, they will mirror helping behavior back to the world. They learn from what their parents say and do.

14

—◦—

Conscious Parenting

Conscious parenting is informed, thoughtful parenting, in which the mind and heart of the parent resonate to the needs of the child. The findings in fields as diverse as neuroscience, cell biology, and psychology demand that conscious parenting start at conception. Ideally, every child should be a planned and wanted child. Every child deserves to be cherished and loved from the start.

The challenges of parenting are abundantly clear to new mothers and fathers, who may be so exhausted and overwhelmed by care of their infant they barely feel conscious at all. That is precisely why the principles of conscious parenting are so important. We'd all love to be naturals—the sort of intuitive, gifted parents who never get angry or stressed out, never misstep. But since life is sometimes too difficult to handle on autopilot, an awareness and mastery of the parenting tools will kick in when instinct does not. To raise emotionally fit children requires emotionally fit and intelligently prepared parents. Let me preface my remarks about conscious parenting by emphasizing that this is an absolute, a standard of perfection no parent is likely to achieve. However, if we want the best for our children and the future of this planet, it is something we should strive toward with all our might.

You gave birth in a hospital or a birthing center, and now it is time to take your baby home. Or you had a home birth—the midwife, doctor, and other attendants have left, and now it's just you, your partner, and the baby. Suddenly, if you are like most new parents, you realize that you

have no idea how to take care of this tiny child and you feel *scared*.
A hundred questions arise in your mind revolving around diapering,
feeding, sleeping, crying, colic, infections, and so on. What if the baby
doesn't take to the breast; what if I run out of milk? It's hard to be calm
in the face of such an avalanche of worries.

A new mother who has the good fortune to be part of an extended and
closely knit family will benefit immeasurably from the advice and emotional support of her child's grandparents and great-grandparents. If, in
addition, she also has a loving mate who is willing to share in the raising
of their child, then this baby is off to a very good beginning indeed. The
child of a single mother will not be as lucky. A child given up for adoption may have an even harder time.

If you have read this book and considered the evidence, you know that
each child is different at birth—not only because of his or her genetic
code, but also because of the unique journey from conception to crib.
During the passage across the amniotic sea, there are a thousand routes
and detours. Every experience on the road of prenatal life alters the molecules of emotion, the autonomic and central nervous systems, and the
architecture of the brain. As we come into being, rising from a single
cell to an individual with a body and a brain, our experience creates sen-
sitivities, expectations, moods, attitudes, strengths, vulnerabilities, and
predispositions toward optimism or pessimism, trust or distrust, love or
hate. The three years following birth will, to a very large extent, determine how much and in which direction the child's potential and nascent
personality traits develop.

In this respect, the newborn is totally at the mercy of her parents.
Good parenting can gradually overcome enormous prenatal and perinatal difficulties. Abusive parenting can quickly and permanently darken
the brightest and most loving mind.

It is the unseen, often unconscious, interactions and acts of parents
that shape and pattern a child's personality. What she sees and hears,
how she is touched and spoken to, the expression on her father's face
when he changes her diaper, the look in her mother's eyes when she
feeds her—these are the things that count. While ministering to the
physical needs of a child is, of course, essential, meeting her emotional,
intellectual, moral, and spiritual needs is equally crucial, though largely
neglected by the standard parenting literature.

RULE ONE: FACE YOUR DEMONS

In the past, when I have addressed the topic of mothering, I have found some parents resistant. "Isn't mothering natural?" some have asked me. "Every mother instinctively knows what to do," others have said.

But the belief that all mothers automatically love their babies, or that all fathers can let go of past hurts to nurture their offspring, is naive. Without exception, we are all descendants of generations of neurotic parents. This is not a criticism but a fact. The scars on our psyches tend to interfere with our natural capacity to love and respect both ourselves and others.

Let me give you an example of what happens when a person neglects to take inventory of his or her readiness for parenthood. An accomplished actress I know, Genevieve, wanted desperately to get pregnant. Her husband, Patrick, was not particularly keen on having a child. She grew progressively more unhappy and more adamant in her demands. When Genevieve's younger sister had a baby, Genevieve threatened to leave Patrick unless he agreed to start a family. A few months later she conceived and in due course had a beautiful baby boy, whom they named Jason.

All was well at the beginning, but as time progressed Gen turned out to be an extremely anxious mother. The moment Jason cried she would run and pick him up. At the slightest cough, she would rush him to the pediatrician. She would never leave him in the care of another person. Of course, Gen became a nervous wreck. What's worse, she found no pleasure in being with the child. She referred to looking after Jason as "doing Jason." She wanted her husband to take care of Jason more and more. Finally, they got a nanny five days a week. In the evening, when the nanny left and before Patrick came home from the office, Gen still found it too frustrating to be alone with Jason, despite the fact that she did not work. So now they have a live-in nanny and Gen and Patrick spend "quality time" with Jason.

Babies are tremendously demanding of their caretakers, and there isn't a mother or father alive who does not look forward to the moment when their child is finally asleep in the evening and they can have some time to themselves. Some parents must be away from their children during the day because they need to earn a living. But others, like Gen, resent every second they spend with their child, and this is another story altogether. Is there a way that Gen could have known about her mothering attributes before she got pregnant?

I think if she had honestly thought about herself and her relationships, particularly with her mother, she would have recognized that her
motivation for having a child was not pure but was really competition
with her sister. Additionally, her self-image and self-esteem required
some shoring up before she could be the mother she had hoped to become. So the first rule of conscious parenting is this: Courageously con-
front your own and your partner's dark side. Face all the character traits,
fears, and worries that reside in the cellar of your mind lest they interfere with your ability to be a parent.

How will Jason be affected by his "reluctant" but loving parents?
I would venture to say that he will feel diminished, that a part of him
will feel not-good-enough. He may grow into a people-pleaser, with an exaggerated urge to be good and nice; this facade of pleasantness may hide
anxiety, anger, and difficulty with the world. Alternatively, he might become obsessed with seeking power, fame, and fortune and in this way try
to make up for the love he did not have. Whatever course his life takes, it
will reflect the ambivalent mothering and fathering he received.

Unconscious conflicts in the parents will always interfere with normal emotional growth in the child, which in turn will further aggravate
the parents' neuroses. The operation of these processes is further illus-
trated in the case of a mother observed by Rene Spitz. This mother sat
feeding her infant with an expression of deep concern on her face, all the
while pouring far too much milk into his mouth. At the same time, swallowing movements of her throat suggested that she was identifying with
her child, encouraging him to swallow by performing the act herself. It
quickly became clear, however, that her swallowing represented a desperate effort to overcome an overpowering nausea, which soon began to
express itself in her face. The child, of course, was not experiencing nausea; it was only the mother who was nauseated, for neurotic reasons of
her own, at the idea of swallowing milk. Her hope was to save her child
unpleasantness by feeding him his milk as quickly as possible. But while
the milk did not sicken the child, the forced feeding did. As she tried
ever harder to get the feeding over with, he regurgitated the excess milk,
increasing the mother's revulsion and driving her to feed him more rapidly still.

RULE TWO: YOU CAN'T HAVE IT ALL

The second rule of conscious parenting is this: Contrary to popular belief, you cannot have it all. You cannot keep a full-time job, parent your

child or children, work out regularly at a fitness club, entertain your friends, be a sexual acrobat for your spouse, and not become exhausted and irritable. Before you know it, you will be taking a ton of Prozac, and getting sick to boot. Choices must be made. The birth of a baby will change your life forever. It is foolish to expect to live after you have had a baby the way you did before.

RULE THREE: YOUR CHILDREN KNOW WHAT YOU ARE FEELING

Studies on children up to 3 years of age during the London blitz demonstrated that they did not become anxious unless their mothers began to feel anxious. From this follows the third rule of conscious parenting: Your children know what you are feeling.

It is generally accepted that infants and their parents are both active agents in a reciprocal system of interaction. By the time children are born, they already have definite tastes and predilections. Some are more outgoing, others are shy. Some smile and coo more while others are reserved; some like to be cuddled while others don't; and so on. Likewise, parents themselves often prefer certain physical features, behaviors, and temperaments. Whether consciously or not, they will treat boys differently from girls, and a calm baby differently from an anxious one.

When the parent is anxious, he or she will be less able to recognize the emotional or medical needs of the baby. Scientists have found that inconsistent and inappropriate parental responsiveness may permanently compromise an infant's mental health. Mothers' negative perceptions of the behavior of their 1-month-old infants, for instance, were highly predictive of social and emotional problems in these children at 4½ years and 10 years of age.

Recent advances in neuroscience point to the importance of "contingent responsiveness"—parental behavior directly and immediately related to the infant's signals. It involves a caretaker's capacity to observe her infant's cues, to interpret them accurately, and to respond to them appropriately. Contingent responsiveness has been specifically associated with the development of good cognitive and motor functions, language ability, self-esteem and security, and overall competence in social and emotional realms.

RULE FOUR: DON'T STEREOTYPE YOUR CHILD

The "fit" between babies and parents often depends not so much on the child's characteristics as on the parent's preconceptions or attitudes. To study the subtle stereotyping that takes place in most families, a group of parents were asked to fill out a questionnaire rating their babies by choosing from such adjectives as firm/soft, big/little, relaxed/nervous, and so on. The researchers also obtained from the hospital records the doctors' ratings of the infants' color, muscle tone, reflex irritability, weight, height, and so forth. None of the hospital scores showed significant differences between fifteen male and fifteen female infants. But this was not the case with the parents. They saw their daughters as softer, finer-featured, smaller, and more inattentive. Fathers and mothers agreed on these points. However, mothers rated sons as cuddlier than daughters, while fathers rated daughters as cuddlier than sons—a finding the researchers dubbed the Oedipal effect.

Sex-typing begins at birth and becomes magnified with time. Eleven mothers in one study were observed as they played with a 6-month-old boy in a nursery. Five of them saw the baby dressed in blue pants and were told his name was Adam. The other six saw the same baby, introduced as Beth, in a pink dress. The mothers were observed through a one-way mirror as they played with the child. Three toys—a fish, a doll, and a train—were placed on the table in front of the baby and the mothers. The women who thought the baby was a girl handed "her" the doll more often; those who thought he was a boy gave him the train more frequently. There was no difference in the handling of the fish, a sex-neutral toy. The mothers also smiled more at the girl. Two mothers said they could tell Beth was a girl because "she" was sweeter and showed softer crying; one said she could tell Adam was a boy because he had a little boy's face.

There is no doubt that children are influenced by their parents' expectations and perceptions, whether positive or negative. Therefore, the fourth rule of conscious parenting is this: Know your negative expectations, fears, and stereotyped ideas about babies. Then try to talk about them frankly with your spouse, a trusted friend, or a professional counselor. Airing these preconceived notions will greatly help to dissipate their hold on you and your child.

RULE FIVE: TUNE INTO AND RESOLVE THE INNER CONFLICTS THAT ARISE IN THE COURSE OF PARENTING

Many parents become so focused on what the baby is feeling that they neglect to consider their own feelings. As the parents are exposed to the infantile behavior of the child—as they feed him, diaper him, cuddle him, take pictures of him—their own hidden fears may be activated. The father may become anxious at the thought of having to compete for his wife's love with the baby, or he may become depressed because of the added financial responsibilities imposed by the new arrival, or because of a sense of entrapment. In the mother, the baby may mobilize similar feelings, in addition to concerns about permanent damage to her body, loss of youthful good looks, and the perception of breast-feeding as somehow animalistic.

For some parents, cleaning a baby triggers repressed feelings of shame about excretory functions or sex. The most common way in which parents unconsciously defend themselves from their own unacceptable feelings is by an overconcern for the welfare of the child. Gen's story earlier in this chapter is a case in point.

Remember, just as an infant reacts to the parent's unresolved conflicts, so, too, parents can be affected by the infant's feelings about them. Not all children take automatically to their parents and vice versa. But with patience, mutual love, and empathy, conflicts can be resolved and everyone grows as a result. Therefore, this is the fifth rule of parenting: Anticipate not only giving to and instructing your child, but also receiving and learning from him or her. Most of the time you are the teacher and the child is the student. But from the moment of conception and throughout her life, your child presents you with an unparalleled opportunity to become a wiser, kinder, and more fulfilled human being.

RULE SIX: FATHER LOVE IS JUST AS IMPORTANT AS MOTHER LOVE

After millennia of being spooked and perplexed by childbirth and feeling incompetent around and often uninterested in infants, men have, over the past twenty to thirty years, charged into fatherhood with an almost messianic fervor. They attend Lamaze classes and crowd into delivery rooms. They are willing to "coparent." Some choose to relocate their business to their home, while others give up their outside jobs to become full-time parents.

At the same time, the United States and Canada are becoming increasingly fatherless societies. Tonight, about 40 percent of American children will go to sleep in homes in which the father is absent. Before they reach the age of 18, more than half of this continent's children are likely to spend at least a significant portion of their childhoods separated from their father. According to some credible estimates, this figure is likely to rise to 60 percent of American children born in the 1990s.

The absence of fathers is even more pronounced in black communities than in the rest of America. The female-headed household is the dominant family form among African Americans today. African American couples have a divorce rate higher than whites, are more likely to separate but not obtain a legal divorce, and are less likely to remarry. The 48 percent overall national divorce rate masks the fact that 38 percent of white children but 75 percent of black children will experience at least one parental divorce. Thus black children are more likely than white children to spend longer periods of time in a household with a single or divorced mother.

This trend is alarming, given the findings of hundreds of studies over the past thirty years: the presence of a father enhances self-esteem, economic security, and physical and emotional health. The absence of a father puts children at greater risk for abuse when young, and violent and dysfunctional behavior as adults.

Do fathers affect children differently from mothers? Most researchers seem to think so. For example, many studies have shown that fathers influence the development of sex-role and gender identity, especially in boys. American fathers speak to, touch, and react to their firstborn sons more frequently than to their firstborn daughters, and similar tendencies are evident among English fathers. Fathers are warmer and more sensitive with 3-month-old sons than with daughters. Even among the nomadic !Kung bushmen, fathers spent more time with sons than with daughters.

Some studies suggest that sex-differentiated treatment intensifies during the second year of life, when fathers often take a special interest in their sons. Robert Bly, the American poet and a leader of the men's movement, describes this stage beautifully:

"At about age one and a half, the son begins to switch his intense gaze over to the father. Mothers have to be prepared for this. The rowdy play of the father suddenly seems much more attractive. Probably before one and a half, the infant boy sees the father as simply an alternative mother; but now he feels strangely drawn to this different energy and different body mood. The father throws him up in the air, or rolls around and imitates a bear. The son knows that the vibrations of the molecules here are different, and the boy sometimes gets high on this new vibration, too. A love affair with the father now starts; it will be one of the most crucial events in his whole life, but he will not be able to speak of it, because it takes place mostly before speech. It is a noncompetitive, ecstatic relationship with an idealized father."

Mother love, no matter how pure and generous, cannot make up for the lack of father love. Of course, the opposite is equally true. It is from our fathers and mothers that we first learn about masculinity and femininity, about roles, expectations, and relationships. From whom are children in a fatherless home going to learn about men and manhood or relationships with men?

For boys, the most socially acute manifestation of paternal absence is juvenile violence. For girls, it is juvenile and out-of-wedlock childbearing. Which brings us back to the sixth and final rule of conscious parenting: Child-rearing is not a solo act. Children need to be raised by a mother and a father who work together, complementing each other's differences.

THE CORROSIVE EFFECT OF CRITICISM

As a psychiatrist, I have listened for more than thirty years as my patients recalled, often with tears and rage, parental criticisms and putdowns, and I can tell you with absolute certainty that the catchy little schoolyard chant, "Sticks and stones can break my bones, but words can never hurt me," is not true.

Here is my Top Ten list of what to avoid saying or doing:

1. Holding outdated beliefs:
   If a child cries or otherwise acts up, "all she wants is attention," so it's best to ignore her.
   If you show too much affection or interest, or respond too quickly to your child, you will "spoil him rotten."
   To provide your children with material goods, extra piano les-

sons, soccer camps, or an Ivy League education you should put off vacations and other sources of personal enjoyment.

Even if you and your spouse argue constantly, sleep in separate rooms, and have not made love for years, it's best to stay together for the sake of the children.

2. Pay attention to your children only if they cry or do something wrong, like stealing or setting fires.

3. Make your children play sports even if they hate it. If they refuse, call them by an unflattering name, preferably in front of their friends.

4. Treat your child as if your life depended on her success. This is especially pronounced in parents whose artistic careers were interrupted by marriage. They will often make a child study music or dance, then have her perform in front of their friends.

5. Poke "good-natured fun" at some physical attribute or disability your child may have, such as being near-sighted, overweight, or having red hair.

6. In the event that your son cries, tell him that soldiers don't cry and he better shape up or you will ship him out.

7. Compare your child unfavorably with his sibling, one of the neighbors' children, or with yourself at his age.

8. Turn a trait that you lack or secretly envy into a liability. For example, say to a child who is boisterous and inquisitive that he is full of "nervous energy," or to one who is smarter than you, "When will you stop asking so many dumb questions?" or to a daughter who likes animals, "I wonder who she got *that* from" (not from me, that's for sure), or to a son who likes cooking, "Look at the little housewife."

9. A child who spends too much time reading, drawing, or doing homework will become sort of a nerd. Keep him or her busy with such chores as answering the phone, feeding the cat, shoveling the snow, washing the car, cleaning his room, mowing the lawn, taking out the garbage, helping with the groceries. That will teach the child the sort of practical things actually required to navigate the world.

10. Fathers are especially fond of issuing the following macho lines:

When I tell you to jump, just ask how high.

I owe you nothing.

Smarten up, bud; I don't like your attitude and it better change.

This is not your room. This is my room, my house. I pay the rent on this place.

Okay, if you don't like it, get out. You don't have to wait until you've finished school. Leave right now.

Do it right the first time.

THE TRUTH ABOUT SPANKING

In *The Taming of the Shrew,* Shakespeare has great fun in showing that nothing succeeds more with a headstrong woman than a proper thrashing by her husband. This behavior is no longer acceptable (at least as public policy) in the West. You may be angry at your spouse, but no matter how provocative (to your mind) his or her behavior is, you are not allowed to threaten or use physical force against him or her. Children deserve the same protection.

More than fifty years ago, the noted anthropologist Ashley Montagu argued, "Spanking the baby may be the psychological seed of war." On the basis of studying eight nonviolent preliterate societies, he concluded that what they all had in common was nonviolent child-rearing practices; that is, they did not spank children.

Murray A. Straus, a University of New Hampshire sociologist, has conducted extensive research on the effects of spanking both on individuals and on societies. Straus and his colleagues studied the degree to which parents and teachers in ten European countries approved of corporal punishment. They found that the greater the degree of approval of corporal punishment, the higher the overall homicide rate and also the rate of infanticide.

According to Straus, one out of four American parents will strike an infant, and virtually all spank their children by age 4. Other studies show that over half of children age 13 and 14 are still being hit. What are the measurable consequences of such cruel and coercive practices?

Adults who employ corporal punishment teach children what to do when someone crosses them or does not do their bidding. Instead of learning how to express feelings or wishes verbally, children learn to lash out impulsively against anyone who frustrates them.

A child who is repeatedly, harshly, and unfairly punished is very likely as an adult to:

- severely assault a child
- assault a spouse
- become depressed
- demonstrate a high level of marital conflict

- if female, suffer a drop of eight points in IQ scores (and if that girl's mother also lacked warmth, her IQ score drops an additional four points)

In Canada and the United States corporal punishment of children by their parents is exempt from prosecution under the criminal code. Research by Harriet L. MacMillan and her colleagues adds to the mounting evidence that the time has come to end that exemption. They studied a large sample of Ontario residents and found that adults who remembered being slapped or spanked as children were twice as likely to report current alcohol abuse or dependence or to have antisocial problems (for example, illicit drug abuse or dependence, or stealing) compared with adults who did not report being slapped or spanked as children. A study by MacMillan and colleagues and five recent longitudinal studies provide much more definitive evidence than existed even three years ago on the potential benefits of not spanking, including decreased lifetime risk of mental health problems and enhanced cognitive ability.

What alternatives for discipline should be used when parents stop spanking? Some psychologists fear that parents will replace physical attacks with verbal attacks or that they will give up and abandon all rules. Although some parents will take those routes, in my opinion ending spanking will, in general, have the opposite effect. It will sensitize parents to the vulnerability of children and result in fewer verbal attacks.

Despite all the evidence, the harsh treatment of children continues in our homes and schools. There are several reasons for this. For one, most children who were spanked, like most smokers, do not suffer visible damage. As adults they can say, and most do, "I was spanked but, hey, I turned out all right." The troubling consequences are slow to develop, and when they do, in the form of marital discord or spousal abuse, for instance, no one makes the connection. It took several hundred years to establish a relationship between smoking and an increased incidence of heart and lung disease among smokers. I hope it will take less time to establish a link between corporal punishment and self-destructive and violent behavior.

Another reason so many people ignore the corrosive impact of spanking is the idealization of parents in adulthood; most people have trouble admitting that their parents did some awful things to them in the past. Similarly, a lot of parents would rather forget the times they "lost it" and treated their children harshly.

To add fuel to the fire, deep-seated aspects of American culture also support the use of violence for what are perceived to be socially desirable ends. The love of contact sports, gangster and brawl TV (Jerry Springer springs to mind), and superheroes in action movies and the emphasis on competition and winning are, unfortunately, the thread and twine that are powerfully woven into the American social fabric.

Conscious parents reason with their children rather than use force. If that fails, as it does from time to time, they punish the child by withdrawing a privilege, such as watching a favorite TV show, or sending them to cool off somewhere. Remember that your role as parent demands that you set standards for what is desirable and what is permitted in your house. Your child will not always agree with your decisions, but parenting is not a popularity contest. It is about doing the right thing for your child.

When you do need to resort to punishment, keep three simple rules in mind:

1. Always make the punishment fit the "crime." Do not go overboard and withdraw a week's desserts for a minor misdemeanor.
2. Always follow through. Never make empty threats or forget about the punishment or diminish it as a result of pressure from your child or spouse.
3. Present a united front. Do not countermand your spouse's directions. If you disagree, talk to your partner privately.

To be absolutely clear: children should never be subjected to physical violence or have to witness it. This applies equally to seeing Uncle Charlie drunk at the cottage and to watching gratuitous violence on TV. Of course, it goes without saying that children should never be exposed to sexual activity or be exploited by adults for sexual purposes.

SUMMING UP

To give a baby what he or she needs amid the stresses of modern life requires an awareness of the issues. Affectionate, attentive, and rational parenting is the key. In order to achieve such "conscious parenting," parents must take an honest inventory of their personal demons, their marital relationship, and the parenting they themselves received. Empowered by this knowledge, they must then prepare themselves for the challenges of pregnancy, labor, childbirth, and parenting. Conscious parents will meet their children's needs *despite* their own past traumas and the difficulties of everyday life. They will do so because they have taken the time and made the effort to understand their inner feelings and motives and because, unlike their parents before them, they have successfully learned the lessons of raising healthy and happy children.

In the final analysis, our only hope for a better world lies in heightening and deepening our children's innate capacity to care, to nurture, and to feel for others.

Key Parenting Points

PRECONCEPTION

- Obtain information about which physical and chemical toxins to avoid before conception and during pregnancy.
- Honestly assess your readiness for the challenges of pregnancy and raising a child. If problems of a medical, psychological, or financial nature surface, you should avail yourself of professional help.

CONCEPTION

- Every child, ideally, should be a wanted child.
- Every child should be created as an expression of the love the parents feel for each other.

PREGNANCY

- Mothers and fathers should become as aware as possible of their births, their childhoods, and their relationships to their parents.
- Parents should explore their relationship to each other, honestly discussing their hopes and fears.
- Parents must learn to appreciate the fundamental humanity of the unborn child and to communicate their love to him.
- Parents ought to strive to bond with their unborn child prenatally and postnatally through talking, singing, dancing, visualization, and play.
- The pregnant mother must do all in her power to reduce stress during pregnancy. If there is a threat of or actual violence, she must remove herself from it.
- The mother should attend prenatal classes—if possible, with her partner.
- The pregnant mother must abstain from alcohol, tobacco, and all "recreational" drugs.

LABOR AND DELIVERY

- If at all possible, the mother's partner should be present. If she is giving birth in a hospital, it is advisable that she be accompanied by a professional support person such as a midwife or doula.
- Unless there is a medical problem, the birth should be free of medical interventions. That means no unnecessary fetal heart monitors, anesthetics, or analgesics, and no episiotomies, forceps, inductions, or C-sections unless medically necessary.
- Only friends and relatives that the parents know and trust should be present during labor and delivery.
- Only professionals who love and respect babies should birth them.

AFTER BIRTH

- Say only complimentary things about your newborn. Remember, your child is listening.
- Insist on holding your baby right away and rooming in with her.
- Resist the administering of silver nitrate eyedrops to your newborn and other routine medications and tests, or at least delay them for a few hours after birth so the two of you have a better chance to bond.
- Oppose circumcision or any form of genital mutilation unless required for religious reasons. This is a practice that is no longer medically indicated or psychologically desirable.
- Leave the hospital as soon as possible.
- Nurse your baby for at least three months.
- If you cannot breast-feed your baby, bottle-feed her while cradling her in your arms and giving her your full attention.

FIRST FEW MONTHS

- If you are isolated, vulnerable, or depressed, ask for help. Visits by nurses or social workers have a demonstrably positive impact.
- If your baby develops colic or cries a lot or does not sleep much, don't assume that it's your fault or that you are an incompetent parent. But do make sure you get help.
- If the baby becomes ill, don't wait until tomorrow—take him to a doctor today.
- If you are a single mother and you are beginning to lose your pa-

tience with your child, call a friend, a family member, a women's
support group, or a social agency. Whatever you do, don't yell at,
shake, or hit the baby.

- Infants require a lot of attention. They cannot take care of themselves. But they are also a source of great joy. Have fun with your
son or daughter.
- A baby can teach you many important lessons. Be prepared to learn
from your child.

First Few Years

- Talk to your toddler as much as possible.
- If you can manage it, do not send your child to day care until he or
she is at least 2.
- Try to be responsive to the needs of your child rather than your
own.
- Always treat your child the way you would like to be treated in
return.

Appendix

This questionnaire is designed to increase your awareness of your pre-natal and perinatal experiences (that is, before, at the time of, and shortly after your child's birth) and the effect they had on your personality and your behavior patterns. Its function is to provide you with new insights that will be personally meaningful to you. The questionnaire is not, at this time, a scientific instrument. Please answer all questions quickly, without thinking too hard. Circle as many answers as are applicable. If you do not know an answer, let your unconscious guide you. After you have completed the questionnaire, please feel free to seek verification from your parents, your siblings, or your birth records.

1. Age _____ Sex _____ Time of birth _____

2. Birth weight _____

3. Condition at birth:

   a. excellent (alert)
   b. very good
   c. fair

    d. poor

    e. very poor (blue and not breathing)

    f. don't know

4. Birth order:

    a. first

    b. second

    c. third

    d. fourth

    e. fifth

    f. sixth or later

5. Are you a twin?

    a. yes

    b. no

6. Were you adopted?

    a. yes

    b. no

7. Did your mother want to have a baby when you were conceived?

    a. yes

    b. no

8. Your mother wanted

    a. a boy

    b. a girl

    c. didn't matter

9. Did your father want to have a baby when you were conceived?

    a. yes

    b. no

10. Your father wanted

    a. a boy

    b. a girl

    c. didn't matter

11. Did your mother have any major calamities during pregnancy?

    a. yes

    b. no

12. During pregnancy your mother was generally

    a. happy
    b. unhappy

13. During your intrauterine life, did your mother talk or sing to you?

    a. yes
    b. no

14. During your intrauterine life, did your father talk or sing to you?

    a. yes
    b. no

15. During her pregnancy, was your mother exposed to noise from

    a. machinery
    b. planes or trains
    c. loud music
    d. none of the above

16. During your intrauterine life, you felt

    a. wanted
    b. loved
    c. happy
    d. peaceful
    e. connected to your mother
    f. disconnected from your mother
    g. anxious
    h. fearful
    i. guilty
    j. angry
    k. bored
    l. alone
    m. unloved
    n. unwanted
    o. inadequate/not good enough

17. While she was pregnant with you, your mother often felt

    a. angry
    b. fearful
    c. anxious

      d. depressed

      e. happy

      f. content

18. Do you remember dreaming in the womb? If so, what? (Write your dream on a separate sheet of paper.)

      a. yes

      b. no

19. During her pregnancy your mother generally

      a. smoked cigarettes

      b. smoked marijuana

      c. consumed excessive amounts of alcohol

      d. drank more than two cups of regular coffee or tea per day

      e. used speed

      f. used drugs such as cocaine, crack, and heroin

      g. used painkillers

      h. used tranquilizers

      i. used antidepressants

      j. none of the above

20. You were born

      a. in a hospital

      b. at home

      c. elsewhere

21. During delivery your mother received

      a. painkillers

      b. local anesthesia

      c. general anesthesia

      d. none of the above

22. Your birth was

      a. vaginal

      b. forceps used

      c. episiotomy performed

      d. cesarean section performed

      e. induced with Pitocin

      f. breech

      g. delayed (doctor not available)

h. premature
i. postmature

23. After your birth, you were

    a. placed on your mother's breast
    b. put in a baby nursery
    c. put in an incubator
    d. taken to the neonatal intensive care unit

24. During birth you and your mother were probably

    a. in sync
    b. at odds

25. You are primarily

    a. heterosexual
    b. bisexual
    c. homosexual

26. You like touching, hugging, and cuddling

    a. an inordinate amount
    b. very much
    c. an average amount
    d. very little
    e. not at all

27. With food, you tend to

    a. overeat
    b. eat until full
    c. nibble
    d. have trouble eating or undereat
    e. cause yourself to vomit after eating

28. In regard to sex, you

    a. can't get enough of it
    b. have it on your mind all the time
    c. consider it important
    d. find it a problem
    e. think you'd be better off without it
    f. are uninterested

29. In regard to money, you

   a. can't get enough of it
   b. have it on your mind all the time
   c. consider it important
   d. find it a problem
   e. think you'd be better off without it
   f. are uninterested

30. You have at some point been dependent on

   a. tranquilizers
   b. antidepressants
   c. sleeping pills
   d. painkillers
   e. speed
   f. cigarettes/tobacco
   g. alcohol
   h. marijuana
   i. cocaine
   j. heroin
   k. crack
   l. none of the above

31. Are you attracted to large, fat people?

   a. yes
   b. no

32. Are you attracted to small, thin people?

   a. yes
   b. no

33. You suffer from

   a. a learning disability
   b. panic attacks
   c. phobias
   d. depression
   e. manic-depression
   f. schizophrenia
   g. antisocial behavior
   h. ADD or ADHD
   i. none of the above

34. You sometimes dream of

    a. falling or tumbling
    b. floating in water
    c. tunnels or openings
    d. quicksand or swamps
    e. shipwrecks or breaking into pieces

35. Are you or would you like to be employed by a major organization offering good benefits and a pension plan?

    a. yes
    b. no

36. You describe yourself as

    a. optimistic
    b. outgoing
    c. people-oriented
    d. pessimistic
    e. withdrawn
    f. shy
    g. introverted
    h. assertive
    i. rootless
    j. cautious
    k. passive
    l. reckless
    m. aggressive
    n. adventurous
    o. prudent
    p. extroverted

37. You enjoy

    a. getting ahead
    b. diving into things
    c. exploring new horizons
    d. none of the above

38. You fear

    a. losing your temper
    b. going crazy
    c. becoming violent and destructive

       d. becoming helpless
       e. making a mistake
       f. being wrong
       g. being a failure
       h. being successful
       i. being raped
       j. being abandoned
       k. none of the above

39. You often experience

       a. an inability to get into what you are doing
       b. inexplicable fatigue
       c. lack of willpower
       d. intellectual stagnation
       e. the feeling that something is missing
       f. none of the above

40. You try to avoid wearing

       a. scarves
       b. hats
       c. turtlenecks
       d. neckties
       e. none of the above

41. You have a fear of

       a. open spaces
       b. closed spaces
       c. water
       d. traveling
       e. the dark
       f. heights
       g. animals
       h. none of the above

42. You react to stress with

       a. increased activity
       b. decreased activity
       c. immobilization
       d. confusion
       e. anxiety

f. anger
g. none of the above

43. Did any trauma occur to you or your family when you were in your mother's womb?

    a. yes
    b. no

44. Did any trauma occur to you or your family at the time of your birth?

    a. yes
    b. no

45. Did any trauma occur to you or your family within the first few weeks or months after your birth?

    a. yes
    b. no

46. Did any trauma occur to you or your family within the first two years of your life?

    a. yes
    b. no

47. Were you and your mother separated for any period of time exceeding a few hours within the first few weeks or months after your birth?

    a. yes
    b. no

48. Did you have any surrogate mothers? If so, who?

    a. nurse
    b. housekeeper/nanny
    c. baby-sitter
    d. sister
    e. cousin
    f. aunt
    g. grandmother
    h. family friend
    i. neighbor
    j. teacher

    k. doctor
    l. dentist
   m. clergy
    n. none

49. Did you have any surrogate fathers? If so, who?

    a. nurse
    b. housekeeper/nanny
    c. baby-sitter
    d. brother
    e. cousin
    f. uncle
    g. grandfather
    h. family friend
    i. neighbor
    j. teacher
    k. doctor
    l. dentist
   m. clergy
    n. none

50. Did your mother have any miscarriages before you were conceived?

    a. yes
    b. no

51. Did your mother ever have an abortion before you were conceived?

    a. yes
    b. no

52. Did your mother ever have a stillborn before you were conceived?

    a. yes
    b. no

53. Did your mother ever give a child up for adoption before you were conceived?

    a. yes
    b. no

54. If your mother had a miscarriage, abortion, stillborn, or gave a child up for adoption before you were conceived, how many times?

    a. once
    b. twice

    c. three or more times

    d. not applicable

55. Did your mother ever have a miscarriage, abortion, stillborn, or give a child up for adoption after you were born?

    a. yes

    b. no

56. Did any of your siblings die while you were an infant or very young child?

    a. yes

    b. no

57. Did either of your parents die while you were an infant or very young child?

    a. mother

    b. father

    c. both mother and father

    d. neither

58. Did anyone in your immediate family commit suicide while you were an infant or very young child?

    a. yes

    b. no

59. Did your mother take DES during her pregnancy?

    a. yes

    b. no

60. What length of time was your mother in labor?

    a. short

    b. average

    c. long

61. Do you think you were ever emotionally abused as an infant or very young child? If so, by whom?

    a. mother/father

    b. sister/brother

    c. aunt/uncle

    d. cousin (male/female)

    e. grandmother/grandfather

    f. nurse (male/female)
    g. housekeeper/nanny (male/female)
    h. baby-sitter (male/female)
    i. family friend (male/female)
    j. neighbor (male/female)
    k. doctor (male/female)
    l. clergy (male/female)
    m. stranger (male/female)
    n. none

62. Do you think you were ever physically abused as an infant or very young child? If so, by whom?

    a. mother/father
    b. sister/brother
    c. aunt/uncle
    d. cousin (male/female)
    e. grandmother/grandfather
    f. nurse (male/female)
    g. housekeeper/nanny (male/female)
    h. baby-sitter (male/female)
    i. family friend (male/female)
    j. neighbor (male/female)
    k. doctor (male/female)
    l. clergy (male/female)
    m. stranger (male/female)
    n. none

63. Do you think you were ever sexually abused as an infant or very young child? If so, by whom?

    a. mother/father
    b. sister/brother
    c. aunt/uncle
    d. cousin (male/female)
    e. grandmother/grandfather
    f. nurse (male/female)
    g. housekeeper/nanny (male/female)
    h. baby-sitter (male/female)
    i. family friend (male/female)
    j. neighbor (male/female)
    k. doctor (male/female)
    l. clergy (male/female)

m. stranger (male/female)

n. none

64. Record all of your memories of your intrauterine life, birth, and early childhood on a separate sheet of paper.

65. Record all experiences or stories reported by others about your intrauterine life, birth, and early childhood on a separate sheet of paper.

KEY TO ROOTS OF PERSONALITY QUESTIONNAIRE

The following presents suggestions on the meaning of your answers to the questionnaire. The key may help you discover early influences that shaped your personality.

There are no absolute answers. Each answer represents a small piece of a large jigsaw puzzle that is made up of a continuum of variables from conception to the present. When you have finished with the questionnaire and studied the key to it, what may emerge is a composite picture of you, from conception to early childhood.

1. Age _____ Sex _____ Time of birth _____
   —birth time may be the time of day when creativity is greatest for you or you get most anxious
   —hospital staff and doctors are usually more tired and less efficient at night

2. Birth weight _____ (*average for boys=$7\frac{1}{4}$ lb.; average for girls=7 lb.)
   —if heavier than average, then it may be a more difficult birth and the infant may be postmature (late)
   —if lighter than average, then the infant may be premature, born to a stressed, anxious mother

3. Condition at birth—listed from most desirable to least desirable
   —may indicate the difficulty of labor
   —may indicate patterns of general functioning in life

   a. excellent (alert)—exceptional performance in all relationships
   b. very good—productive performance in most relationships

*Lucille F. Whaley and Donna L. Wong, *Nursing Care of Infants & Children*, 6th ed. (St. Louis, Missouri: Mosby, 1999).

    c. fair—problematic existence

    d. poor—very problematic, struggling existence

    e. very poor (blue and not breathing)—near-death experience may have left a legacy of feeling dead inside

    f. don't know

4. Birth order:

    a. first—has tendency to be more successful than siblings; is usually father's favorite

      —an "only child" is like a firstborn child

    b. second—is usually mother's favorite

      —middle child seems to get the least attention; tends to get lost in the shuffle

      —youngest is the "baby" of family; tends to be infantilized

    c. third—middle child seems to get the least attention; tends to get lost in the shuffle

      —youngest is the "baby" of family; tends to be infantilized

    d. fourth—same as (c)

    e. fifth—same as (c)

    f. sixth or later—same as (c)

5. Are you a twin?

    a. yes—shares either with difficulty or with ease

      —twins tend to be very close throughout lifetime; tend to have a psychic connection

      —twins may marry twins and live in the same house

    b. no—may have a clear sense of individuality

6. Were you adopted?

    a. yes—unplanned, unwanted, abandoned (regardless of how much loved by adoptive parents)

      —child carries the loss of birth mother in memory

      —may feel estranged, feel as if they did not belong, and tend to be sensitive to separation

    b. no—less likelihood of (a)

7. Did your mother want to have a baby when you were conceived?

    a. yes—wanted child is blessed, feels safe and secure

      —being wanted is prime factor in acquiring strong, healthy sense of self; greater tendency to feel accepted and loved

b. no—unwanted child may tend to have low self-esteem and problems feeling accepted and loved

8. Your mother wanted

    a. a boy—if male, then all is well
    —if female, then unwanted as female; may have psychosexual problems; may have problems feeling accepted and loved
    b. a girl—if female, then all is well
    —if male, then unwanted as male; may have psychosexual problems; may have problems feeling accepted and loved
    c. didn't matter—less likelihood of psychosexual problems and problems feeling accepted and loved

9. Did your father want to have a baby when you were conceived?
—father's influence is generally less significant than mother's

    a. yes—same as #7
    b. no—same as #7
    —father's opposition may lead to mother having a more stressful pregnancy

10. Your father wanted
—father's influence is generally less significant than mother's

    a. a boy—same as #8
    b. a girl—same as #8
    c. didn't matter—same as #8

11. Did your mother have any major calamities during pregnancy?

    a. yes—stress factor
    —unborn child may have identified with calamity and may be born sensitized to future difficulties
    —child's life susceptible to trauma
    b. no—child's life less susceptible to trauma

12. During pregnancy your mother was generally
—mother provides model for child's outlook on life

    a. happy—child tends to develop positive/optimistic attitude
    b. unhappy—child tends to develop negative/pessimistic attitude

13. During your intrauterine life, did your mother talk or sing to you?

    a. yes—presence of prenatal communication and bonding
    b. no—lack of prenatal communication and bonding

14. During your intrauterine life, did your father talk or sing to you?

    a. yes—same as #13
    b. no—same as #13

15. During her pregnancy, your mother was exposed to noise from .

    a. machinery—may be strongly attracted to or try to avoid such sounds
    b. planes or trains—same as (a)
    c. loud music—same as (a)
    d. none of the above

16. During your intrauterine life, you felt
    —these feelings may have originated in your mother's womb and then become more pronounced with subsequent experiences that strengthened and supported them
    —may relate to similar conditions during child's life experiences

17. While she was pregnant with you, your mother often felt
    —mother provides model for child's life experiences

18. Do you remember dreaming in the womb? If so, what? Please write on a separate sheet of paper.

    a. yes—any recalled dreams may be useful
    b. no—very few people remember prebirth dreams

19. During her pregnancy your mother generally
    —all substances listed may dull thoughts, feelings, and creativity in mother and child
    —child may become substance abuser
    —if mother was a substance abuser, (according to statistics) she was probably single, poor, uneducated, anxious and/or depressed, received inadequate prenatal medical care, and communicated very little with unborn child either verbally or nonverbally

20. You were born

    a. in a hospital—greater likelihood for medical interventions and drug use (see #21 and #22)
    b. at home—more peaceful surroundings
       —mother probably more comfortable and less stressed
    c. elsewhere—whatever the condition, may relate to life patterns

21. During delivery your mother received

   a. painkillers—dulls thoughts, feelings, and creativity of
   mother and child
   —inhibits natural, spontaneous process of bonding with
   mother and in life relationships
   b. local anesthesia—same as (a)
   c. general anesthesia—same as (a)
   d. none of the above—infant aware, attentive, and responsive at
   birth

22. Your birth was
   —each mode of delivery may be retained in emotional or cellular
   memory, influencing personality and actions throughout lifetime

   a. vaginal—healthy sense of self; feeling in control of one's
   life; optimistic; an active doer
   b. forceps used—child tends to need assistance but often re-
   sists it; life may be perceived as a struggle; tendency for
   headaches, neck and shoulder pain
   c. episiotomy—same as forceps, plus child may feel guilty for
   pain inflicted upon mother
   d. cesarean section—tendency to feel helpless under stress; often sensitive to being interrupted; may suffer from cuddle
   hunger, that is, an inordinate need for touch
   e. induced with Pitocin—sense of being rushed; resentful of
   controls; may be rebellious
   f. breech—may be very determined, headstrong; likes to do
   things her way; may have difficulty moving forward in life
   g. delayed (doctor not available)—may feel held back in life; react violently to perceived unfair treatment; may be inhibited
   h. premature—child tends to be early and fast in life; may feel
   rushed, always in a hurry
   i. postmature—child tends to be late and slow in life; tendency
   to procrastinate

23. After your birth, you were

   a. placed on your mother's breast—ideal option: child nurtured;
   enhanced relationships between child and mother, and between child and others in life
   b. put in a baby nursery—child may feel cut off, abandoned,
   and rejected by mother

    c. put in an incubator—child may feel as if an invisible wall separates him or her from others; this may persist into adult life

    d. taken to the neonatal intensive care unit—most threatening option—all of the above

24. During birth you and your mother were probably
—your relationship to your mother during birth may determine relationships between you and others

    a. in sync—child tends to be congenial, agreeable

    b. at odds—child tends to be argumentative, disagreeable

25. You are primarily
—sexual orientation may be related to other variables in this questionnaire (genetics and prenatal/perinatal environment; #8 and #10, being wanted as opposite sex; #38, being wrong or a mistake; and other physical and psychological factors, such as stress)

26. You like touching, hugging, and cuddling
—degree of physical contact infant experienced during and after birth may determine child's patterns of giving and receiving affection

    a. an inordinate amount—insecure; seeks other's approval for validation

    b. very much—somewhat insecure yet demonstrative/affectionate

    c. an average amount—comfortable with sense of self; concerned for others

    d. very little—reluctant to receive attention

    e. not at all—resistant to receiving attention

27. With food, you tend to
—relates to feelings of being loved; may substitute food for love; tendency to compensate for feeling empty inside

    a. overeat—obesity; unhealthy condition.

    b. eat until full—healthy condition

    c. nibble—feelings of boredom, mild depression

    d. have trouble eating or undereat—anorexia

    e. cause yourself to vomit after eating—bulimia

28. In regard to sex, you
    —relates to feelings of being loved; may mistake sex for love; tendency to compensate by seeking sex for feelings of low self-esteem

    a. can't get enough of it—addictive behavior
    b. have it on your mind all the time—addictive behavior
    c. consider it important—healthy sexual attitude
    d. find it a problem—probability of negative childhood experiences
    e. think you'd be better off without it—avoidance/denial of pleasure
    f. are uninterested—low libido: may be d) or e) above

29. In regard to money, you
    —relates to feelings of being loved; may unconsciously substitute money for love
    —same answers as 27 and 28; your relationship to food, sex, and money tells a lot about who you are

30. You have at some point been dependent on
    —addictions may relate to mother's perinatal condition and the drugs she received
    —addictions are also a means of filling a vast sense of emptiness stemming from lack of love during formative years
    —same as #19

31. Are you attracted to large, fat people?

    a. yes—insecurity: wants to be attached to mother
       —may indicate unresolved feelings toward mother
    b. no—when attracted to average-size people, then comfortable in relationship with mother

32. Are you attracted to small, thin people?

    a. yes—overpowering mother: seeks detachment from mother
    b. no—when attracted to average-size people, then comfortable in relationship with mother

33. You suffer from
    —additional conditions may be related to genetics and other variables in this questionnaire

34. You sometimes dream of
    —may be reenactments of very early memories of lurching down

the fallopian tube, implanting in the uterus, or floating in the amniotic fluid

    a. falling or tumbling—fallopian tube journey

    b. floating in water—memories of being in amniotic fluid

    c. tunnels or openings—passing through the cervix; fallopian
        tube to uterus

    d. quicksand or swamps—implantation (foothold in posterior
        wall of uterus); insecure; fear of engulfment

    e. shipwrecks or breaking into pieces—same as (d) above

35. Are you or would you like to be employed by a major organization
    offering good benefits and a pension plan?

    a. yes—may feel unsafe and insecure in outside world
        —may seek to recapture safety and security of womb

    b. no—may feel safe and secure in outside world

36. You describe yourself as
    —prenatal and perinatal experiences may relate to dominant out-
    look on life

    a. optimistic—comfortable womb life/birth/early life
        successful postnatal bonding

    b. outgoing—same as (a) above
        —trusting/confident relationship with parent(s)

    c. people-oriented—same as (a) and (b)

    d. pessimistic—impaired womb life/birth/early life
        —faulty postnatal bonding
        —distrusting/insecure relationship with parent

    e. withdrawn—same as (d)

    f. shy—same as (d)

    g. introverted—same as (d)
        —parent(s) encouraged thoughtfulness and discouraged ex-
        pressiveness

    h. assertive—same as (a)
        —parent(s) supported child's expressiveness, may be unas-
        sisted vaginal birth, firstborn

    i. rootless—floating in life, has difficulty with settling down
        —unattached to parents/insecure, faulty prenatal or postna-
        tal bonding
        —difficulty developing strong bond/insecure

    j. cautious—some constructive attachments and some betrayals

k. passive—mother anesthetized/epidural at birth: difficulty feeling; tendency to suffer or feel threat of suffering

l. reckless—seeking stimulation and excitement
—excited/hyper mother: scared, fussing; child overstimulated/becomes addicted to high level of stimulation

m. aggressive—rejection by parent(s) because of unwanted pregnancy or unwanted gender
—neglect/abuse after birth: antisocial behavior, anger, hostility

n. adventurous—reckless, optimistic: combination of destructive and constructive early experiences

o. prudent—cautious; same as (j)

p. extroverted—same as (a)

37. You enjoy

a. getting ahead—natural, unassisted vaginal birth: tendency to become successful

b. diving into things—same as (a)

c. exploring new horizons—same as (a)

d. none of the above

38. You fear

a. losing your temper—mother lost control at birth

b. going crazy—mother lost control at birth

c. becoming violent and destructive—mother lost control at birth

d. becoming helpless—mother anesthetized at birth

e. making a mistake—unplanned/unwanted pregnancy or unwanted gender: child not living up to expectations; may feel unaccepted and may receive conditional love

f. being wrong—same as (e) plus, may have been a breech

g. being a failure—same as (e)

h. being successful—child may feel guilty for hurting mother during birth

i. being raped—feeling helpless at birth
—mother/baby may have been exposed to painful medical procedures
—things may have been done to infant, for example, eyedrops or suck-out mouth

j. being abandoned—infant was probably taken from mother immediately after birth, before infant had chance to establish close contact with her

k. none of the above—relatively easy, comfortable birth

39. You often experience
—(a) to (d) indicate some unresolved problems that may have started around birth

    a. an inability to get into what you are doing—assisted birth (cesarean, forceps, breech)
    b. inexplicable fatigue—anesthetics, sedatives, painkillers —long labor: helplessness
    c. lack of willpower—assisted birth: can't do it on my own —helplessness: dependence
    d. intellectual stagnation—anesthetics, sedatives, painkillers: dull the mind
    e. the feeling that something is missing—twin died in utero
    f. none of the above—relatively easy, comfortable birth

40. You try to avoid wearing
—any of (a) to (d) may indicate cord around neck at birth: will avoid clothing that fits tightly around neck; tendency to feel inhibited or choked by people and under pressure

    a. scarves
    b. hats
    c. turtlenecks
    d. neckties
    e. none of the above—unobstructed birth

41. You have a fear of
—due to fearful perinatal experience that the child then identifies with

    a. open spaces—agoraphobia (*agora*=Greek for "market/out of home")
    b. closed spaces—claustrophobia (elevators, closets, basements)
    c. water—may associate with drowning at birth
    d. traveling—may associate with birth in car, bus, train, plane, or boat
    e. the dark—may associate with anxiety in womb or birth canal

f. heights—may associate with being suddenly lifted up after birth
g. animals—mother frightened during pregnancy
     —infant frightened during birth or postnatally
h. none of the above—relatively easy, comfortable birth

42. You react to stress with

a. increased activity—mother's anxiety during labor
b. decreased activity—anesthetics to mother during labor
c. immobilization—anesthetics to mother during labor
d. confusion—anesthetics to mother during labor
e. anxiety—mother worried/anxious during labor
f. anger—delivery held back during labor
g. none of the above—absence of trauma during labor

43. Did any trauma occur to you or your family when you were in your
mother's womb?

a. yes—child may develop decreased stress tolerance
b. no—child may tolerate stress well

44. Did any trauma occur to you or your family at the time of your
birth?

a. yes—same as #43 (a): may fear giving birth as adult
b. no—same as #43 (b): may look forward to giving birth as
     adult

45. Did any trauma occur to you or your family within the first few
weeks or months after your birth?

a. yes—same as #43 (a): may increase anxiety about first few
     weeks or months after giving birth as adult
b. no—same as #43 (b): may decrease anxiety about first few
     weeks or months after giving birth as adult

46. Did any trauma occur to you or your family within the first two
years of your life?

a. yes—same as #43 (a): may increase anxiety about the first two
     years of your child's life
b. no—same as #43 (b): may decrease anxiety about the first two
     years of your child's life

47. Were you and your mother separated for any period of time exceeding a few hours within the first few weeks or months after your birth?

    a. yes—may increase fear of abandonment
    b. no—may decrease fear of abandonment

48. Did you have any surrogate mothers? If so, who?
 —the surrogate's role or occupation may provide a role model for and influence the child's relationships and career choices
 —the more surrogates, the less likely the child truly bonded to one or two persons: may have problems with trust and intimacy

49. Did you have any surrogate fathers? If so, who?
 —same as #48

50. Did your mother have any miscarriages before you were conceived?

    a. yes—child may have feelings of loss for the dead sibling, with unexplained depressive tendencies
    b. no—less likelihood of (a)

51. Did your mother ever have an abortion before you were conceived?

    a. yes—child may have unconscious fear of mother
      —if followed by destructive experiences with women, a generalized fear of women as malicious and evil may develop
    b. no—less likelihood of (a)

52. Did your mother ever have a stillborn before you were conceived?

    a. yes—child may have fear of death, sense of loss
    b. no—less likelihood of (a)

53. Did your mother ever give a child up for adoption before you were conceived?

    a. yes—child may have fear of abandonment, sense of loss
    b. no—less likelihood of (a)

54. If your mother had a miscarriage, abortion, stillborn, or gave a child up for adoption before you were conceived, how many times?
 —the more often, the stronger the tendencies described in #50, #51, #52, and #53, respectively

55. Did your mother ever have a miscarriage, abortion, stillborn, or give a child up for adoption after you were born?

    a. yes—more likelihood of #50 (a), #51 (a), #52 (a), #53 (a)

    b. no—less likelihood of #50 (a), #51 (a), #52 (a), #53 (a)

56. Did any of your siblings die while you were an infant or very young child?

    a. yes—child may have deep sense of loss; lifelong fear of losing a person who is close

    b. no—less likelihood of (a)

57. Did either of your parents die while you were an infant or very young child?

    a. mother—pronounced version of #56 (a)

    b. father—pronounced version of #56 (a)

    c. both mother and father—most pronounced version of #56 (a)

    d. neither—less likelihood of #56 (a)

58. Did anyone in your immediate family commit suicide while you were an infant or very young child?

    a. yes—increases tendency for child to think of suicide as a real way out of difficult situations

    b. no—less likelihood of (a)

59. Did your mother take DES during her pregnancy?

    a. yes—if male, then markedly increased stereotypical feminine traits

    —if female, then stereotypical tendency to be more masculine in behavior and outlook; does not carry over to sexual orientation

    b. no—less likelihood of (a)

60. What length of time was your mother in labor?

    —indication of stress both mother and child experienced during delivery

    a. short—minimum traumatic labor

    b. average—medium traumatic labor

    c. long—maximum traumatic labor

61. Do you think you were ever emotionally abused as an infant or very young child? If so, by whom?

—abuse of any kind may have long-lasting, destructive effects on personality; child tends to blame self rather than caretakers for occurrences, which lead to low self-esteem and an enduring sense of shame and guilt and distrust of people

    a. mother/father   .
    b. sister/brother
    c. aunt/uncle
    d. cousin (male/female)
    e. grandmother/grandfather
    f. nurse (male/female)
    g. housekeeper/nanny (male/female)
    h. baby-sitter (male/female)
    i. family friend (male/female)
    j. neighbor (male/female)
    k. doctor (male/female)
    l. clergy (male/female)
    m. stranger (male/female)
    n. none

62. Do you think you were ever physically abused as an infant or very young child? If so, by whom?
    —same as #61

    a. mother/father
    b. sister/brother
    c. aunt/uncle
    d. cousin (male/female)
    e. grandmother/grandfather
    f. nurse (male/female)
    g. housekeeper/nanny (male/female)
    h. baby-sitter (male/female)
    i. family friend (male/female)
    j. neighbor (male/female)
    k. doctor (male/female)
    l. clergy (male/female)
    m. stranger (male/female)
    n. none

63. Do you think you were ever sexually abused as an infant or very young child? If so, by whom?
    —same as #61

64. Record all of your memories of your intrauterine life, birth, and early childhood on a separate sheet of paper.

65. Record all experiences or stories reported by others about your intrauterine life, birth, and early childhood on a separate sheet of paper.

Notes and References

CHAPTER ONE: CROSSING THE AMNIOTIC SEA

page

15 migratory voyage: Arnold B. Scheibel, "Embryological Development of the Human Brain," *New Horizons for Learning Electronic Journal* (September/October 1997), www.newhorizons.org. newsletter14.html.

16 So immense are the challenges: Rima Shore, *Rethinking the Brain* (New York: Families and Work Institute, 1997), 15.

17 "directed evolution": Interviews with John Cairns and Barry Hall, 1990, and J. Cairns, J. Overbaugh, and S. Miller, "The Origin of Mutants," *Nature* 335 (1998):142–145.

17 cracked the human genome: Robert Sapolsky, quoted in *Newsweek*, 10 April 2000, 68.

18 "malleable aspect of gene expression": Bruce H. Lipton, "Nature, Nurture, and the Power of Love," *Pre- and Perinatal Psychology Journal* 13 (1) (1998).

18 Every living organism: Ibid. Lipton's work is on the cutting edge and I am much in awe of his knowledge.

19 Sex on the Brain: Bruce S. McEwen and Harold M. Schmeck, Jr., *The Hostage Brain* (New York: The Rockefeller University Press, 1994).

20 scientists from McGill University: Joyce F. Benenson, Erica R. Liroff, Stacey J. Pascal, and Guiseppe Della Cioppa, "Propulsion: A

page

behavioral expression of masculinity," *British Journal of Developmental Psychology* 15 (1997): 37–50.

20 Researchers from the University of London: Abi Berger, "The Dangers of Blues for a Boy," *New Scientist* 147 (1985):4, 1995.

20 neurobiologist Donald Pfaff: Donald W. Pfaff, *Estrogens and Brain Function: Neural Analysis of a Hormone-Controlled Mammalian Reproductive Behavior* (New York: Springer Verlag, 1980).

21 scientists from Oxford University: G. W. Harris and S. Levine, "Sexual differentiation of the brain and its experimental control," *Journal of Physiology* 181 (2): 379–400 (1965).

21 scientists castrated young male rats: Geoffrey Raisman and Pauline Field, "Sexual dimorphism in the preoptic area of the rat," *Science* 173 (1971): 731–733.

23 prenatal famine: Alan S. Brown, Jim van Os, Corine Driessens, Hans W. Hoek, and Ezra S. Susser, "Further Evidence of Relation Between Prenatal Famine and Major Affective Disorder," *American Journal of Psychiatry* 157:2 (February 2000); Richard Neugebauer, Hans W. Hoek, and Ezra Susser, "Prenatal Exposure to Wartime Famine and Development of Antisocial Personality Disorder in Early Adulthood," *Journal of the American Medical Association* 282 (5): 455–462 (1999).

23 omega-3 fatty acids: A. C. van Houwelingen et al., "Essential fatty acid status in neonates after fish-oil supplementation during late pregnancy," *British Journal of Nutrition* 74 (5): 723–731 (1995).

24 exposure to harmful substances: Jeannette L. Johnson and Michelle Left, "Environmental Agents and the Developing Brain." "Children of Substance Abusers: Overview of Research Findings," *Pediatrics*, part 2 of 2, 103 (5): 1,085–1,900 (1999).

24 Studies of mice: C. P. Ross and T. V. Persaud, "Neural tube defects in early rat embryos following maternal treatment with ethanol and caffeine," *Anatomischer Anzeiger* 169 (4): 247–252 (1989). Susan M. Smith, "Alcohol-induced cell death in the embryo," *Alcohol Health & Research World* 21 (4): 287–296 (1997).

24 When alcohol is administered to rats: Marion Diamond, "The Significance of Enrichment," in *Enriching Heredity* (New York: The Free Press, 1988).

24 the vital left hemisphere: I. A. Janzen, J. L. Nanson, and G. W. Block, "Neuropsychological evaluation of preschoolers with FAS," *Neurotoxical Teratol* 17 (1995): 273–275.

25 In one study in Chicago: L. S. Wakschlag et al., "Maternal Smoking

page

During Pregnancy and the Risk of Conduct Disorder in Boys," *Archives of General Psychiatry* 54 (1997): 670–676.

25 risk of criminal behavior: Patricia A. Brennan, Emily R. Grekin, and Sarnoff A. Mednick, "Maternal Smoking During Pregnancy and Adult Male Criminal Outcomes," *Archives of General Psychiatry* 56 (1999): 215–219.

25 cocaine: N. He, "Cocaine induces cell death within the primate fetal cerebral wall," *Neuropathology Applied Neurobiology* 25 (6): 504–512 (1999).

25 maternal bouts of the flu: Ricardo A. Machón, "Adult major affective disorder after prenatal exposure to an influenza epidemic," *Archives of General Psychiatry* 54 (4): 322–328 (1997).

26 Other diseases and conditions: Ezra B. Susser, Alan Brown, and Thomas D. Matte, "Prenatal Factors and Adult Mental and Physical Health," *Canadian Journal of Psychiatry* 44, May 1999.

CHAPTER TWO: THE DAWN OF CONSCIOUSNESS

29 "emotional reactions": Jason Birnholz, Report on "Sonochromes," *The Medical Post* 25 (19), 16 May 1989.

30 brain structures necessary for learning: Dominick Purpura, "Consciousness," *Behavior Today*, 2 June 1975, 494.

30 dream sleep: Maria Z. Salam and Raymond D. Adams, "New Horizons in the Neurology of Childhood," *Perspectives in Biology and Medicine*, Spring 1966, 364–410.

30 psychology of conception: Sabina Spielrein, "Destruction as a Cause of Coming into Being," *Jahrbuch für psychoanalytische und psychopathologische Forschungen* 4 (1912): 465–503.

31 Isador Sadger: "Preliminary Study of the Psychic Life of the Fetus and the Primary Germ Cell," *The Psychoanalytic Review* 28 (3), 1941.

31 These physiological events: Candace B. Pert, *Molecules of Emotion* (New York: Simon & Schuster, 1999).

31 As the unborn child grows: David Chamberlain, "The Sentient Prenate: What Every Parent Should Know," *Pre- and Perinatal Psychology Journal* 9 (1), 1994.

32 chamber of echoes: Peter G. Hepper and Sara B. Shahidullah, "Development of Fetal Hearing," *Archives of Disease in Children* 71 (1994): 81–87.

32 three children's stories: Anthony J. deCasper and William P. Fifer,

page

"Of Human Bonding: Newborns Prefer Their Mothers' Voices," *Science* 208 (1980): 1,174–1,176.

33 sing a melody: R. K. Panneton, "Prenatal Auditory Experience with Melodies: Effects on Postnatal Auditory Preferences in Human Newborns" (Ph.D. thesis, University of North Carolina, Greensboro, 1985).

33 primed for language: Marshall R. Childs, "Prenatal Language Learning," *Journal of Prenatal and Perinatal Psychology and Health* 13 (2), 1998.

34 fetal pain: K. J. S. Anand and P. R. Hickey, "Pain and Its Effects— the Human Neonate and Fetus," *New England Journal of Medicine* 317 (1987): 1,321–1,329; also, Anne Faddio, Joel Katz, et al.; and Fran Lang Porter, Cynthia N. Zaloff, and L. Philip Miller, "Procedural Pain in Newborn Infants: The Influence of Intensity and Development," *Pediatrics* 104 (1): 13–27 (1999). A. Tadio, J. Katz et al., "Effect of neonatal circumcision on pain response during subsequent routine examination," *The Lancet* 349 (1997): 599–605.

35 Nicholas M. Fisk: Nicholas M. Fisk and V. Glover, "Fetal pain: implications for research and practice," *British Journal of Obstetrical Gynecology* 106 (1999): 881–886.

CHAPTER THREE: MATERNAL STRESSORS

37 "I'm a very unhappy woman": From a letter to T.R.V. Name withheld.

38 Mothers of schizophrenic offspring: P. B. Jones et al., "Schizophrenia as a long-term outcome of pregnancy, delivery, and perinatal complications: a 28-year follow-up of the 1966 North Finland General Population Birth Cohort," *American Journal of Psychiatry*, 155 (1998): 355–364.

38 hyperactivity, motor problems, and attention deficits: B. R. H. Van den Bergh, "The Influence of Maternal Emotions During Pregnancy on Fetal and Neonatal Behavior," *Pre- and Perinatal Psychology Journal* 5 (20): 119–130 (1990).

38 Babies who undergo ultrasound: A good review of the effects can be found in *Birth* 13 (1): March 1986. Also see Susan M. Heidrich and Mecca S. Cranley, "Effects of Fetal Movement, Ultrasound Scans, and Amniocentesis on Maternal-Fetal Attachment," *Nursing Research* 38 (2): 81–84 (1989); also James D. Campbell, Wayne Efford, and Rollin Brannt, "Case-control study of prenatal ultra-

page

sonography exposure in children with delayed speech," *Canadian Medical Association Journal* 149 (10): 1,435–1,440 (1993).

38 irritability: Barry Zuckerman, Howard Bauchner, Steven Parker, and Howard Cabral, "Maternal Depressive Symptoms During Pregnancy and Newborn Irritability," *Developmental and Behavioral Pediatrics* 11 (4): 190–194 (1990).

39 These hormones have: Bruce S. McEwen, "Allostasis and Allostatic Load: Implications for Neuropsychopharmacology," *Neuropharmacology* 22 (3): 108–213 (2000).

39 experiments with animals and in studies of human populations: Charles A. Nelson and Leslie J. Carver, "The effects of stress and trauma on brain and memory: A view from the developmental cognitive neuroscience," *Development and Psychopathology* 10 (1998): 793–809.

39 shocked rats: W. R. Thompson, "Influence of prenatal maternal anxiety on emotionality in young rats," *Science* 125 (1957): 698–699.

40 a variety of stressors: W. R. Thompson, J. Watson, and W. R. Charlesworth, "The effects of prenatal maternal stress on offspring behavior in rats," *Psychological Monographs* 76 (38), 1962.

40 prenatal stress and the outcome of a pregnancy: Pathik D. Wadhwa et al., "The association between prenatal stress and infant birth weight," *American Journal of Obstetrics & Gynecology* 169 (4): 858–865 (1993).

40 low-birth-weight and premature births: P. D. Wadhwa, "Prenatal stress and life-span development," in *Encyclopedia of Mental Health* ed. Howard S. Friedman (San Diego, Calif.: Academic Press, 1998).

41 monetary and family problems: Kathleen M. Kalil, James E. Gruber, Joyce Conley, and Michael Sytniac, "Social and Family Pressures on Anxiety and Stress During Pregnancy," *Pre- and Perinatal Psychology Journal* 8(2), 1993.

41 A study of Danish women: H. C. Lou, M. Nordentoft, and F. Jense, "Psychosocial stress and severe prematurity," *Lancet* 340 (1992): 54.

42 pregnant women in Alabama: Rachel L. Copper and Robert L. Goldenberg, "The preterm prediction study: maternal stress is associated with spontaneous preterm birth at less than thirty-five weeks gestation." *American Journal of Obstetrics & Gynecology* 175 (5): 1,286 (1996).

43 stress affects the physiology of the brain: Curt A. Sandman, Pathik D. Wadhwa, Aleksandra Chicz-DeMet, Christine Dunkel-Schetter,

page

and Manuel Porto, "Maternal Stress, HPA Activity, and Fetal/ Infant Outcome," *Annals of the New York Academy of Sciences* 814 (1997): 266–275.

43 stress hormones can influence the gender of the brain: Jaak Panksepp, *Affective Neuroscience: The Foundations of Human and Animal Emotions* (New York: Oxford University Press, 1998), 237–239.

44 neuroscientist Jaak Panksepp: ibid.

45 "Under conditions of maternal stress": Jaak Panksepp, *Affective Neuroscience*, 238.

45 "As a seven-month-old unborn child": From a letter to T.R.V. Name withheld.

46 study of 1,123 mothers: Barry Zuckerman, Howard Bauchner, Steven Parker, and Howard Cabral, "Maternal Depressive Symptoms During Pregnancy and Newborn Irritability," *Developmental and Behavioral Pediatrics* 11 (4): 190–194 (1990).

46 another study found elevated levels of norepinephrine: Neuronal excitability: M. Joels and E. Vreugdenhil, "Corticosteroids in the brain," *Molecular Neurobiology* 17 (1998): 87–198; also, C. Pavlides and A. Kimura et al., "Hippocampal homosynaptic long-term depression/depotentiation induced by adrenal steroids," *Neuroscience* 68 (1995): 379–385; and, E. Gould, P. Tanapat et al., "Proliferation of granule cell precursors in the dentate gyrus of adult monkeys is diminished by stress, *Proceedings of the National Academy of Science* 95 (1998): 3,168–3,171.

46 teenage pregnancy: Angelo Ponirakis, Elizabeth J. Susman, Cynthia A. Stifer, "Negative emotionality and cortisol during adolescent pregnancy and its effects on infant health and autonomic nervous system reactivity," *Developmental Psychobiology* 33 (2): 163–174 (1998).

46 Apgar scores: On a scale of 1 to 10, a means of evaluating within 60 seconds the survival probability of a newborn child. It assesses the heart rate, respiratory effort, muscle tone, reflex irritability, and color. A score of 10 is perfect, 7 is quite normal, but 3 or less calls for emergency measures.

47 15 percent of pregnant women: Barbara Parker, Judith McFarlane, and Karen Soeken, "Abuse During Pregnancy: Effects on Maternal Complications and Birth Weight in Adult and Teenage Women," *Obstetrics & Gynecology* 841 (1994): 323–328.

48 "I have for a long time felt": From letter to T.R.V. Name withheld.

49 infants born of unwanted pregnancies: Muhammad N. Bustan and

page

Ann L. Coker, "Maternal Attitude Toward Pregnancy and the Risk of Neonatal Death," *American Journal of Public Health* 4 (3): 411–414 (1994).

49   Scientists in Prague: Henry P. David, Zilenek Dybrich, Zilenek Matejcek, and Vratislav Schuller, *Born Unwanted—Developmental Effects of Denied Abortion* (New York: Spring Publishing, 1988).

49   examining self-esteem: William G. Axinn, Jennifer S. Barber, and Arland Thornton, "The Long-Term Impact of Parents' Childbearing Decisions on Children's Self-Esteem," *Demography* 35 (4): 435–443 (1998).

49   Loss During Pregnancy: Gayle Peterson, "Chains of Grief: The Impact of Prenatal Loss on Subsequent Pregnancy," *Pre- and Perinatal Psychology Journal* 9 (2) 1994.

CHAPTER FOUR: THE WOMB AS CLASSROOM

54   Brigitte Bardot: From the memoirs of Brigitte Bardot, as reported by Kirsty Lang in *The Sunday Times*, 27 October, 1996.

55   Addressing the issue, William Axinn: William G. Axinn, Jennifer S. Barber, and Arland Thornton, "The Long-Term Impact of Parents' Childbearing Decisions on Children's Self-Esteem," *Demography* 35 (4): 435–443 (1998).

56   manager to nurturer: Robbie E. Davis-Floyd, "Mind Over Body: The Pregnant Professional," *Pre- and Perinatal Psychology Journal* (3): 201–227 (1994).

57   "cobweb-cleaning session": Candace Fields Whitridge, "The Power of Joy: Pre- and Perinatal Psychology as Applied by a Mountain Midwife," *Pre- and Perinatal Psychology Journal* 2 (3), 1988.

63   "Meeting to sing": Rosario N. Rozada Montemurro, "Singing Lullabies to Unborn Children: Experience in Village Vilamarxant, Spain," *Pre- and Perinatal Psychology Journal* 11 (1): 9–16 (1996).

64   Baroque music: Michele Clements, in Dorothy Trainor, "Newborns Love Womb Sounds—Vivaldi, Mozart," *Medical Tribune*, 23 March 1978.

64   Mozart's Sonata in D Major: F. H. Rauscher, "Improved Maze Learning Through Early Music Exposure in Rats," *Neurological Research* 20 (1998): 427–432.

65   college students: F. H. Rauscher, "Listening to Mozart enhances spatial-temporal reasoning towards a neurophysical basis," *Neuroscience Letter* 185 (1): 44–47 (1995).

page

65 preschool children exposed to the music: F. H. Rauscher et al., "Music training causes long-term enhancement of preschool children's spatial-temporal reasoning," *Neurological Research* 19 (1): 218 (1997).

65 Other research has shown: Don Campbell, *The Mozart Effect for Children* (New York: William Morrow, 2000).

65 superior language skills: D. J. Shetler, "The Inquiry into Prenatal Music Experience; a Report of the Eastman Project," *Pre- and Perinatal Psychology Journal* 3 (3): 171–189 (1980–1987).

65 Rene Van de Carr: Rene Van de Carr, "Enhancing Early Speech, Parental Bonding and Infant Physical Development Using Prenatal Intervention in Standard Obstetric Practice," *Pre- and Perinatal Psychology Journal* 1 (1): 20–29 (1986).

66 enriched and varied environments: Marion Diamond, "Mother's Enriched Environment Alters Brains of Unborn Rats," *Brain/Mind Bulletin* 12 (7): 1 and 5 (1987). Also, M. C. Diamond, "The Significance of Enrichment," in *Enriching Heredity* (New York: The Free Press, 1988).

67 exposed to too much stimulation: T. Berry Brazelton, as quoted in Susan Quinn, "The Competence of Babies," *Atlantic Monthly*, January 1982, 54–62.

CHAPTER FIVE: BIRTH AND PERSONALITY

70 "Inside the womb, fetuses can hear": Chairat Panthuraamphorn, "How to Maximize Human Potential at Birth," *Pre- and Perinatal Psychology Journal* (winter 1994): 117–126.

72 Cross-cultural studies reveal: James W. Prescott, "Body of Pleasure and the Origins of Violence," *Pulse of the Planet* 3 (1991): 17–25. Also, James DeMeo, "The Origins and Diffusion of Patrism in Saharasia, c. 4000 BCE: Evidence for a Worldwide, Climate-Linked Geographical Pattern in Human Behavior," *Pulse of the Planet* 3 (1991): 3–16.

73 The high-tech, low-tech: Ruth Dianne Rice, "Neurophysiological Development in Premature Infants Following Stimulation," *Developmental Psychology* 13 (1): 69–76 (1997).

73 hormones released during labor: Michel Odent, "Why Laboring Women Don't Need Support," *Mothering* 80 (fall 1996), 46.

74 To facilitate ease of labor: Gayle Peterson, *Birthing Normally* (Berkeley: Mindbody Press, 1984), 15, 16, 35, 115, 161, 186, 194.

page

Also, Marshall H. Klaus, John H. Kennell, and Phyllis H. Klaus, *Mothering the Mother* (Reading, Mass.: Addison-Wesley Publishing Company, 1993), 13, 17–22, 25–30.

75 modes of birth: William R. Emerson, "Birth Trauma: The Psychological Effects of Obstetrical Interventions," *Journal of Prenatal and Perinatal Psychology and Health* (fall 1998), 11.

79 birth timing: Roger Smith, "The Timing of Birth," *Scientific American* 280 (3): 68 (1999).

81 traumatic births: L. Salk, Lewis P. Lipsitt et al., "Relationships of Maternal and Perinatal Conditions to Eventual Adolescent Suicide," *The Lancet* 1 (1985): 624–627.

81 In a related study: B. Jacobsen, and G. Eklund, et al., "Perinatal Origin of Adult Self-Destructive Behavior," *Acta Psychiatrica Scandinavia* 76 (1987): 364–371.

81 aggressive acts: Elizabeth Kandel and Sarnoff Mednick, "Perinatal Complications Predict Violent Offending," *Criminology* 29 (3): 519–527 (1991).

82 Writing in the *Archives of General Psychiatry:* Adrian Raine, Patricia Brenman, and Sarnoff A. Mednick, "Birth Complications Combined with Early Maternal Rejection at Age 1 Year Predispose to Violent Crime at Age 18 Years," *Archives of General Psychiatry,* 51 (1994): 984–988.

83 birth order: Frank Sulloway, *Born to Rebel.* (New York: Vintage Books, 1996).

83 birth weight increases with each pregnancy: Michel Odent, "Birth Order and Intrauterine Life," *Primal Health Research* 4 (3): 1–4 (1996).

CHAPTER SIX: SENSE AND SENSIBILITY OF THE NEWBORN

85 Pediatricians' misconceptions about newborn babies: Susan Quinn, "The Competence of Babies," *Atlantic Monthly,* January 1982, 54–62.

86 lip movements: Patricia Kuhl and A. N. Meltzoff, "The bimodal perception of speech in infancy," *Science* 218 (1982): 1,138–1,241, and Meltzoff and Kuhl "Faces and speech" in D. J. Lewkowicz and R. Lickliter, eds., *The Development of Intersensory Perception* (Hillsdale, N.J.: Erlbaum, 1994).

86 Sensory Explosion: S. Begley, "Your Child's Brain," *Newsweek,* February 1996, and Sheila Anne Feeney, "Babies' Amazing Skills," *New York Daily News,* 26 March 1999.

page

87 Jacob E. Steiner of the Hebrew University in Jerusalem: J. E. Steiner, "Discriminative Human Facial Expressions to Taste and Smell Stimulation," *Annals of the New York Academy of Sciences* 237 (1974): 229–233.

88 out of the line of vision: as previous, Meltzoff and Kuhl.

88 special attention to their fathers: "What Do Babies Know," *Time* 15 August 1983.

90 neonate's reaction to pain: K. J. S. Anand and P. R. Hickey, "Pain and its effects in the human neonate and fetus," *New England Journal of Medicine* 317 (1987): 1,321–1,329.

91 lasting pain reflex: Anna Taddio, Joel Katz, A. Lane Ilersich, and Gideon Koren, "Effect of neonatal circumcision on pain response during subsequent routine vaccination," *Lancet* 349 (9,052): 599–603 (1997).

91 victimized parents: Madeleine H. Shearer, editorial, "Surgery on the Paralyzed, Unanesthetized Newborn," *Birth* 13 (2): 79 (1986). Also Jill R. Lawson, Letters, *Birth* 13 (2), 1986, and Helen Harrison, Letters, *Birth* 13 (2), 1986.

93 newborns experience severe pain: J. Winberg, "Do Neonatal Pain and Stress Program the Brain's Response to Future Stimuli?" *Acta Paediatrica Scandinavica* 87 (1998): 723–725.

93 brain plasticity is highest: Fran Lang Porter, "Pain in the Newborn," in J. Volpe, ed., *Clinics in Perinatology: Neonatal Neurology*, Vol. 16 (Philadelphia: W. B. Saunders, 1989), 549–564. Also, Fran Lang Porter, "Pain Assessment in Children: Infants," in N. L. Schecter, C. B. Berde, and M. Yaster, eds., *Pain in Infants, Children, and Adolescents* (Baltimore: Williams & Wilkins, 1993), 87–96.

93 windows of critical brain development: K. J. S. Anand and F. M. Scalzo, "Can adverse neonatal experiences alter brain development and subsequent behavior?" *Biology of the Neonate* 77 (2): 69–82 (2000).

93 Managing pain: Children of all ages have the right to receive the most effective pain relief that can safely be provided. In February 1992, the U.S. Department of Health and Human Services, Public Health Service, Agency for Health Care Policy and Research published *Acute Pain Management: Operative or Medical Procedures and Trauma. Clinical Practice Guideline*. The goals of this guideline are as follows:

    1. Reduce the incidence and minimize the severity of postoperative and post-traumatic pain.

2. Educate patients and families about the importance of communicating unrelieved pain to facilitate prompt evaluation and treatment.

3. Promote patient comfort and satisfaction.

4. Reduce the frequency of potential postoperative complications and possibly decrease the length of stay after surgical procedures.

These goals apply to all patient populations, including neonates.

The guideline emphasizes an individualized, team approach to pain management that focuses on the prevention of pain through assessment and frequent reassessment and the use of both pharmacologic and nonpharmacologic strategies. Persistence of misconceptions surrounding neonatal pain and its management make the application of the guideline and meeting the defined goals difficult at best.

Is it safe to anesthetize newborns and young infants? Absolutely. See: Susan Givens Bell, "The National Pain Management Guideline: Implications for Neonatal Intensive Care," *Neonatal Network* 13 (3): 9–17 (April 1994).

94 A team of American and Canadian researchers studying stress: M. J. Meany et al., "Individual Differences in the Hypothalamic-Pituitary-Adrenal Stress Response and the Hypothalamic CRF System," *Annals of the New York Academy of Sciences* 697 (1993): 70–85.

94 a Seattle pediatrician: Louis D. Pollack, M.D.

96 deprivation of stimulation: L. Salk, "The role of the heartbeat in the relations between mother and infant," *Scientific American* 228 (1973): 24–29.

96 In the womb, the baby receives continual tactile and kinesthetic stimulation: Ruth Dianne Rice, *Developmental Psychology* 13 (1): 69–76 (1997).

96 infant massage: T. Field, N. Grizzle, F. Scafidi, S. Abrams, and S. Richardson, "Massage therapy for infants of depressed mothers," *Infant Behavior and Development* 19 (1996): 109–114.

97 infant massage training groups: Tiffany M. Field, *Touch in Early Development* (Mahwah, N.J.: Lawrence Erlbaum Associates, 1995).

97 fathers who massaged and bathed infants: K. Scholtz and C. A. Samuels, "Neonatal bathing and massage intervention with fathers, behavioral effects 12 weeks after birth of the first baby: The Sunraysia Australia Intervention Project," *International Journal of Behavioral Development* 15 (1), 67–81 (1992).

page

97 mouthing, grimacing, and clenching fists: F. Scafidi et al., "Massage stimulates growth in preterm infants: A replication," *Infant Behavior and Development* 13 (1990): 167–188.

97 catecholamines—norepinephrine and epinephrine: C. Kuhn et al., "Tactile-kinesthetic stimulation effects on sympathetic and adrenocortical function in preterm infants," *Journal of Pediatrics* 119 (1991): 434–440.

97 food absorption: K. Uvnas-Moberg, A. M. Widstrom, G. Marchine, and J. Windberg, "Release of GI Hormone in Mothers and Infants by Sensory Stimulation," *Acta Paediatrica Scandinavia* 76 (1987): 851–860.

97 cocaine-exposed and HIV-exposed infants: Tiffany M. Field, op. cit.

98 Music was also shown to shorten labor: M. A. Winokur, "The use of music as an audio-analgesia during childbirth" (master's thesis, Florida State University, Tallahassee, 1984).

98 decrease pain in mother and baby alike: C. H. McKinney, M. H. Antoni, A. M. Kumar, and M. Kumar, "The effect of selected classical music and spontaneous imagery on plasma beta-endorphin," *Journal of Behavioral Medicine* 20 (1): 85–99 (1997). Also, S. B. Hanser, S. C. Larson, and A. S. O'Connell, "The effect of music on relaxation of expectant mothers during labor," *Journal of Music Therapy* 20 (2): 5–58 (1983).

99 nurses at the NICU: Sharon K. Collins and Kay Kuck, "Music Therapy in the Neonatal Intensive Care Unit," *Neonatal Network*, March 1991.

99 prerecorded intrauterine sounds combined with female singing: S. K. Collins and K. Kuck, "Music therapy in the neonatal intensive care unit," *Neonatal Network* 9 (6): 23–26 (1997).

99 music therapy: When lullaby music was played in the NICU there were fewer episodes of oxygen desaturation: J. Caine, "The effects of music on the selected stress behaviors, weight, caloric and formula intake, and length of hospital stay of premature and low-birth-weight neonates in a newborn intensive care unit," *Journal of Music Theory* 28(4): 180–192 (1991).

Other studies have shown a doubled daily weight gain when premature babies in the NICU were exposed to music: Ibid. Also, J. M. Coleman, R. R. Pratt, and H. Abel, "The effects of male and female singing and speaking voices on selected behavioral and physiological measures of premature infants in the intensive care unit," Presented at the International Society for Music in Medicine Symposium in San Antonio, Texas, October 1996.

page

The above researchers plus Standley, have shown a 3- to 5-day earlier discharge from the NICU when babies were exposed to music: J. M. Standley, "The effect of music and multimodal stimulation of physiologic and developmental responses of premature infants in neonatal intensive care," Presented at the International Society for Music in Medicine Symposium in San Antonio, Texas, October 1996.

Exposing newborns to soothing classical music resulted in fewer high arousal states and less liability in behavioral states: June Kaminski and Wendy Hall, "The Effect of Soothing Music on Neonatal Behavioral States in the Hospital Newborn Nursery," *Neonatal Network* 15 (1): 45–54 (1996).

100 "When she is awake and alert": Louise J. Kaplan, *No Voice Is Ever Wholly Lost* (New York: Simon & Schuster, 1996), 26.

CHAPTER SEVEN: THE ALCHEMY OF INTIMACY

103 now classic work: Marshall H. Klaus, and John H. Kennell, *Maternal-Infant Bonding* (Saint Louis, C. V. Mosby, 1976), 1–2.

105 psychologist Rene Spitz studied two groups of children: Rene A. Spitz, "Anaclitic depression," *Psychoanalytic Study of the Child* 2 (1946): 313–342, and Rene A. Spitz, "Hospitalism: An inquiry into the genesis of psychiatric conditions in early childhood," *Psychoanalytic Study of the Child* 1 (1945): 53–74.

106 The Harlows and their students separated infant monkeys from their mothers: A good summary may be found in *Primate Perspective* (1979). Also, see Stephen J. Suomi and C. Ripp. "A History of Motherless Monkey Mothering," in M. Rerte and N. Caine (eds.), *Child Abuse: The Nonhuman Primate Data* (New York: Alan R. Liss, 1983), 49–78.

106 maternal deprivation syndrome: John Bowlby, *Attachment and Loss*, vol. 1, *Attachment* (New York: Basic Books, 1969). Also recommended are his next two volumes, published in 1973 and 1980.

106 the Strange Situation: Mary Ainsworth, M. C. Blehar, et al., *Patterns of Attachment* (Hillsdale, N.J.: Erlbaum, 1978).

108 the benefits of breast-feeding for physical health: the American Academy of Pediatrics' Committee on Nutrition declared already in 1978 that:

• Despite technological advances in infant formulas, breast milk is "the best food for every newborn infant";

- All doctors need to become "much more knowledgeable" about infant nutrition in general and breast-feeding in particular;
- Attitudes, practices, and instruction in prenatal clinics and maternity wards should be changed to encourage breast-feeding;
- In hospitals, mothers and infants should be kept together after birth so babies can be fed on demand;
- Not only should information about breast-feeding be supplied to all schoolchildren but nursing should be portrayed as natural on television and other media;
- To prevent conflict between breast-feeding and employment, legislation should mandate three- or four-month postdelivery leaves so that working mothers can breast-feed.

The statement, issued jointly with the Canadian Paediatric Society, was five years in the making, says nutrition committee chairman Lewis A. Barness, head of pediatrics at the University of Southern Florida in Tampa. Recent findings indicate that "breast-feeding supplies more than nutrition," he says. Its anti-infective properties are "impressive." It contributes to a lower incidence of pneumonia, bronchiolitis, and gastrointestinal disorders. He is impressed that necrotizing enterocolitis occurs rarely, if at all, among low-birth-weight infants who are breast-fed. Dr. Myron Winick, committee member and director of Columbia University's Institute of Human Nutrition, notes, "Breast-fed infants are not as heavy as bottle-fed infants after a year. We used to think this was bad. But in light of obesity today, we recognize the breast-fed infant controls his own food intake."

"Pediatricians back breast-feeding," *Medical World News*, November 13, 1978, 23.

109 higher IQ: Justin Call, John Kennell, and Marshall Klaus, *Frontiers in Psychiatry* (New York: Basic Books).

109 Australian research: Wendy Oddy, as quoted on *CBS News*, September 28, 1999, referring to a paper published in the *British Medical Journal*, July 23, 1999.

109 reduces breast cancer risk: J. L. Freudenheim, J. R. Marshall, S. Graham, R. Laughlin, J. E. Vena, and E. Bandera, "Exposure to breastmilk in infancy and the risk of breast cancer," *Epidemiology* 5 (3): 324–31 (1994).

page

110 brain cells change and grow in response to trains of stimuli: Rima Shore, *Rethinking the Brain: New Insights into Early Development* (New York: Families and Work Institute, 1997). An excellent and easily accessible book by leading neuroscientists.

110 Harry Chugani: Harry T. Chugani, "Critical Importance of Emotional Development: Biological Basis of Emotions: Brain Systems and Brain Development," *Pediatrics* 102 (5, Supplement November 1998): 1,225–1,229.

110 the orbitofrontal cortex: Allen N. Schore, "The experience-dependent maturation of a regulatory system in the orbital prefrontal cortex and the origin of developmental psychopathology," *Development and Psychopathology* 8 (1996): 59–87. A remarkable paper.

111 "the social nervous system": Stephen W. Porges, "Orienting in a defensive world: Mammalian modifications of our evolutionary heritage. A Polyvagal Theory," *Psychophysiology* 32 (1995): 301–318.

112 called the vagus: Stephen W. Porges, "Love: An Emergent Property of the Mammalian Autonomic Nervous System," *Psychoneuroendocrinology* 23 (8): 837–861 (1998).

What has formed is a powerful auxiliary nervous system. Susan A. Greenfield, *The Human Brain: A Guided Tour* (New York: Basic Books, 1997).

113 yin and yang of brain construction: Daniel L. Siegel, "Relationships and the Developing Mind: An Interpersonal Neurobiology of Attachment," The Childhood Information Exchange, (1999).

116 My second son was damaged twice in utero: letter to T.R.V., name withheld.

118 dramatic changes in family life in the latter half of the twentieth century: Sharon Hays, "The Fallacious Assumptions and Unrealistic Prescriptions of Attachment Theory: A Comment on Parents' Socioemotional Investment in Children," *Journal of Marriage & the Family* 60 (3), 1998.

CHAPTER EIGHT: ADOPTION AND THE SEARCH FOR IDENTITY

123 "*I am adopted*": B. J. Lifton, *Twice Born* (New York: McGraw-Hill, 1975).

123 In a recent issue of *Adoption News*: Connie Dawson, lecture given at the 1994 American Adoption Congress.

124 "why separation from a birth mother would affect a newborn

page

baby": Nancy Verrier, *The Primal Wound: Understanding the Adopted Child* (Baltimore: Gateway Press, 1997).

124 newborns from diverse cultures arrive with unique expectations: T. Berry Brazelton, "On Adoption: Zero to Three," 10 (5): 5–8.

124 researchers at the Listening Centre: Paul Madaule, "Left Out: The Rejection Complex of the Adopted," Presentation at the 4th International Congress on Pre- and Perinatal Psychology, August 1989. The Listening Centre is a private clinic that follows the teachings of Dr. Alfred Tomstis. They treat a variety of disorders, from autism to learning difficulties, in children and adults.

125 referred to therapy far more frequently: Sotiris Kotsopoulos, Selena Walker, Winona Copping, Andre Corte, and Chryssoula Stavrakaki, "A Psychiatric Follow-Up Study of Adoptees," *Canadian Journal of Psychiatry* 38 (1993): 391–396.

126 adoptees and non-adoptees referred for psychiatric care: Ibid.

126 a book about Cinderella: David Kirk, in *Shared Fate* (Port Angeles, Wash.: Ben Simon Publications, 1984), 163.

129 advises adoptive parents to verbally acknowledge: Marcy Axness, "A Therapist Counsels Adoptive Parents: Interview with Wendy McCord, M.F.C.C., Ph.D.," birthpsychology.com. Also in *Roots and Wings*, Winter 1994.

131 children with deep brain "spiking": J. W. Prescott, "The Origins of Human Love and Violence," *Pre- and Perinatal Psychology Journal* 10 (3): 143–188 (1996). Also, NIH Violence Research Initiatives: Is Past Prologue, and The Prescott Report, Parts I and II, testimony before the NIH Panel on Violence Research, 23 September, 1993.

132 the Golden Cradle Adoption Agency: Margaret Doris, *New Age Journal*, April 1985, 43–79.

132 "When I got engaged": letter to T.R.V.; name withheld.

133 "It's not an accident": Marlou Russell, "Meeting My Mother," *Whole Life Times*, January 1995, 18–19.

133 a major study conducted in Los Angeles: R. Pannor, A. Baran, and A. D. Sorosky, "Birth Parents Who Relinquished Babies for Adoption Revisited," *Family Process*, 1978, vol. 17: 329–337.

134 the birth father: R. Pannor, F. Massarik, and B. Evans, *The Unmarried Father* (New York: Springer, 1967).

134 advocates open adoptions: Suzanne Arms, *To Love and Let Go* (New York: Alfred A. Knopf, 1983). A good contact is Michael

page

Trout, director of the Infant-Parent Institute, in Champaign, Ill.; e-mail: mtrout@infant-parent.com.

CHAPTER NINE: EXPERIENCE AS ARCHITECT OF THE BRAIN

137 Swiss psychologist Jean Piaget: J. Piaget, *Play, Dreams, and Imitation in Childhood* (New York: W. W. Norton, 1962).

138 Roll the Videotape: A. Meltzoff and M. K. Moore, "Imitation of facial and manual gestures by human neonates," *Science* 198 (1977): 75–78. Also, A. Gopnik, A. Meltzoff, and P. Kuhl, *The Scientist in the Crib: Minds, Brains, and How Children Learn* (New York: William Morrow and Company, 1999).

139 Affirmative Action: Rima Shore, *Rethinking the Brain: New Insights Into Early Development* (New York: Families and Work Institute, 1997).

142 Chugani has shown that there are specific "prime" months: Harry T. Chugani, "Biological Basis of Emotions: Brain Systems and Brain Development," *Pediatrics* 102 (5), Supplement: 1,225–1,229 (1998).

144 babies as young as 3 months of age can detect maternal depression: E. Z. Tronick and A. Gianino, "The Transmission of Maternal Disturbance to the Infant," in *Maternal Depression and Infant Disturbance*, ed. E. Tronick and T. Field (New York: Jossey-Bass, 1986).

145 In general, Tronick's studies: E. Z. Tronick, "On the primacy of social skills," in *The exceptional infant: Psychosocial risks in infant environment transaction*, ed. D. B. Sawin, L. O. Walker, and J. H. Penticuff (New York: Bruner/Mazel, 1980), 144–158; E. Z. Tronick, "Affectivity and sharing," in *Social interchange in infancy: Affect, cognition and communication*, ed. E. Z. Tronick (Baltimore: University Park Press, 1982), 1–6; E. Z. Tronick, "Emotions and emotional communication in infants," *American Psychologist* 44 (1989): 112–128; E. Z. Tronick, H. Als and L. Adamson, "Structure of early face-to-face communicative interactions," in *Before speech: The beginning of interpersonal communication*, ed. M. Bullowa (New York: Cambridge University Press, 1979), 349–372.

145 offspring of happy mothers generally communicate a sense of joy: E. Z. Tronick and A. Gianino, "Interactive mismatch and repair: Challenges to the coping infant," *Zero to Three* 6 (3): 1–6 (1986).

148 When the infant becomes a toddler: Allen Schore, "The experience-dependent . . ." p. 68.

page

148 if parents have done their job well: Allen N. Schore, "The experience-dependent maturation of a regulatory system in the orbital prefrontal cortex and the origin of developmental psychopathology," *Development and Psychopathology* 8 (1996): 59–87. Also, A. N. Schore, "Early organization of the nonlinear right brain and development of a predisposition to psychiatric disorders," *Development and Psychopathology* 9 (1997): 595–631.

149 42 children born to professional, working-class, and welfare parents: B. Hart and T. Risley, *Meaningful Differences in the Everyday Experience of Young American Children* (Baltimore: Brookes, 1995).

150 parents from different cultures impart different styles of thought: Erica Goode, "How Culture Molds Habits of Thought," *New York Times*, 8 August 2000.

CHAPTER TEN: THE MYSTERY AND POWER OF EARLY MEMORY

153 recollections of my life in the womb: letter to author, May 1983.

154 If we push our memory back: Frances J. Mott, "World Transformation," *Journal of Psychohistory* 4 (3): 319–335 (1997).

156 cells read their environment: Bruce Lipton, "Adaptive Mutation: A New Look at Biology," *Touch the Future*, Summer 1997 (4350 Lime Avenue, Long Beach, Calif. 90807).

157 If you doubt the potential for cells to remember: Bruce S. McEwen and Harold M. Schmeck, Jr., *The Hostage Brain* (New York: Rockefeller University Press, 1994).

157 neurobiologist Candace Pert: Candace B. Pert, *Molecules of Emotion* (New York: Simon & Schuster, 1999).

157 Past studies have shown: Robert Ader, David Felton, and Richard Cohen, *Psychoneuroimmunology*, 2d ed. (San Diego: Academic Press, 1991).

157 Howard Hall of Case Western Reserve University: as quoted in Candace B. Pert, op. cit., 191.

160 Psychologists specializing in the study of memory: J. Douglas Bremner, John H. Krystal, Dennis S. Charney, and Steven Southwick, "Neural Mechanisms in Dissociative Amnesia for Childhood Abuse: Relevance to the Current Controversy Surrounding the 'False Memory Syndrome,'" *American Journal of Psychiatry* 153 (1996): 7.

161 unborn children may literally absorb the mother's experience: Alice M. Givens, "The Alice Givens Approach to Prenatal and Birth

page

Therapy," *Pre- and Perinatal Psychology Journal* 1 (3): 223–229
(1987).

162   Australian researchers: Inez Correia, "The impact of television
stimuli on the prenatal infant" (Ph.D. diss., University of New
South Wales, Sydney, Australia, 1994).

162   One of the first people to study the birth memory phenomenon:
David Cheek, interview by author, 1989. Also, D. B. Cheek, "Sequential head and shoulder movement appearing with age regression from hypnosis to birth," *American Journal of Clinical Hypnosis*
16 (4): 261–266 (1974).

163   years collecting birth memories: David Chamberlain, interview by
author, May 1989. Also, D. B. Chamberlain, "The Expanding
Boundaries of Memory," *Pre- and Perinatal Psychology Journal* 4 (3):
171–189 (1990).

163   increased flow of the peptide oxytocin: Bela Bohus et al., "Oxytocin, Vasopressin and Memory: Opposite Effects on Consolidation and Retrieval Processes," *Brain Research* 157 (1978): 414–417.

164   a mobile attached to one of their legs: Carolyn Rovee-Collier, "The
Memory System of Prelinguistic Infants," in *Annals of the New York
Academy of Sciences.* "The Development of and Neural Bases of
Higher Cognitive Functions," vol. 608, ed. A. Diamond, (1993)
517–42.

164   6-month-old infants retain impressions of events for years: E. Perris, N. Meyers, and R. Clifton, "Long-term memory for a single infancy experience," *Child Development* 61 (1990): 1,796–1,807.

165   Meltzoff had researchers bang the top of a plastic box with their
foreheads: A. N. Meltzoff, "Infant Imitation After a 1-week Delay:
Long-term Memory for Novel Acts and Multiple Stimuli," *Developmental Psychology* 24 (1988): 470–476. Also, P. J. Klein and A. N.
Meltzoff, "Long-term Memory, Forgetting and Deferred Imitation
in 12-month-old Infants," *Developmental Science* 2 (1989): 102–113.

165   how to assemble a gong: Patricia Bauer, in Daniel L. Schacter,
Searching for Memory: The Brain, the Mind, and the Past (New York:
Basic Books, 1996).

165   when a mouse entered a new environment: Matthew Wilson and
Bruce McNaughton, "Memory Building," *The Economist*, 29 August 1998.

166   Flashbulb memories: J. Douglas Bremner, John H. Krystal, Dennis
S. Charney, and Steven Southwick, "Neural Mechanisms in Dissociative Amnesia for Childhood Abuse: Relevance to the Current

page

Controversy Surrounding the 'False Memory Syndrome,'" *American Journal of Psychiatry* 153 (1996): 7.

166 Intense, long-term memories are also forged by fear: "Memory Building," Wilson and McNaughton, op. cit.

166 False Memory or Total Recall: J. Douglas Bremner, John H. Krystal, Dennis S. Charney, and Steven Southwick, "Neural Mechanisms in Dissociative Amnesia for Childhood Abuse: Relevance to the Current Controversy Surrounding the 'False Memory Syndrome,'" *American Journal of Psychiatry* 153 (1996): 7.

167 lying flat on her back with a feeding tube inserted in her stomach: Lynda Share, *Dreams and the Reconstruction of Infant Trauma* (Hillsdale, N.J.: Analytic Press, 1994).

168 cycle of family patterns: Averil Earnshaw, "The Inheritance of Life Events: A Synopsis of *Time Will Tell*," *Pre- and Perinatal Psychology Journal* 10 (3), 1996.

CHAPTER ELEVEN: DEPENDING ON THE KINDNESS OF STRANGERS

172 22 million youngsters age 6 and under who must be watched: National Institute of Child Health and Human Development, Early Child Care Research Network, (NICHD), "The effect of infant child care on infant-mother attachment security: Results of the NICHD of early child care," *Child Development*, 69, 860–879 (1997).

172 Early Child Care Research Network of the NICHD in 1997: op. cit.

174 When it comes to day care centers: Kate Fillon, "The Day Care Decision," *Saturday Night*, January 1989, 23–30.

174 "Quality 2000": Sharon L. Kagan and Nancy E. Cohen, "Not by Chance: Creating an Early Care and Education System for America's Children: The Quality 2000 Initiative" (New Haven: Bush Center in Child Development and Social Policy at Yale University, 1997).

174 20 percent of day care is poor: J. Belsky, "Infant day care: A cause for concern?" *Zero to Three: Bulletin of the National Center for Clinical Infant Programs* (Washington, D.C., Superintendent of Documents, 1986.

175 family factors combine: National Institute of Child Health and Human Development Early Child Care Research Network (NICHD), *The NICHD Study of Early Child Care* (available on-line

page

at: http://www.nichd.nih.gov/publications/pubs/earlycare.htm,
1998).

175   child-care centers are a major source of infection: Michael T. Os-
terholm, "Infectious disease in child day care: An overview," *Pediatrics* 6: 987 (1994).

175   meningitis: A. K. Takala, J. Jero, E. Kela, P. R. Ronnberg; E. Kos-
kenniem; J. Eskola, "Risk factors for primary invasive pneu-
mococcal disease among children in Finland," *Journal of the
American Medical Association* 273 (11): 859–864 (1995).

175   twice as likely to develop asthma: Wenche Nystad, "Asthma linked
to day care, researchers say," *Toronto Star*, 24 September 1987,
A29.

175· Researchers from the University of Montreal: Michel Pircard presented his findings at an acoustics conference in Berlin in 1999.
Reported by Margaret Munro, "Daycare may harm hearing, affect
ability to learn: Study," *The National Post* (February 23, 1999).

176   chaos takes its toll on the developing brain: Andrea C. Dettling,
Megan R. Gunnar, and Bonny Donzella, "Cortisol Levels of Young
Children in Full-Day Childcare Centers: Relations with Age and
Temperament," *Psychoneuroendocrinology* 24 (5): 514–536 (1999).

177   Claudio Violato and Clare Russell: "Effects of nonmaternal care on
child development: A meta-analysis of the published research," in
The Changing Family and Child Development, edited by C. Violato,
E. Oddone-Paolucci, and M. Genuis (Aldershot, UK: Ashgate,
2000).

177   males fared more poorly than females in every domain: Henry
Brandtjen and Thomas Verny, "Long-Term Effects of Daycare Centers on Infants and Toddlers" (master's thesis, St. Mary's University, Minneapolis, 2000). To be published in *Pre- and Perinatal
Psychology Journal*, 15 (4) Summer 2001.

178   associate director of the famous Gesell Institute: Louise Bates
Ames, "Day Care for Infants May Cause Psychological Harm," *Behavior Today Newsletter*, 16 March 1987, 5.

179   One mother rhapsodized to a reporter about her son's day care:
Kate Fillon, "The Day Care Decision," *Saturday Night*, January
1989, 23–30.

182   Child Care and TV: "Fantasy, TV and crime," publication of the
Group for the Advancement of Psychiatry, 1983.

182   Excessive time in front of the TV damages children: See Joseph

page

Chilton Pearce, *Evolution's End: Claiming the Potential of Our Intelligence* (San Francisco and New York: Harper and HarperCollins, 1992); Jane M. Healy, *Endangered Minds: Why Our Children Don't Think* (New York: Simon & Schuster, 1990); and Keith A. Buzzell, "The Neurophysiology of Television Viewing." Available from Dr. Keith A. Buzzell, 14 Portland Street, Fryeburg, Maine 04037.

CHAPTER TWELVE: WHEN THINGS GO WRONG: SAD CHILDREN, ANGRY CHILDREN

189 eight suicidal children: Perihan Rosenthal, "Suicide Among Preschool Children Found More Prevalent Than Commonly Believed," talk presented at the American Psychiatric Association, Toronto, 1982. Reported in *Psychiatric News*, 6 April 1984.

190 a conference at New Children's Hospital in Sydney: Louise Newman, lecture reported by Chris Pritchard, *Medical Post*, 8 October 1996.

191 seriously self-destructive or suicidal: Morris Paulson, quoted in *Time*, 25 September 1978, 76.

191 quality of home life subsequent to early parental loss: A. Breier, J. R. Kelsoe, and P. D. Kirwin, "Early parental loss and development of adult psychopathology," *Archives of General Psychiatry* 45 (1998): 987–993.

192 Abused and neglected children have a higher likelihood of arrests: Dorothy Otnow Lewis, "From Abuse to Violence: Psychophysiological Consequences of Maltreatment," *Journal of the American Academy of Child and Adolescent Psychiatry* 31 (3): 383–391 (1992); and "Child delinquents who later commit murder," reported in *Psychiatric News*, 21 June 1985.

192 "killing for kicks": Moira Martingale, *Cannibal Killers: The History of Impossible Murders* (New York: Carrol & Graf, 1993).

193 a 9-year-old boy was charged with aggravated battery and domestic violence: *Globe and Mail*, 18 July 1996.

193 In Tokyo, meanwhile, police arrested a 14-year-old boy: *Toronto Star*, 29 June 1997.

194 The Origins of Violence: B. D. Perry, "Incubated in Terror: Neurodevelopmental Factors in the 'Cycle of Violence,'" in *Children, Youth and Violence: The Search for Solutions*, ed. J. Osofsky (New York: Guilford Press, 1997), 124–148.

195 The Cycle of Violence: Bruce Perry, "The Vortex of Violence: How

page

Children Adapt and Survive in a Violent World," ChildTrauma Academy, Parent and Caregiver Education Series, ed. B. D. Perry, CIVITAS Child Trauma Programs, Dept. of Psychiatry and Behavioral Sciences, Baylor College of Medicine, Texas Children's Hospital. Adapted in part from *Maltreated Children: Experience, Brain Development and the Next Generation* (New York: W. W. Norton, 2000).

195 Thirty percent of children living in high-crime neighborhoods of cities: James Garbarino, "The American War Zone: What Children Can Tell Us About Living with Violence," *Developmental and Behavioral Pediatrics,* 16 (3): 431–435 (1995).

195 National Institute of Mental Health study: L. Richters and W. Salzman, "Survey of children's exposure to community violence" (Bethesda, Maryland: National Institute of Mental Health, 1990).

196 Dorothy Otnow Lewis has studied violent youth for years: Dorothy Otnow Lewis, "From Abuse to Violence: Psychophysiological Consequences of Maltreatment," *Journal of the American Academy of Child and Adolescent Psychiatry* 31 (3): 383–391 (1992).

196 a twenty-year study of 875 primary school children in rural New York: Leonard D. Eron, L. M. Gentry, and P. Schlegel, eds., *Reasons to Hope: A psychosocial perspective on violence & youth* (Washington, D.C.: American Psychological Association, 1994).

197 "I first met Buddie when he was 13 years old": Roger Tonkin, "Sorting out the 'bad apples.'" *Medical Post,* 2 April 1966, 30.

198 The path from terrorized infant to terrorizing adolescent: B. D. Perry, "Incubated in Terror: Neurodevelopmental Factors in the 'Cycle of Violence,'" in *Children, Youth and Violence: The Search for Solutions,* ed. J. Osofsky (New York: Guilford Press, 1997), 124–148.

198 a wide range of studies: Bruce Perry, "How Persisting Fear Can Alter the Developing Child's Brain," a special Child Trauma Academy Web site version of "The Neurodevelopmental Impact of Violence in Childhood," The Child Trauma Academy, Department of Psychiatry and Behavioral Sciences, Baylor College of Medicine and Texas Children's Hospital, http://www.bcm.tmc.edu/cta/; also, B. D. Perry, R. Pollard, T. Blakely, W. Baker, D. Vigilante, "Childhood trauma, the neurobiology of adaptation and 'use-dependent' development of the brain: How 'states' become 'traits,'" *Infant Mental Health Journal* 16 (4): 271–291 (1995); and B. D. Perry, and R. Pollard, "Homeostasis, stress, trauma, and adaptation: A neurodevelopmental view of childhood trauma,"

page

Child and Adolescent Psychiatric Clinics of North America 7 (1): 33–51 (1998); and B. D. Perry, and I. Azad, "Post-traumatic stress disorder in children and adolescents," Current Opinion in Pediatrics 11 (1999): 121–132.

201 eating disorders and self-mutilation: Todd F. Heatherton and Roy F. Baumeister, "Binge Eating As Escape From Self-Awareness," Psychological Bulletin 110 (10): 86–108 (1991).

201 the most violent among us emerge not just from early abuse: Remi Cadoret, William R. Yates, Ed Troughton, George Woodworth, and Mark Stewart, "Genetic-Environmental Interaction in the Genesis of Aggressivity and Conduct Disorders," Archives General Psychiatry 52: November 1995.

203 system of belief: Bruce D. Perry, Ronnie A. Pollard, et al, "Childhood Trauma, the Neurobiology of Adaptation, and 'Use-dependent' Development of the Brain: Now 'States' Become 'Traits'," Infant Mental Health Journal 16 (4): 271–289 (Winter 1995).

203 Emotional Battering: J. Garbarino, E. Guttmann, and J. Seeley, The Psychologically Battered Child: Strategies for Identification, Assessment, and Intervention (San Francisco: Jossey-Bass, 1986).

204 Cognitive Deprivation: C. A. Rohrbect and C. T. Twentyman "Neglect and Abuse," Journal of Consulting Clinical Psychology 54 (1986): 231. Also, Carla Rivera, "Report to the U.S. Congress," The Advisory Board of Child Abuse and Neglect, Los Angeles Times, 26 April 1995.

204 The Roots of Psychopathology: Child Abuse and Multiple Personality Disorder, Philip M. Coons, A. Browne, and D. Finkelhor, "Impact of child sexual abuse: A review of the research," Psychological Bulletin 99 (1986): 66–77; J. H. Beitchman et al, "A review of the long-term effects of child sexual abuse," Child Abuse and Neglect 16 (1992): 101–118; J. Bigras, P. Leichner, M. Perreault, and R. Lavoie, "Severe paternal sexual abuse in early childhood and systematic aggression against the family and the institution," Canadian Journal of Psychiatry 36 (1991): 527–529; S. Bjorkly, "Trauma and violence: The role of early abuse in the aggressive behavior of two violent psychotic women," Bulletin of the Menninger Clinic 59 (1995): 205–220; J. Briere and M. Runtz, "Childhood sexual abuse: Long-term sequelae and implications for psychological assessment," Journal of Interpersonal Violence 8 (1993): 312–330; C. G. Curtis, "Violence Breeds Violence Perhaps?" American Journal of Psychiatry 120

page

(1963): 386; D. David, A. Giron, and T. Mellman, "Panic-phobic patients and developmental trauma," *Journal of Clinical Psychiatry* 56 (1995): 113–117; A. H. Green, "Child sexual abuse: Immediate and long-term effects and interventions," *Journal of the American Academy of Child and Adolescent Psychiatry* 32 (1993): 890–902; A. B. Gross and H. R. Keller, "Long-term consequences of childhood physical and psychological maltreatment," *Aggressive Behavior* 18 (1992): 171–185; T. Heins, A. Gray, and M. Tennant, "Persisting hallucinations following childhood sexual abuse," *Australian and New Zealand Journal of Psychiatry* 24 (1990): 561–565; C. Mancini, M. Van Ameringen, and H. MacMillan, "Relationship of childhood sexual and physical abuse to anxiety disorders," *Journal of Nervous and Mental Disease* 183 (1995): 309–314; R. Parke and C. Collmer, "Child Abuse: An Interdisciplinary Review," *Review of Child Development Research*, vol. 5, ed. E. M. Hetherington (Chicago: Chicago University Press, 1975); Adrian Raine et al, "Relationships Between Central and Autonomic Measures of Arousal at Age 15 Years and Criminality at Age 24 Years," *Archives of General Psychiatry* 47 (1990): 1,003–1,007; A. B. Rowan and D. W. Foy, "Post-traumatic stress disorder in child sexual abuse survivors: A literature review," *Journal of Traumatic Stress* 6 (1993): 3–20; C. Swett and M. Halpert, "High rates of alcohol problems and history of physical and sexual abuse among women inpatients," *American Journal of Drug and Alcohol Abuse* 20 (1994): 263–272; E. G. Triffleman, C. R. Marmar, K. L. Delucchi, and H. Ronfeldt, "Childhood trauma and post-traumatic stress disorder in substance abuse inpatients," *Journal of Nervous and Mental Disease* 183 (1995): 172–176.

207 television programs featuring gratuitous violence: Lynette Friedrich-Cofer and Aletha C. Houston, "Television Violence and Aggression: The Debate Continues," *Psychological Bulletin* 100 (3) (1986): 364–371. Also, Linda Heath, Candace Kruttschmitt, David Ward, "Television and Violent Criminal Behavior: Beyond the Bobo Doll," *Victims and Violence* 1 (3): 177–190 (1986).

CHAPTER THIRTEEN: CULTIVATING BASIC GOODNESS: HOW TO ENHANCE EMPATHY, COMPASSION, AND ALTRUISM

211 Auguste Comte: quoted in Phillip Rushton and Richard Sorentino (1984). *Altruism and Human Behavior* (Hillsdale, N.J.: Erlboum, 1984).

page

212   the human brain is associated with light: Robert Bly, *Sibling Society* (Reading, Mass.: Addison-Wesley Publishing Company, 1996), 20.

212   The Triune Brain: Paul MacLean, *A Triune Concept of the Brain and Behavior,* ed. D. Campbell and T. J. Boag (Toronto: University of Toronto Press, 1973), and Karl Pribram, "What the Fuss Is All About," in *The Holographic Paradigm,* ed. Ken Wilber (Boulder, Colo., and London: Shambhala, 1982). Also, Wilder Penfield, *The Mystery of the Mind* (Princeton, N.J.: Princeton University Press, 1977).

212   Animal experiments in which the neocortex was surgically disconnected from the mesocortex: V. H. Mark and F. R. Ervin, *Violence and the Brain* (Hagerstown, Md.: Harper and Row, 1970).

213   removal of the amygdala: V. H. Mark and F. R. Ervin, *Violence and the Brain* (Hagerstown, Md.: Harper and Row, 1970).

213   oxytocin injected into the brain: C. A. Pederson and A. J. Prange, Jr., "Induction of Maternal Behavior in Virgin Rats After Intracerebroventricular Administration of Oxytocin," *Proceedings of the National Academy of Sciences* 76 (1979): 6,661–6,665. Also, J. T. Winslow and T. R. Lisel, "Social status of male squirrel monkey determines response to central oxytocin administration," *Journal of Neuroscience* 11 (1991): 2,032–2,038.

213   vasopressin brings out the paternal impulse: Z. X. Wang, C. F Ferris, and G. H. L. De Vries, "The role of septal vasopressin innervation in paternal behavior in prairie voles," *Proceedings of the National Academy of Sciences* 91 (1993): 400–404.

214   ultrasound studies of twins: Alessandra Piontelli, "Infant Observation from Before Birth," *International Journal of Psycho-Analysis* 68 (1987): 453–463.

214   "a deep connectedness to other beings": Alison Gopnick and Andrew N. Meltzoff, *Words, Thoughts, and Theories* (Cambridge, Mass: A Bradford Book, MIT Press, 1997), 133.

214   in response to the crying of another infant: M. L. Simner, "Newborn's response to the cry of another infant," *Developmental Psychology* 5 (1971): 136–150. Also, A. Sagi and J. L. Hoffman, "Empathic distress in the newborn," *Developmental Psychology* 12 (1976): 175–176.

215   reactive cry is the mark of empathy: J. Phillipe Rushton and Richard M. Sorrentino, *Altruism and Helping Behavior: Social, Personality, and Developmental Perspectives* (Hillsdale, N.J.: Lawrence Erlbaum, 1981).

page

215 early manifestations of altruistic and aggressive behavior: Maya Pines, "Good Samaritans at Age Two?", *Psychology Today*, June 1979, and the chapter by E. Mark Cummings, Barbara Hollenbeck, Ronald Iannotti, Marian Radke-Yarrow, and Carolyn Zahn-Waxler, 165–188; in Carolyn Zahn-Waxler, E. Mark Cummings, and Ronald Iannotti, *Altruism and Aggression: Biological and Social Origins* (Cambridge: Cambridge University Press, 1984). Also, M. R. Radke-Yarrow, C. Zahn-Waxler, and M. Chapman, "Children's prosocial dispositions and behavior," in P. H. Mussen, ed., *Carmichael's Manual of Child Psychology*, 4th ed., vol. IV (New York: Wiley, 1984).

215 goldfish crackers and a plate of broccoli: Gopnik and Meltzoff, *Words, Thoughts, and Theories*. 149–150.

216 children who form secure attachments: L. A. Sroufe, "The coherence of individual development: Early care, attachment, and subsequent developmental issues," *American Psychologist* 34 (1979): 834–841.

217 "an expression of ethical principles": Samuel P. Oliver and Pearl M. Oliver, *The Altruistic Personality: Rescuers of Jews in Nazi Europe* (New York: Free Press, 1988).

217 a prenatal bonding custom practiced by a tribe in East Africa: Jack Kornfield, *A Path with Heart: A Guide Through the Perils and Promises of Spiritual Life* (New York: Bantam, 1996).

218 love hormone: Michel Odent, *The Scientification of Love* (London: Free Association Books, 1999).

CHAPTER FOURTEEN: CONSCIOUS PARENTING

224 a mother observed by Rene Spitz: Rene Spitz, *The First Year of Life* (New York: International Universities Press, 1965), 238.

225 "contingent responsiveness": M. Lewis and S. Goldberg, "Perceptual Cognitive Development in Infancy: A Generalized Expectancy Model As a Function of Mother-Infant Interaction," *Merrill-Palmer Quarterly* 15 (1969): 81–100.

226 To study the subtle stereotyping: Jeff Rubin, Frank Provenzano, and Luria Zelba, "Sex typing in the delivery room," *American Journal of Orthopsychiatry* 44 (4): 512–519 (1974).

226 mothers in one study were observed as they played with a six-month-old boy: Jerry Will, Patricia Self, and Nancy Dratan, "Nursery Stereotypes," paper presented at the American Psychology Association meeting, 1974.

page

228 fatherless societies: L. L. Bumpass and J. A. Sweet, "Children's experience in single-parent families: Implications of cohabitation and marital transitions," *Family Planning Perspectives* 21(6e): 256–260 (1989). Also, David Blankenhorn, 40 percent of American children: Wade F. Horn, *Father Facts*, 3rd Edition (Gaithersburg, MD: The National Fatherhood Initiative, 1998).

228 likely to rise to 60 percent: Frank F. Furstenberg Jr. and Andrew J. Cherlin, *Divided Families: What Happens to Children When Parents Part* (Cambridge, Mass: Harvard University Press, 1991).

228 female-headed household: Bumpass and Sweet, "Children's experience."

228 fathers speak to, touch, and react to their firstborn sons more frequently: P. Bronstein, "Father-child interaction: Implications for gender role socialization," in *Fatherhood Today: Men's Changing Role in the Family*, ed. P. Bronstein and G. P. Cowan (New York: Wiley & Sons, 1988), 107–124.

228 Fathers are warmer: R. D. Parke and S. E. O'Leary, "Family interaction in the newborn period: Some findings," in *The Developing Individual in a Changing World*, vol. 2, *Social and Environmental Issues*, ed. K. Riegel and J. Meacham (The Hague: Morton, 1976), 653–663. Also, A. D. White Woolett and L. Lyon, "Observations of fathers at birth," in *Fathers: Psychological Perspectives*, ed. N. Beail and J. McGuire (London: Junction, 1982), 72–94, and M. J. Cox, M. T. Owen, et al, "Marriage, adult adjustment and early parenting," *Child Development* 60 (1989): 1,015–1,024.

228 !Kung bushmen: David Blankenhorn, *Fatherless America: Confronting Our Most Urgent Social Problems* (New York: Basic Books, 1995).

228 sex-differentiated treatment intensifies during the second year of life: Michael E. Lamb, *The Father's Role: Applied Perspectives* (New York: John Wiley & Sons, 1986).

228 "the son begins to switch his intense gaze over to the father": Robert Bly, *The Sibling Society* (Reading, Mass.: Addison-Wesley, 1996), 119.

229 the most socially acute manifestation of paternal absence: David Blackenhorn, *Fatherless America*.

231 the noted anthropologist Ashley Montagu: Ashley Montagu quoted in Murray A. Straus, "Spanking and the Mating of a Violent Society," *Pediatrics* 98 (4): 837–844 (1996).

page

231 Murray A. Straus: Murray A. Straus, op. cit.

232 if female, suffer a drop of eight points: J. R. Smith and J. Brooks-Gunn, "Correlates and consequences of harsh discipline for young children," *Archives of Pediatrics and Adolescent Medicine* 151 (1997): 777–786.

232 research by Harriet L. MacMillan: Harriet L. MacMillan, Michael H. Boyle, et al., "Slapping and spanking in childhood and its association with lifetime prevalence of psychiatric disorders in a general population," *Canadian Medical Association Journal* 161(7) (1999): 805–809.

Bibliography

Ader, Robert, David Felton, and Richard Cohen. *Psychoneuroimmunology.* 2d ed. San Diego: Academic Press, 1991.

Ainslie, R. C., ed. *The Child and Day Care Setting.* New York: Praeger, 1984.

Ainslie, R. C., and C. W. Anderson. "Day care children's relationships to their mothers and caregivers: An inquiry into the conditions for the development of attachment." In Ainslie, *The Child and Day Care Setting.*

Ainsworth, Mary, M. C. Blehar, et al. *Patterns of Attachment.* Hillsdale, N.J.: Erlbaum, 1978.

Ainsworth, M., S. Bell, and D. Stanton. "Individual differences in strange situation behavior of one-year-olds." In *The Origins of Human Social Relations,* edited by H. Schaffer. London: Academic Press, 1971.

Ames, Louise Bates. "Day Care for Infants May Cause Psychological Harm." *Behavior Today Newsletter,* 16 March 1987: 5.

Amighi, Janet Kestenberg. "Some Thoughts on the Cross Cultural Study of Maternal Warmth and Detachment." *Pre- and Perinatal Psychology Journal* 5 (2): Winter.

Anand, K. J. S. and P. R. Hickey. "Pain and its effects in the human neonate and fetus." *Pre- and Perinatal Psychology Journal* 3(2): 103–123 (1988).

———. "Pain and its effects in the human neonate and fetus." *New England Journal of Medicine* 317 (1987): 1,321–1,329.

Arms, Suzanne. *To Love and Let Go.* New York: Alfred A. Knopf, 1983.

Axinn, William G., Jennifer S. Barber, and Arland Thornton. "The Long-Term Impact of Parents' Childbearing Decisions on Children's Self-Esteem." *Demography* 35 (4): 435–443 (1998).

Axness, Marcy. "A Therapist Counsels Adoptive Parents: Interview with Wendy McCord, M.F.C.C., Ph.D." birthpsychology.com; also in *Roots and Wings*, Winter 1994.

Baker, R. A. "Technologic intervention in obstetrics." *Obstetrics and Gynecology* 51 (2): 241–244 (1978).

Barnett, E. A. "The Role of Prenatal Trauma in the Development of the Negative Birth Experience." *Pre- and Perinatal Psychology Journal* 1 (3): 191–207 (1987).

Batchelor, Ervin S., et al. "Classification Rates and Relative Risk Factors for Perinatal Events Predicting Emotional/Behavioral Disorders in Children." *Pre- and Perinatal Psychology Journal* 5 (4): 327–341 (summer 1991).

Bauer, Patricia. In *Searching for Memory: The Brain, the Mind, and the Past*, edited by Daniel L. Schacter. New York: Basic Books, 1996.

Begley, S. "Your Child's Brain." *Newsweek*, 19 February 1996.

Beitchman, J. H., K. J. Zucker, J. E. Hood, G. A. DaCosta, D. Akman, and E. Cassavia. "A review of the long-term effects of child sexual abuse." *Child Abuse & Neglect* 16 (1992): 101–118.

Belsky, J. "Infant day care: A cause for concern?" *Zero to Three: Bulletin of the National Center for Clinical Infant Programs*. Washington, D.C.: Superintendent of Documents, 1986.

Benenson, Joyce F., Erica R. Liroff, et al. "Propulsion: A behavioural expression of masculinity." *British Journal of Developmental Psychology* 15 (1997): 37–50.

Bigras, J., P. Leichner, M. Perreault, and R. Lavoie. "Severe paternal sexual abuse in early childhood and systematic aggression against the family and the institution." *Canadian Journal of Psychiatry* 36 (1991): 527–529.

Birnholz, J., J. C. Stephens, and M. Faria. "Fetal movement patterns." *American Journal of Roentgenology* 130 (1978): 537–540.

Birnholz, Jason. Report on "Sonochromes." *Medical Post* 25 (19): 16 May 1989, Toronto, Canada.

Bjorkly, S. "Trauma and violence: The role of early abuse in the aggressive behavior of two violent psychotic women." *Bulletin of the Menninger Clinic* 59 (1995): 205–220.

Blankenhorn, David. *Fatherless America: Confronting Our Most Urgent Social Problems*. New York: Basic Books, 1995.

Blomberg, S. "Influence of Maternal Distress During Pregnancy on

Postnatal Development." *Acta Psychiatrica Scandinavia* 62 (1980): 405–417.

Blum, Thomas, ed. *Prenatal Perception, Learning and Bonding*. Seattle, Wash.: Leonardo Publishing, 1993.

Bly, Robert. *Iron John: A Book About Men*. Reading, Mass.: Addison-Wesley, 1990.

———. *The Sibling Society*. Reading, Mass.: Addison-Wesley, 1996.

Bohman, M., and Anne-Lils von Knorring. "Psychiatric illness among adults adopted as infants." *Acta Psychiatrica Scandinavia* 60 (1): (1979).

Bohus, Bela, et al. "Oxytocin, Vasopressin and Memory: Opposite Effects on Consolidation and Retrieval Processes." *Brain Research* 157 (1978): 414–417.

Bonovich, Leah. "The Influence of Mother-Daughter Communications on Anxiety During Labor." *Pre- and Perinatal Psychology Journal* 2 (4): 242–248 (1988).

Bower, Thomas G. R. *The Rational Infant: Learning in Infancy*. New York: W. K. Freeman, 1989.

Bowlby, John. *Attachment*. Vol. 1 of *Attachment and Loss*. New York: Basic Books, 1969.

Brandtjen, Henry, and Thomas Verny. "Long-Term Effects of Daycare Centers on Infants and Toddlers." *Pre- and Perinatal Psychology Journal* 15 (4): 239–285 (Summer 2001).

Brassard, M., R. Germain, and S. Hart. *Psychological Maltreatment of Children and Youth*. New York: Pergamon Press, 1987.

Brazelton, T. Berry. "On Adoption." *Zero to Three* 10 (5): 5–8 (1990).

———. *On Becoming a Family: The Growth of Attachment Before and After Birth*. New York: Delacorte Press, 1992.

———. *Touchpoints: Your Child's Emotional and Behavioral Development*. Reading, Mass.: Addison-Wesley, 1992.

———. Differences in response to fathers and mothers in newborns quoted in Otto Friedrich, "What Do Babies Know?" *Time*, 15 August 1983.

Breier, A., J. R. Kelsoe, and P. D. Kirwin. "Early parental loss and development of adult psychopathology." *Archives of General Psychiatry* 45 (1998): 987–993.

Bremner, J. Douglas, Meena Narayan, Lawrence H. Staib. "Neural Mechanisms in Dissociative Amnesia for Childhood Abuse: Relevance to the Current Controversy Surrounding the 'False Memory Syndrome.'" *American Journal of Psychiatry* 153 (7): 71–82 (1996).

Brennan, Patricia A., Emily R. Grekin, and Sarnoff A. Mednick. "Maternal Smoking During Pregnancy and Adult Male Criminal Outcomes." *Archives of General Psychiatry* 56 (March 1999): 215–219.

Brezinka, C., O. Huter, W. Biebl, and J. Kinzl. "Denial of Pregnancy: Obstetrical Aspects." *Journal of Psychosomatic Obstetrics and Gynecology* 15 (1994): 1–8.

Briere, J., and M. Runtz. "Childhood sexual abuse: Long-term sequelae and implications for psychological assessment." *Journal of Interpersonal Violence* 8 (1993): 312–330.

Bronstein, P. "Father-child interaction: Implications for gender role socialization." In *Fatherhood Today: Men's Changing Role in the Family,* edited by P. Bronstein and G. P. Cowan, 107–124. New York: Wiley & Sons, 1988.

Broussard, E. "Neonatal prediction and outcome at 10/11 years." *Child Psychiatry and Human Development* 7 (2): 85–93 (1976).

Broussard, E., and M. Kortner. "Maternal perception of the neonate as related to development." *Child Psychiatry and Human Development* 1 (1): 16–25 (1970).

Brown, Alan S., Jim van Os, Corine Driessens, Hans W. Hoek, and Ezra S. Susser. "Further Evidence of Relation Between Prenatal Famine and Major Affective Disorder." *American Journal of Psychiatry* 157 (2), February 2000.

Brown, Gary F. Short-Term Impact of Fetal Imaging on Paternal Stress and Anxiety." *Pre- and Perinatal Psychology Journal* 3 (1): 25–40 (1988).

Browne, A., and D. Finkelhor. "Impact of child sexual abuse: A review of the research." *Psychological Bulletin* 99 (1986): 66–77.

Buber, Martin. *Good and Evil.* New York: Charles Scribner's Sons, 1952.

Bumpass, L. L., and J. A. Sweet. "Children's experience in single-parent families: Implications of cohabitation and marital transitions." *Family Planning Perspectives* 21 (6e): 256–260 (1989).

Burns, M. M., and M. A. Straus. *Cross-National Differences in Corporal Punishment, Infant Homicide, and Socioeconomic Factors.* Durham: University of New Hampshire Press, 1987.

Bustan, Muhammad N., and Ann L. Coker. "Maternal Attitude Toward Pregnancy and the Risk of Neonatal Death." *American Journal of Public Health* 84 (4): 411–414 (1994).

Buzzell, Keith A. "The Neurophysiology of Television Viewing." Available from Dr. Keith A. Buzzell, 14 Portland St., Fryeburg, ME 04037.

Byrd, Randolph. "Positive Therapeutic Effects of Intercessory Prayer in a Coronary Care Unit Population." *Southern Medical Journal* 81 (7): 826–829 (1988).

Cadoret, Remi, William R. Yates, Ed Troughton, George Woodworth, and Mark Stewart. "Genetic-Environmental Interaction in the Genesis of Aggressivity and Conduct Disorders." *Archives of General Psychiatry* 52 (November 1995).

Caine, J. "The effects of music on the selected stress behaviors, weight, caloric and formula intake, and length of hospital stay of premature and low-birth-weight neonates in a newborn intensive care unit." *Journal of Music Theory* 28 (4): 180–192 (1991).

Cairns, J., J. Overbaugh, and S. Miller. "The Origin of Mutants." *Nature* 335 (1998): 142–145.

Campbell, James D., R. Wayne Efford, and Rollin F. Brant. Case control study of prenatal ultrasonography exposure in children with delayed speech." *Canadian Medical Association Journal* 149 (10): 1,435–1,490. (15 November 1993).

Campbell, S. "Mother-infant interaction as a function of maternal ratings of temperament." *Child Psychiatry and Human Development* 10 (1970): 67–76.

Campbell, S., et al. "Ultrasound scanning in pregnancy." *Journal of Psychosomatic Obstetrics Gynecology* 1 (2): 57–61 (1982).

Carruthers, Peter. *Language, Thought and Consciousness: An Essay in Philosophical Psychology.* Cambridge: Cambridge University Press, 1996.

Caspi, Avshalom, et al. "Behavioral Observations at age 3 years Predict Adult Psychiatric Disorders." *Archives of General Psychiatry* 53 (1996): 1,033–1,039.

Catano, James W., and Victor M. Catano. "The Infantile Amnesia Paradigm." In *Pre- and Perinatal Psychology: An Introduction,* edited by Thomas R. Verny. New York: Human Sciences Press, 1987.

Chamberlain, Clive. Conversation with author, Toronto, 1996.

Chamberlain, David. "The Expanding Boundaries of Memory." *Pre- and Perinatal Psychology Journal* 4 (3): 171–189 (1990).

———. *Babies Remember Birth.* Los Angeles: Jeremy P. Tarcher, 1988.

———. "Is There Intelligence Before Birth?" *Pre- and Perinatal Psychology Journal* 6 (3): 217–237 (1992).

———. "What Babies Are Teaching Us About Violence." *Pre- and Perinatal Psychology Journal* 10 (2): 57–74 (1995).

———. *The Mind of Your Newborn Baby.* Berkeley, Calif.: North Atlantic Books, 1998.

———. "The Sentient Prenate: What Every Parent Should Know." *Pre- and Perinatal Psychology Journal* 9 (4): 9–32 (1994).

Cheek, D. B. "Sequential head and shoulder movement appearing with age regression from hypnosis to birth." *American Journal of Clinical Hypnosis* 16 (4): 261–266 (1974).

Cheek, David B. "Prenatal and Perinatal Imprints: Apparent Prenatal Consciousness as Revealed by Hypnosis." *Pre- and Perinatal Psychology Journal* 2 (2): 97–110 (1986).

Childs, Marshall R. "Prenatal Language Learning." *Journal of Prenatal and Perinatal Psychology and Health* 13 (2): Winter 1998.

Chugani, Harry T. "Biological Basis of Emotions: Brain Systems and Brain Development." *Pediatrics* 102 (5), Supplement: 1,225–1,229 (1998).

———. As chronicled on ABC's *Turning Point*, on Romanian adoptees, 16 January 1997.

Clarke-Stewart, K. "Interactions Between Mothers and Their Young Children: Characteristics and Consequences." *Monograph of Social Resources in Child Development* 38 (6–7, serial number 153), 1973.

Clements, Michele. In Dorothy Trainor, "Newborns Love Womb Sounds—Vivaldi, Mozart." *Medical Tribune*, 23 March 1978.

Coleman, J. M., R. R. Pratt, and H. Abel. "The effects of male and female singing and speaking voices on selected behavioral and physiological measures of premature infants in the intensive care unit." Presented at the International Society for Music in Medicine symposium in San Antonio, October 1996.

Collins, S. K., and K. Kuck. "Music therapy in the neonatal intensive care unit." *Neonatal Network* 9 (6): 23–26 (1997).

Comte, August. Quoted in Phillip Rushton and Richard Sorentino, *Altruism and Human Behavior*. Hillsdale, N.J.: Lawrence Erlbaum Associates, 1984.

Constantino, John N. "Early Relationships and the Development of Aggression in Children." *Harvard Review of Psychiatry* 2 (5): 259–273 (1966).

Copper, Rachel L., et al. "The preterm prediction study: Maternal stress is associated with spontaneous preterm birth at less than thirty-five weeks gestation." *American Journal of Obstetrics and Gynecology* 175 (5): 1,286–1,292 (1996).

Cox, M. J., M. T. Owen, J. M. Lewis, and U. K. Henderson. "Marriage, adult adjustment and early parenting." *Child Development* 60 (1989): 1,015–1,024.

Crittenden, Patricia M. "Attachment and Risk for Psychopathology: The Early Years." *Developmental and Behavioral Pediatrics* 16 (3): S12–S16 (1995).

Cunningham, Alastair. Quoted by Brad Evenson. "Meditation boosts life expectancy in terminally ill: Study." *National Post*, 5 September 2000.

Curtis, C. G. "Violence Breeds Violence Perhaps?" *American Journal of Psychiatry* 120 (1963): 386.

Dahmer, Lionel. *A Father's Story*. New York: William Morrow & Company, 1994.

David, D., A. Giron, and T. Mellman. "Panic-phobic patients and developmental trauma." *Journal of Clinical Psychiatry* 56 (1995): 113–117.

David, Henry P., Zilenek Dybrich, Zilenek Matejcek, and Vratislav Schüller. *Born Unwanted—Developmental Effects of Denied Abortion.* New York: Spring Publishing Company, 1988.

Davis-Floyd, Robbie "Mind Over Body: The Pregnant Professional." *Pre- and Perinatal Psychology Journal* 8 (3): 201–227 (1994).

———. *Birth As an American Rite of Passage.* Berkeley: Univ. of California Press, 1992.

Dawson, Connie. Lecture given at the American Adoption Congress, 1994, Atlanta, GA.

DeCasper, Anthony J., and William P. Fifer. "Of Human Bonding: Newborns Prefer Their Mothers' Voices." *Science* 208 (6 June 1980): 1,174–1,176.

DeMause, Lloyd. *Foundations of Psychohistory.* New York: Creative Roots Inc., 1982.

———. "The Personality of the Fetus." In *Donald Winnicott: A Memorial Volume for Mental Health Professionals,* edited by Brett Kahr and Ved P. Varma. London: Karmac Books, 1995.

DeMeo, James. "The Origins and Diffusion of Patrism in Saharasia, c. 4000 BCE: Evidence for a Worldwide, Climate-Linked Geographical Pattern in Human Behavior," *Pulse of the Planet* 3 (1991): 3–16.

Dennis, L. J., E. L. Dennis, and R. K. Newcomb. "Music training causes long-term enhancement of preschool children's spatial-temporal reasoning." *Neurological Research* 19 (1): 218 (1997).

Department of Justice. Crime in the United States: Washington, D.C.: Government Printing Office, 1986, 166–167 and 182–184.

Dettling, Andrea C., Megan R. Gunnar, and Bonny Donzella. "Cortisol Levels of Young Children in Full-Day Childcare Centers: Relations with Age and Temperament." *Psychoneuroendocrinology* 24 (5): 514–536 (1999).

———. "Mother's Enriched Environment Alters Brains of Unborn Rats." *Brain/Mind Bulletin* 2 (7): 1 and 5 (1987).

Diamond Marion. "The Significance of Enrichment," in *Enriching Heredity.* New York: The Free Press, 1988.

Douglas, John, and Mark Olshaker. *Mindhunter: Inside the FBI's Elite Serial Crime Unit.* New York: Scribner's, 1995.

Driscoll, Margarette. "Hands of Fate." *London Sunday Times,* 9 March 1997, 1–13.

Drover, Jack W., and Robert F. Casper. "Initiation of parturition in humans." *Canadian Medical Association Journal* 128 (1983): 387–392.

Dubowitz, Howard, Susan Zuravin, Raymond H. Starr, Jr., Susan Feigelman, and Donna Harrington. "Behavior Problems of Children in Kinship Care." *Developmental and Behavioral Pediatrics* 14 (6): 386–393 (1993).

Earnshaw, Averil. "The Inheritance of Life Events: A Synopsis of *Time Will Tell.*" *Pre- and Perinatal Psychology Journal* 10 (3): Spring 1996.

Edelman, Gerald M. *Bright Air, Brilliant Fire: On the Matter of the Mind.* New York: Basic Books, 1992.

Eichelman, Burr. "Aggressive Behavior: From Laboratory to Clinic. Quo Vadis?" *Archives of General Psychiatry* 49 (1992): 485–486.

Ellis, Lee, and William Peckham. "Prenatal Stress and Handedness Among Offspring." *Pre- and Perinatal Psychology Journal* 6 (2): 135–143 (winter 1991).

Emerson, William R. "Birth Trauma: The Psychological Effects of Obstetrical Interventions." *Journal of Prenatal and Perinatal Psychology and Health,* Fall 1998, 11.

———. "Psychotherapy with infants and children." *Pre- and Perinatal Psychology Journal* 3 (3): 190–317 (1989).

Eron, Leonard D., J. H. Gentry, and P. Schlegel, eds. *Reason to Hope: A Psychosocial Perspective on Violence and Youth.* Washington, D.C.: American Psychological Association, 1994.

Faddio, Anna, Joel Katz, et al. "Effect of neonatal circumcision on pain response during subsequent routine vaccination." *The Lancet* 394 (1997): 599–603.

Feeney, Sheila Anne. "Babies' Amazing Skills." *New York Daily News,* March 26, 1999.

Ferguson, David M., L. John Horwood, and Michael T. Lynskey. "Maternal Smoking Before and After Pregnancy: Effects on Behavioral Outcomes in Middle Childhood." *Pediatrics* 92 (6): 815–822 (1993).

Field, T., N. Grizzle, F. Scafidi, S. Abrams, and S. Richardson. "Massage therapy for infants of depressed mothers." *Infant Behavior and Development* 19 (1996): 109–114.

Field, Tiffany. *Touch in Early Development.* Mahwah, N.J.: Lawrence Erlbaum Associates, 1995.

———. *Infancy.* Cambridge, Mass.: Harvard University Press, 1990.

Fields, Whitridge, Candace. "The Power of Joy: Pre- and Perinatal Psychology as Applied by a Mountain Midwife." *Pre- and Perinatal Psychology Journal* 2 (3): Spring 1988.

Fillon, Kate. "The Day Care Decision." *Saturday Night,* January 1989, 23–30.

Freedman, Daniel X. Editorial: "Violence (and a Message for the 90's)." *Archives General Psychiatry* 49 (1992): 485–486.

Friedrich-Cofer, Lynette, and Aletha C. Houston. "Television Violence and Aggression: The Debate Continues." *Psychological Bulletin* 100 (3): 364–371 (1986).

Fromm, Erich. *The Heart of Man.* New York: Harper and Row, 1964.

Garbarino, J., E. Guttmann, and J. Seeley. *The Psychologically Battered Child: Strategies for Identification, Assessment, and Intervention.* San Francisco: Jossey-Bass Publishers, 1986.

Gardner, Howard. *Creating Minds.* New York: Basic Books, 1993.

Garland, Keldwyn R. "Psychological Effects of Neonatal Management." *Pre- and Perinatal Psychology Journal* 7 (1): 73–83 (1992).

Garmezy, N. "Children under stress: Perspectives on antecedents and correlates of vulnerability and resistance to psychopathology." In *Further Explorations in Personality,* edited by A. I. Rabin, J. Aronoff, A. M. Barclay, and R. A. Zucker, 196–269. New York: Wiley & Sons, 1981.

———. "Stress Resistant Children: The Search for Protective Factors." In *Recent Research in Developmental Psychopathology,* edited by J. E. Stevenson. Oxford: Pergamon Press, 1985.

Gershon, Judy. "Adoptive Breastfeeding." *Infertility Network* 2 (2): 1–3 (1997).

Gianino, A., and E. Z. Tronick. "The mutual regulation model: The infant's self and interactive regulation and coping and defensive capacities." In *Stress and Coping,* edited by R. Field, P. McCabe, and N. Schneiderman, 47–68. Hillsdale, N.J.: Erlbaum, 1985.

Gilligan, James. *Violence.* New York: G.P. Putnam's Sons, 1996.

Givens, Alice. "The Alice Givens Approach to Prenatal and Birth Therapy." *Pre- and Perinatal Psychology Journal* 1 (3): 223–229 (1987).

Gladwell, Malcolm. "Damaged." *New Yorker,* 24 February and 3 March 1997.

Goldenberg, Robert L., et al. "Medical, psychosocial, and behavioral risk factors do not explain the risk for low birth weight among black women." *American Journal of Obstetrics and Gynecology* 175 (5): 1,317–1,324 (1996).

Goode, Erica. "How Culture Molds Habits of Thought." *New York Times,* 8 August 2000.

Goodlin, Robert C. *Care of the Fetus.* New York: Masson Publishing, 1979.

Gopnik, A., A. Meltzoff, and P. Kuhl. *The Scientist in the Crib: Minds, Brains, and How Children Learn.* New York: William Morrow, 1999.

Gopnik, Alison, and Andrew N. Meltzoff. *Words, Thoughts, and Theories.* Cambridge, Mass.: MIT Press, A Bradford Book, 1997.

———. *The Other Socratic Method.* Cambridge, Mass.: MIT Press, 1997.

Gottlieb, Gilbert. *Synthesizing Nature-Nurture: Prenatal Roots of Instinctive Behavior.* Mahwah, N.J.: Erlbaum Associates, 1997.

Gould, E., P. Tanapat, et al. "Proliferation of granule cell precursors in the dentate gyrus of adult monkeys is diminished by stress." *Proceedings of the National Academy of Science* 95 (1998): 3, 163–168, 171.

Gray, Jane D., Christie A. Cutler, et al. "Prediction and Prevention of Child Abuse and Neglect." *Child Abuse and Neglect* 1 (1977): 45–58.

Green, A. H. "Child sexual abuse: Immediate and long-term effects and interventions." *Journal of the American Academy of Child and Adolescent Psychiatry* 32 (1993): 890–902.

Greenfield, Susan A. *The Human Brain: A Guided Tour.* New York: Basic Books, 1997.

Grimm brothers. *The Complete Fairy Tales of the Brothers Grimm.* Translated by Jack Zipes. New York: Bantam Books, 1987.

Grof, Stanislav. "Planetary Survival and Consciousness Evolution: Psychological Roots of Human Violence and Greed." *Primal Renaissance: The Journal of Primal Psychology* 2 (1): 3–26 (spring 1996).

———. *Realms of the Human Unconscious: Observations from LSD Research.* New York: Dutton, 1985.

———. "Perinatal Roots of Wars, Totalitarianism, and Revolutions: Observations from LSD Research." *Journal of Psychohistory* 4 (3): 271–308 (1977).

Gross, A. B., and H. R. Keller. "Long-term consequences of childhood physical and psychological maltreatment." *Aggressive Behavior* 18 (1992): 171–185.

Hanser, S. B., S. C. Larson, and A. S. O'Connell. "The effect of music on relaxation of expectant mothers during labor." *Journal of Music Therapy* 20 (2): 5–58 (1983).

Harlow, Harry F. "Love in Infant Monkeys." *Scientific American* 200 (6): 68–74 (1959).

———. "The Nature of Love." *American Psychologist* 13 (1958): 673–685.

———. "The Heterosexual Affectional System in Monkeys." *American Psychologist* 17 (1962): 1–9.

————. "Primary Affectional Patterns in Primates." *American Journal of Orthopsychiatry* 30 (1960): 676–684.

Harrison, Helen. Letters. *Birth* 13 (2): 79 (1986).

Harrison, Lynda, et al. "Effects of Gentle Human Touch on Preterm Infants: Pilot Study Results." *Neonatal Network* 15 (2): 35–42 (1996).

Hart, Betty, and Todd R. Risley. Meaningful Differences in the Everyday Experience of Young American Children. Baltimore and Toronto: P.H. Brooks, 1995.

Haverkamp, A. D., et al. "The evaluation of continuous fetal heart rate monitoring in, high-risk pregnancy." *American Journal of Obstetrics and Gynecology* 125 (1976): 310–317.

Hay, D. F., and H. S. Ross. "The social nature of early conflict." *Child Development* 53 (1982): 105–113.

He, N. "Cocaine induces cell death within the primate fetal cerebral wall." *Neuropathology and Applied Neurobiology* 25 (6): 504–512 (1999).

Healy, Jane M. *Endangered Minds: Why Our Children Don't Think.* New York: Simon & Schuster, 1990.

Heath, Linda, Candace Kruttschmitt, and David Ward. "Television and Violent Criminal Behavior: Beyond the Bobo Doll." *Victims and Violence* 1 (3): 177–190 (1986).

Heatherton, Todd F., and Roy F. Baumeister. "Binge Eating as Escape From Self-Awareness." *Psychological Bulletin* 110 (10): 86–108 (1991).

Heidrich, Susan M., and Mecca S. Cranley. "Effects of Fetal Movement, Ultrasound Scans, and Amniocentesis on Maternal-Fetal Attachment." *Nursing Research* 38 (2): 81–84 (1989).

Heins, T., A. Gray, and M. Tennant. "Persisting hallucinations following childhood sexual abuse." *Australian and New Zealand Journal of Psychiatry* 24 (1990): 561–565.

Hepper, Peter G., and Sara B. Shahidullah. "Development of Fetal Hearing." *Archives of Disease in Children* 71 (1994): 81–87.

Hillman, James. *The Soul's Code.* New York: Random House, 1996.

Hollinger, Paul C., Daniel Offer, James T. Barter, and Carl C. Bell. *Suicide and Homicide Among Adolescents.* New York: Guilford Press, 1994.

Holt, Luther Emmett. *The Care and Feeding of Children.* Washington, D.C.: U.S. Government Printing Office, 1935.

Huttunen, Mathi O. "Maternal Stress During Pregnancy and the Behavior of the Offspring." In *Early Influences Shaping the Individual*, edited by Spyros Doliadis. New York and London: Plenum Press, 1988.

Ianniruberto, A., and E. Tajani. "Ultrasonographic Study of Fetal Movements." *Seminars in Perinatology* 5 (2): 175–181 (1981).

Irving, Michael C. *Sexual Abuse and the Trauma of Birth: Interrelated Issues.* Toronto: Carriage House Studios, 1995.

Jacobsen, B., G. Eklund, et al. "Perinatal Origin of Adult Self-Destructive Behavior." *Acta Psychiatrica Scandinavia* 76 (1987): 364–371.

Janov, A. *The Feeling Child.* New York: Simon & Schuster, 1973.

Janus, Ludwig. *The Enduring Effects of Prenatal Experience: Echoes from the Womb.* Northvale, N.J.: Aronson, 1997.

Joels, M., and E. Vreugdenhil, "Corticosteroids in the brain." *Molecular Neurobiology* 17 (1998): 87–198.

Johnson, Jeannette L., and Michelle Left. "Children of Substance Abusers: Overview of Research Findings," part 2 of 2. *Pediatrics* 103 (5): 1,085–1,900 (1999).

Kafkalides, Athanassios. *The Knowledge of the Womb.* Heidelberg: Mattes, 1995.

Kaminski, June, and Wendy Hall. "The Effect of Soothing Music on Neonatal Behavioral States in the Hospital Newborn Nursery." *Neonatal Network* 15 (1): 45–54 (1996).

Kandel, Elizabeth, and Sarnoff Mednick. "Perinatal Complications Predict Violent Offending." *Criminology* 29 (3): 519–527 (1991).

Kaplan, Louise J. *No Voice Is Ever Wholly Lost.* New York: Simon & Schuster, 1996.

Kaufman, I. C., and L. A. Rosenblum. "The reaction to separation in infant monkeys: Anaclitic depression and conservation withdrawal." *Psychosomatic Medicine* 29 (1967): 648–675.

Kaufman, Joan, and Edward Zigler. "Do Abused Children Become Abusive Parents?" *American Journal of Orthopsychiatry* 57 (2): 186–192 (1987).

Kigginger, D. O., G. S. Rozycki, J. A. Morris, Jr., et al. "Trauma in Pregnancy Outcome." *Archives of Surgery* 126 (1991): 1,079–1,086.

Kinzel, August E. "Body-Buffer Zone in Violent Prisoners." *American Journal of Psychiatry* 127 (1): 59–64 (1970).

Kipnis, Laura. *Bound and Gagged: Pornography and the Politics of Fantasy in America.* New York: Grove Press, 1996.

Kitzinger, Sheila. *The Complete Book of Pregnancy and Childbirth.* New York: Alfred A. Knopf, 1996.

Klaus, Marshall, John Kennell, and Phyllis Klaus. *Bonding: Building the Foundations of Secure Attachment and Independence.* Reading, Mass.: Addison-Wesley, 1995.

Klaus, Marshall H., and Phyllis H. Klaus. *The Amazing Newborn.* Reading, Mass.: Addison-Wesley, 1985.

Klein, P. J., and A. N. Meltzoff. "Long-term memory, forgetting and deferred imitatión in 12-month-old infants." *Developmental Science* 2 (1989): 102–113.

Kluft, Richard P. "Childhood multiple personality disorder: Predictors, clinical findings and treatment results." *Childhood Antecedents of Multiple Personality*, edited by R. P. Kluft, 167–196. Washington, D.C.: American Psychiatric Press, 1985.

Kolata, Gina. "Studying learning in the womb." *Science* 225 (20 July 1984): 302–303.

Konner, M. S., and M. W. West. "The role of the father: An anthropological perspective." In *The Role of the Father in Child Development*, edited by M. Lamb. New York: John Wiley, 1996.

Kornfield, Jack. *A Path with Heart: A Guide Through the Perils and Promises of Spiritual Life*. New York: Bantam Books, 1996.

Kornheiser, Tony. *The Baby Chase*. Toronto: McClelland and Stewart, 1983.

Kotsopoulos, Sotiris, Selena Walker, Winona Copping, Andre Corte, and Chryssoula Stavrakaki. "A Psychiatric Follow-Up Study of Adoptees." *Canadian Journal of Psychiatry* 38 (1993): 391–396.

Kraemer, Gary W., Michael H. Ebert, et al. "Strangers in a Strange Land: A Psychobiological Study of Infant Monkeys Before and After Separation from Real or Inanimate Mothers." *Child Development* 62 (1991): 548–566.

Kruse, F. *Die Anfänge des Menschlichen Seelenlebens*. Stuttgart: Enre, 1969.

Kuhl, P. K., and A. N. Meltzoff. "The bimodal perception of speech in infancy." *Science* 218 (1982): 1,138–1,141.

Kuhn, C., S. Scahnberg, T. Field, R. Symanski, E. Zimmerman, F. Scafidi, and J. Roberts. "Tactile-kinesthetic stimulation effects on sympathetic and adrenocortical function in preterm infants." *Journal of Pediatrics* 119 (1991): 434–440.

Lagoy, L. "The Loss of a Twin in Utero: Effect on Prenatal and Postnatal Bonding." *International Journal of Pre- and Perinatal Psychology and Medicine* 5 (4): 439–444 (1993).

Laibow, Rima E. "Toward a Developmental Psychology Based on Attachment Theory." *Pre- and Perinatal Psychology Journal* 3 (1): 5–24 (1988).

Laing, R. D. *The Facts of Life: An Essay in Feelings, Facts, and Fantasy*. New York: Pantheon Books, 1976.

Lamb, Michael E. "The development of parental preferences in the first two years of life." *Sex Roles* 3 (1977): 495–497.

————. *The Father's Role: Applied Perspectives*. New York: John Wiley &
Sons, 1986.

————. ed. *The Role of the Father in Child Development*. New York: John
Wiley & Sons, 1997.

Lang, Kirsty. "Bardot's billets-doux take the heat out of her hate." *Sunday
Times*, 27 October 1996.

Lawson, Jill R. Letters. *Birth* 13 (2): 79 (1986).

Leboyer, Frederick. *Birth Without Violence*. Rochester, N.Y.: Healing Arts,
1996.

Leibenluft, Ellen. "Sex Is Complex." *American Journal of Psychiatry* 153
(8): 969–972 (August 1996).

Lewis, Dorothy Otnow. "From Abuse to Violence: Psychophysiological
Consequences of Maltreatment." *Journal of the American Academy of
Child and Adolescent Psychiatry* 31 (3): 383–391 (1992).

Lewis, M., and S. Goldberg, "Perceptual Cognitive Development in Infancy: A Generalized Expectancy Model as a Function of Mother-
Infant Interaction." *Merrill-Palmer Quarterly* 15 (1969): 81–100.

Libet, Benjamin. "Brain 'decides' before intention becomes conscious."
Brain/Mind Bulletin 9 (3): 1 (1984).

Lifton, B. J. *Twice Born*. New York: McGraw-Hill, 1975.

Lifton, R. J., and E. Markusen. *The Genocidal Mentality: Nazi Holocaust
and Nuclear Threat*. London: Macmillan, 1990.

Liley, A. W. "The foetus as a personality." *Pre- and Perinatal Psychology
Journal* 5 (3): 191–202 (1991).

Linden, Kathleen, and Robert B. McFarland. "Community parenting
centers in Colorado." *Journal of Psychohistory* 21 (1): 7–19 (1993).

Lindholm, Byron W., and John Touliatos. "Psychological Adjustment of
Adopted and Non-Adopted Children." *Psychol Rep* 46 (1980): 307–310.

Linnoila, M., and M. Virkaunen. "Biologic correlates of suicidal risk and
aggressive behavioral traits." *Journal of Clinical Psychopharmacology* 12
(1992): 519–520.

Lipovenko, Dorothy. "Psychiatrist assails day care." *Toronto Globe and
Mail*, 23 December 1983.

Lipton, Bruce H. "Adaptive Mutation: A New Look at Biology." *Touch the
Future*, Summer 1997. 4350 Lime Ave., Long Beach, CA 90807.

————. "Nature, Nurture and the Power of Love." *Pre- and Perinatal Psychology Journal* 13 (1): 3–10 (1998).

Litt, S. "Perinatal Complications and Criminality." In *Proceedings*, 80th
Annual Convention, Amer. Psych. Assoc., Washington, D.C., 1972.

MacFarlane, Aiden. In *Infants: The New Knowledge*, edited by Robert Mc-
Call. Cambridge, Mass.: Harvard University Press, 1979.

Machón, Ricardo. A. "Affective Disorder Linked to Prenatal Influenza." *Clinical Psychiatry News*, 1987.

MacLean, Paul. "A Triune Concept of the Brain and Behavior." *Hincks Memorial Lectures*, edited by D. Campbell and T. J. Boag. Toronto: University of Toronto Press, 1973.

MacMillan, Harriet L., Michael H. Boyle, et al. "Slapping and spanking in childhood and its association with lifetime prevalence of psychiatric disorders in a general population." *Canadian Medical Association Journal* 161 (7): 805–809 (1999).

Madaule, Paul. "Left Out: The Rejection Complex of the Adopted." Presented at the 4th International Congress on Pre- and Perinatal Psychology, August 1989.

Magid, Ken, and Carole A. McKelvey. *High Risk: Children Without Conscience*. New York: Bantam Books, 1987.

Maholmes, Valerie. "The Moral Intelligence of Children: How to Raise a Moral Child." *American Journal of Psychiatry* 156 (1999): 1,827–1,828.

Maliphant, Rodney, et al. "Autonomic Nervous System (ANS) Activity, Personality Characteristics and Disruptive Behavior in Girls." *Journal of Child Psychology* 11 (4): 619–628 (1989).

Mancini, C., M. Van Ameringen, and H. MacMillan. "Relationship of childhood sexual and physical abuse to anxiety disorders." *Journal of Nervous and Mental Disease* 183 (1995): 309–314.

Mark, V. H., and F. R. Ervin. *Violence and the Brain*. Hagerstown, Md.: Harper and Row, 1970.

Martingale, Moira. *Cannibal Killers: The History of Impossible Murders*. New York: Carrol & Graf, 1993.

Masten, A. S., et al. "Competence and stress in schoolchildren: The moderating effects of individual and family qualities." (In preparation.)

Mathison, Linda. "Birth Memories: Does Your Child Remember?" *Mothering* (fall 1981): 103–107.

McCarthy, Terry. "One Mother's Story." *Time*, 24 November 1997, 32–33.

McCartney, Kathleen, and Anastasia Galanopoulos. "Child Care and Attachment: A New Frontier the Second Time Around." *American Journal of Orthopsychiatry* 58 (1): 16–24 (1988).

McCord, John. "A Forty-Year Perceptive on Effects of Child Abuse and Neglect." *Child Abuse and Neglect* 7 (1983): 265–270.

McEwen, Bruce, and Harold M. Schmeck. *The Hostage Brain*. New York: Rockefeller Press, 1994.

McIntosh, Lisa J., Nabil E. Roumayah, and Sidney F. Bottoms. "Perinatal Outcome of Broken Marriage in the Inner City." *Obstetrics & Gynecology* 85 (2): 233–236 (1995).

McKinney, C. H., M. H. Antoni, A. M. Kumar, and M. Kumar. "The effect of selected classical music and spontaneous imagery on plasma beta-endorphin." *Journal of Behavioral Medicine* 20 (1): 85–99 (1997).

McKinney, W. T., S. J. Suomi, and H. F. Harlow. "Experimental psychopathology in non-human primates." In *New Psychiatric Frontiers*, edited by D. A. Hamburg and H. K. Brodie. Vol. 6 of *American Handbook of Psychiatry*, 2d ed. New York: Basic Books, 1975.

McLanahan, S., and G. Sandefur. *Growing Up with a Single Parent*. Cambridge, Mass.: Harvard University Press, 1994.

McWhinnie, Alexina Mary. *Adopted Children—How They Grow Up*. London: Routledge and Kegan Paul, 1967.

Meany, M. J., S. Bhatnager, et al. "Individual Differences in the Hypothalamic-Pituitary-Adrenal Stress Response and the Hypothalamic CRF System." *Annals of the New York Academy of Sciences* 697 (fall 1993): 70–85.

Mednick, S. A., and F. Schulsinger. "Some premorbid characteristics related to breakdown in children with schizophrenic mothers." In *The Transmission of Schizophrenia*, edited by D. Rosenthal and S. S. Kety. Oxford: Pergamon Press, 1968.

Mednick, Sarnoff A. "Breakdown in individuals at high risk for schizophrenia." *Mental Hygiene* 54 (January 1970): 50–61.

———. "Birth Defects and Schizophrenia." *Psychology Today* 4 (11): 48–50, 80–81 (1971).

Mehl, Lewis E. "Women's Birth Experience and Subsequent Infant Motor Development." *Pre- and Perinatal Psychology Journal* 6 (4): 295–315 (1992).

Meltzoff, A. "Molyneux's babies: Cross-modal perception, imitation, and the mind of the preverbal infant." In *Spatial Representation: Problems in Philosophy and Psychology*, edited by N. Eilan, R. McCarthy, and B. Brewer, 219–235. Oxford: Basil Blackwell, 1993.

———. "Infant imitation and memory: Nine-month-olds in immediate and deferred tests." *Child Development* 59 (1988): 217–225.

———. "Infant imitation after a 1-week delay: Long-term memory for novel acts and multiple stimuli." *Developmental Psychology* 24 (1988): 470–476.

———. "Foundations for developing a concept of self: The role of imitation in relating self to other and the value of social mirroring, social modeling, and self-practice in infancy." In *The Self in Transition: Infancy to Childhood*, edited by D. Cicchetti and M. Beeghly, 139–164. Chicago: University of Chicago Press, 1990.

————. "Towards a developmental cognitive science: The implications of cross-modal matching and imitation for the development of representation and memory in infancy." In *The Development and Neural Bases of Higher Cognitive Functions. Annals of the New York Academy of Sciences* 608 (1990): 1–31.

Meltzoff, A., and A. Gopnik. "The role of imitation in understanding persons and developing a theory of mind." In *Understanding Other Minds: Perspectives from Autism*, edited by S. Baron-Cohen, H. Tager-Flusberg, and D. Cohen, 335–366. New York: Oxford University Press, 1993.

Meltzoff, A. N., and P. K. Kuhl. "Faces and speech: Intermodal processing of biologically relevant signals in infants and adults." In *The Development of Intersensory Perception: Comparative Perspectives*, edited by D. J. Lewkowicz and R. Lickliter. Hillsdale, N.J.: Erlbaum, 1994).

————. "Newborn infants imitate adult facial gestures." *Child Development* 54 (1983): 702–709.

————. "Imitation in newborn infants: Exploring the range of gestures imitated and the underlying mechanisms." *Developmental Psychology* 25 (1989): 954–962.

Meltzoff, A., and M. K. Moore. "Imitation, memory, and the representation of persons." *Infant Behavior and Development* 17 (1994): 83–99.

————. "Infants' understanding of people and things: From body imitation to folk psychology." In *The Body and the Self*, edited by J. Bermudez, A. Marcel, and N. Eilan, 43–69. Cambridge, Mass.: MIT/Bradford Press, 1995.

————. "Imitation of facial and manual gestures by human neonates." *Science* 198 (1977): 75–78.

————. "Early imitation within a functional framework: The importance of person identity, movement, and development." *Infant Behavior and Development* 15 (1992): 479–505.

Moffit, T. "Adolescence-limited and life-course-persistent antisocial behavior: A developmental taxonomy." *Psychology Review* 100 (1993): 674–701.

Montagu, Ashley, editor. *Learning Non-Aggression: The Experience of Non-Literate Societies.* New York: Oxford University Press, 1978.

Montemurro, Rosario N. Rozada. "Singing Lullabies to Unborn Children: Experience in Village Vilamarxant, Spain." *Pre- and Perinatal Psychology Journal* 11 (1): 9–16 (1996).

Mott, Frances J. *The Nature of the Self.* London: Allen Vingate, 1959.

————. *The Universal Design of Creation.* Edenbridge, U.K.: Mark Beech, 1964.

————. "World Transformation." *Journal of Psychohistory* 4 (3): 319–335 (1997).

Myhman, A. "Longitudinal Studies on Unwanted Children." *Scandinavian Journal of Social Medicine* 14 (1986): 57–59.

Nathanielsz, Peter. *Life Before Birth and a Time to Be Born.* Ithaca, N.Y.: Promethean Press, 1992.

National Institute of Child Health and Human Development. "Child Care and Mother-Child Interaction in the First 3 Years of Life." Early Child Care Research Network, The American Psychological Association, 1999.

National Institutes of Health. Report of the Panel in NIH Research on Antisocial, Aggressive and Violence-Related Behaviors and Their Consequences. Bethesda, Maryland, 1994.

Neugebauer, Richard, Hans W. Hoek, and Ezra Susser. "Prenatal Exposure to Wartime Famine and Development of Antisocial Personality Disorder in Early Adulthood." *Journal of the American Medical Association* 282 (5): 455–62 (1999).

Newman, Louise. Lecture reported by Chris Pritchard, in *The Medical Post,* 8 October 1996.

Nilsson, Lennart. *A Child Is Born.* New York: Delacorte Press, 1990.

Nover, Aimee, Milron F. Shore, et al. "The Relationship of Maternal Perception and Maternal Behavior: A Study of Normal Mothers and Their Infants." *American Journal of Orthopsychiatry* 54 (2): 210–223 (1984).

Nystad, Wenche. "Asthma linked to day care, researchers say." *Toronto Star,* 24 September 1987, A29.

Odent, Michel. "Preventing Violence or Developing the Capacity to Love?" *Primal Health Research* 2 (3): 1–7 (1994).

————. "One Perspective on Violence." Published on the Association for Pre- and Perinatal Psychology and Health home page, www.birthpsychology.com 1997.

————. "Why Laboring Women Don't Need Support." *Mothering* 80 (fall 1996): 46.

Oliver, Samuel P., and Pearl M. Oliver. *The Altruistic Personality: Rescuers of Jews in Nazi Europe.* New York: Free Press, 1988.

Orr, L., and S. Ray. *Rebirthing in the New Age.* Millbrae, Calif.: Celestial Arts, 1977.

Osofsky, L. D. "The effects of exposure to violence on young children." *American Psychologist* 50: 782–788 (1995).

Paanksepp, Jaak. *Affective Neuroscience: The Foundations of Human and Animal Emotions*. New York and Oxford: Oxford University Press, 1998.

———. "The Neural Basis of the Basic Emotions in the Mammalian Brain." In *Encyclopedia of Human Emotions*, edited by D. Levinson et al., 475–478. New York: Macmillan, 1999.

Pagels, Elaine. *Adam, Eve and the Serpent*. London: Weidenfeld and Nicolson, 1988.

Panneton, R .K. "Prenatal Auditory Experience with Melodies: Effects on Postnatal Auditory Preferences in Human Newborns." Doctoral thesis, University of North Carolina, Greensboro, 1985.

Pannor, R., A. Baran, and A. D. Sorosky. "Birth Parents Who Relinquished Babies for Adoption Revisited." *Family Process* 17 (1978): 329–337.

Pannor, R., F. Massarik, and B. Evans. *The Unmarried Father*. New York: Springer, 1967.

Pantakallio, Paula, Markku Koiranen, and Jyri Mottonen. "Association of perinatal events, epilepsy, and central nervous system trauma with juvenile delinquency." *Archives of Disease in Childhood* 67 (1992): 1,459–1,461.

Panthuraamphorn, Chairat. "How to Maximize Human Potential at Birth." *Pre- and Perinatal Psychology Journal* (winter 1994): 117–126.

Parke, R., and C. Collmer. "Child Abuse: An Interdisciplinary Review." *Review of Child Development Research* 5, edited by E. M. Hetherington. Chicago: University of Chicago Press, 1975.

Parke, R. D., and S. E. O'Leary. "Family interaction in the newborn period: Some findings." In *Social and Environmental Issues*, vol. 2 of *The Developing Individual in a Changing World*, edited by K. Riegel and J. Meacham, 653–663. The Hague: Morton, 1976.

Parker, Faith Lamb, et al. "Head Start as a Social Support for Mothers: The Psychological Benefits of Involvement." *American Journal of Orthopsychiatry* 57 (2): 220–233 (1987).

Pearce, Joseph Chilton. *Evolution's End: Claiming the Potential of Our Intelligence*. San Francisco: Harper; New York: HarperCollins, 1992.

Peck, M. Scott. *People of the Lie: The Hope for Healing Human Evil*. New York: Simon & Schuster, 1983.

Pederson, C. A., and A. J. Prange, Jr. "Induction of Maternal Behavior in Virgin Rats After Intracerebroventricular Administration of Oxytocin." *Proceedings of the National Academy of Sciences* 76 (1979): 6,661–6,665.

Perris, E., N. Meyers, and R. Clifton. "Long-term memory for a single infancy experience." *Child Development* 61 (1990): 1,796–1,807.

Perry, B. D. "Incubated in Terror: Neurodevelopmental Factors in the 'Cycle of Violence.'" In *Children, Youth and Violence: The Search for Solutions*, edited by J. Osofsky, 124–148. New York: Guilford Press, 1997.

———. "The Vortex of Violence: How Children Adapt and Survive in a Violent World." Child Trauma Academy, Interdisciplinary Education Series, adapted in part from *Maltreated Children: Experience, Brain Development and the Next Generation*. New York: W. W. Norton, 1996.

———. "How Persisting Fear Can Alter the Developing Child's Brain." A Special Child Trauma Academy Web site of Baylor College of Medicine and Texas Children's Hospital, 1998, http://www.bcm. tmc.edu/cta/.

Perry, B. D., and I. Azad. "Post-traumatic stress disorder in children and adolescents." *Current Opinion in Pediatrics* 11 (1999): 121–132.

Perry, B. D., and R. Pollard. "Homeostasis, stress, trauma, and adaptation: A neurodevelopmental view of childhood trauma. *Child and Adolescent Psychiatric Clinics of North America* 7 (1): 33–51 (1998).

Perry, B. D., R. Pollard, T. Blakely, W. Baker, and D. Vigilante. "Childhood trauma, the neurobiology of adaptation and 'use-dependent' development of the brain: How 'states' become 'traits.'" *Infant Mental Health Journal* 16 (4): 271–291 (1995).

Pert, Candace B. *Molecules of Emotion*. New York: Simon & Schuster, 1999.

Peterson, Gayle. *Birthing Normally*. Berkeley, Calif.: Mindbody Press, 1984.

———. "Prenatal Bonding, Prenatal Communication, and the Prevention of Prematurity. *Pre- and Perinatal Psychology Journal* 2 (2): 87–92 (1987).

Pfaff, D. W. *Estrogens and Brain Function: Neural Analysis of a Hormone-Controlled Mammalian Reproductive Behavior*. New York: Springer-Verlag, 1980.

Phillips, D., K. McCartney, and S. Scorr. "Child care quality and children's social development. *Developmental Psychology* 23 (1987): 537–543.

"Physical health compromised by daycare." *Pediatrics* supplement, June 1986.

Piaget, J. *Play, Dreams, and Imitation in Childhood*. New York: Norton, 1962.

———. "The Mental Development of the Child." In *Six Psychological Studies*. New York: Vintage, 1968.

Pines, Maya. "Good Samaritans at Age Two?" *Psychology Today*, June 1979: 66–74.

Piontelli, Alessandra. "Infant Observation from Before Birth." *International Journal of Psycho-Analysis* 68 (1987): 453–463.

———. *From Fetus to Child: An Observational and Psychoanalytic Study*. London: Routledge, 1992.

———. "A Study on Twins Before and After Birth." *International Review of Psycho-Analysis* 16 (1989) 413–425.

Pomeroy, Wendy. "A Working Model for Trauma: The Relationship Between Trauma and Violence." Paper delivered at the 7th International Congress on Pre- and Perinatal Psychology, San Francisco, 1995.

Poole, Galen V., et al. "Trauma in Pregnancy: The Role of Interpersonal Violence." *American Journal of Obstetrics and Gynecology* 174 (6): 1,973–1,978 (1996).

Porges, Stephen W. "Orienting in a defensive world: Mammalian modifications of our evolutionary heritage. A Polyvagal Theory." *Psychophysiology* 32 (1995): 301–318.

———. "Love: An Emergent Property of the Mammalian Autonomic Nervous System." *Psychoneuroendocrinology* 23 (8): 837–861 (1998).

Porter, Fran Lang. "Pain in the Newborn." In *Clinics in Perinatology*. Vol. 16 of *Neonatal Neurology*, edited by J. Volpe, 549–564. Philadelphia: W. B. Saunders, 1989.

———. "Pain Assessment in Children: Infants." In *Pain in Infants, Children, and Adolescents*, edited by N. L. Schecter, C. B. Berde, and M. Yaster. Baltimore: Williams & Wilkins, 1993.

Porter, Fran Lang, R. E. Grunau, and K. J. S. Anand. "Long-Term Effects of Pain in Infants." *Developmental and Behavioral Pediatrics* 20 (4): 253–261 (1999).

Prescott, James W. "Affectional Bonding for the Prevention of Violent Behaviors: Neurobiological, Psychological and Religious/Spiritual Determinants." In *Violent Behaviors*, Vol. 1, *Assessment and Intervention*, edited by Leonard Hertzberg et al., 95–124. Great Neck, N.Y.: PMA Publishing, 1990.

———. "Body of Pleasure and the Origins of Violence." *Pulse of the Planet* 3 (1991): 17–25.

———. "The Origins of Human Love and Violence." *Pre- and Perinatal Psychology Journal* 10 (3): 143–188 (1996). Also, NIH Violence Research Initiatives: Is Past Prologue, and the Prescott Report, parts I and II, testimony before the NIH Panel on Violence Research, 23 September 1993.

———. "The Origins of Human Love and Violence." Background Monograph, 7th International Congress, the Association for Pre- and Perinatal Psychology and Health, San Francisco, 1995.

"Problem: The Neglect of Neglect." *American Journal of Orthopsychiatry* 54 (4): 530–543 (1984).

Provence, S., and R. Lipton. *Infants in Institutions*. New York: International Universities Press, 1962.

Purpura, Dominick. "Consciousness." *Behavior Today*, 2 June 1975, 494.

Quinn, Susan. "Your Baby's Smarter Than You Believe." *Atlantic Monthly*, January 1982.

Radke-Yarrow, M. R., C. Zahn-Waxler, and M. Chapman. "Children's prosocial dispositions and behavior. In *Carmichael's Manual of Child Psychology*, 4th ed., vol. IV, edited by P. H. Mussen. New York: John Wiley & Sons, 1984.

Raikov, V. "Age regression to infancy by adult subjects in deep hypnosis." *American Journal of Clinical Hypnosis* 22 (3): 156–163 (1998).

Raine, Adrian, et al. "Relationships Between Central and Autonomic Measures of Arousal at age 15 years and Criminality at age 24 years." *Archives of General Psychiatry* 47 (1990): 1,003–1,007.

Raine, Adrian, et al. "Birth Complications Combined with Early Maternal Rejection at age 1 Predispose to Violent Crime at age 18 years." *Archives of General Psychiatry*, 51 (1994): 984–988.

Raphael-Leff, Joan. "Facilitators and Regulators; Participators and Renouncers: Mothers' and Fathers' Orientations Towards Pregnancy and Parenthood." *Journal of Psychosomatic Obstetrics and Gynecology* 4 (1985): 169–184.

Rauscher, F. H. "Improved Maze Learning Through Early Music Exposure in Rats." *Neurological Research* 20 (1998): 427–432.

———. "Listening to Mozart enhances spatial-temporal reasoning towards a neurophysical basis." *Neuroscience Letter* 185 (1): 44–47 (1995).

Ray, Sondra, and Bob Mandel. *Birth and Relationships*. Berkeley, Calif.: Celestial Arts, 1987.

Rice, Ruth Dianne. "Neurophysiological Development in Premature Infants Following Stimulation." *Developmental Psychology* 13 (1): 69–76 (1997).

Rivera, Carla. "Report to the U.S. Congress, the Advisory Board of Child Abuse and Neglect." *Los Angeles Times*, 26 April 1995.

Roedding, Jude. "Birth Trauma and Suicide: A Study of the Relationship between Near-Death Experiences at Birth and Later Suicidal Behavior." *Pre- and Perinatal Psychology Journal* 6 (2): 145–169 (winter 1991).

Rohrbect, C. A., and C. T. Twentyman. "Neglect and Abuse." *Journal of Consulting Clinical Psychology* 54 (1986): 231.

Rosenblith, Judy F. *In the Beginning: Development from Conception to Age Two.* Newbury Park, Calif.: Sage Publications, 1992.

Rosenthal, Perihan. "Suicide Among Preschool Children Found More Prevalent Than Commonly Believed." Paper presented at APA, Toronto, 1982. Reported in *Psychiatric News*, 6 April 1984.

Ross, C. P., and T. V. Persaud. "Neural tube defects in early rat embryos following maternal treatment with ethanol and caffeine." *Anatomischer Anzeiger* 169 (4): 247–252 (1989).

Rossi, Ernest Lawrence, and David B. Cheek. *Mind-Body Therapy.* New York: W. W. Norton, 1988.

Rossi, Nicolino, et al. "Maternal Stress and Fetal Motor Behavior: A Preliminary Report." *Pre- and Perinatal Psychology Journal* 3 (4): 311–328 (1989).

Rovee-Collier, Carolyn. "The Memory System of Prelinguistic Infants." In *The Development of and Neural Bases of Higher Cognitive Functions,* edited by A. Diamond. *Annals of the New York Academy of Sciences* 608: 517–542. New York: New York Academy of Sciences, 1993.

Rowan, A. B., and D. W. Foy. "Post-traumatic stress disorder in child sexual abuse survivors: A literature review." *Journal of Traumatic Stress* 6 (1993): 3–20.

Rubin, A. J., Joel Aronoff, Andrea M. Barclay, and Robert A. Zucker. *Further Explorations in Personality.* New York: Wiley & Sons, 1981.

Rubin, Jeff, Frank Provenzano, and Luria Zelba. "Sex typing in the delivery room." *American Journal of Orthopsychiatry* 44 (4): 512–519 (1974).

Rubinow, David R., and Peter J. Schmidt. "Androgens, Brain and Behavior." *American Journal of Psychiatry* 153 (8): 974–984 (1996).

Rushton, J. P., L. H. Russell, and P. A. Wells. "Genetic similarity theory: Beyond kin selection." *Behavior Genetics* 14 (1984): 179–193.

Rushton, J. Phillipe, and Richard M. Sorrentino. *Altruism and Helping Behavior: Social, Personality, and Developmental Perspectives.* Hillsdale, N.J.: Lawrence Erlbaum Associates, 1981.

Russell, Marlou. "Meeting My Mother." *Whole Life Times,* January 1995, 18–19.

Rutter, M. "Protective factors in children's responses to stress and disadvantage." In *Primary Prevention of Psychopathology,* Vol. III, *Social*

Competence in Children, edited by M. W. Kent and J. Rolf. Hanover, N.H: University Press of New England, 1979.

Rutter, M., et al. "Attainment and adjustment in two geographical areas: The prevalence of psychiatric disorder." *British Journal of Psychiatry* 126 (1975): 493–509.

———. *Fifteen Thousand Hours: Secondary Schools and Their Effects on Children*. Cambridge, Mass.: Harvard University Press, 1979.

Sadger, Isadore. "Preliminary Study of the Psychic Life of the Fetus and the Primary Germ Cell." *Psychoanalytic Review* 28 (3): July 1941.

Sagi, A., and J. L. Hoffman. "Empathic distress in the newborn." *Developmental Psychology* 12 (1976): 175–176.

Salk, L. "The role of the heartbeat in the relations between mother and infant." *Scientific American* 228 (1973): 24–29.

Salk, L., L. P. Lipsitt, et al. "Relationships of Maternal and Perinatal Conditions to Eventual Adolescent Suicide." *The Lancet* 1 (1985): 624–627.

Sanger, Maureen. William E. MacLean, Jr., and Deborah A. Van Slyke. "Relation Between Maternal Characteristics and Child Behavior Ratings." *Clinical Pediatrics*, August 1992: 461–466.

Sapolsky, Robert. Quoted in *Newsweek*, 10 April 2000, 68.

Saudino, Kimberly, and Robert Plominy. Tester-rated temperament at 14, 20 and 24 months: Environmental change and genetic continuity." *British Journal of Developmental Psychology* 14 (1996): 129–144.

Scafidi, F., T. Field, S. Schanberg, C. Bauer, K. Tucci, J. Robens, C. Morrow, and C. M. Kuhn. "Massage stimulates growth in preterm infants: A replication." *Infant Behavior and Development* 13 (1990): 167–188.

Schacter, Daniel L. *Searching for Memory: The Brain, the Mind, and the Past*. New York: Basic Books, 1996.

Scheibel, Arnold B. "Embryological Development of the Human Brain." *New Horizons for Learning Electronic Journal*, September/October 1997, www.newhorizons.org.newsletter14.html.

Scholtz, K., and C. A. Samuels. "Neonatal bathing and massage intervention with fathers, behavioral effects 12 weeks after birth of the first baby: The Sunraysia Australia Intervention Project." *International Journal of Behavioral Development* 15 (1): 67–81 (1992).

Schore, Allen N. "The experience-dependent maturation of a regulatory system in the orbital prefrontal cortex and the origin of developmental psychopathology." *Development and Psychopathology* 8 (1996): 59–87.

———. "Early organization of the nonlinear right brain and development of a predisposition to psychiatric disorders." *Development and Psychopathology* 9 (1997): 595–631.

Sears, Donald J. *To Kill Again: The Motivation and Development of Serial Murder.* Wilmington, Del.: Scholarly Resources, 1991.

Share, Lynda. *If Someone Speaks, It Gets Lighter: Dreams and the Reconstruction of Infant Trauma.* Hillsdale, N.J.: Analytic Press, 1994.

———. "Dreams and the Reconstruction of Infant Trauma." *International Journal of Prenatal & Perinatal Psychology & Medicine* 8 (3): 295–316 (1996).

Shear, M. Katherine. "Factors in the Etiology and Pathogenesis of Panic Disorder: Revisiting the Attachment-Separation Paradigm." *American Journal of Psychiatry* 153 (7): 125–136 (1996).

Shearer, Madeleine H. Editorial: "Surgery on the Paralyzed, Unanesthetized Newborn." *Birth* 13 (2): 79 (1986).

Shetler, Donald J. "The Inquiry into Prenatal Musical Experience: A Report of the Eastman Project, 1980–1987." *Pre- and Perinatal Psychology Journal* 3 (3): 171–189 (1987).

Shore, Rima. *Rethinking the Brain.* New York: Families and Work Institute, 1997.

Siegel, Daniel J. *The Developing Mind: Toward a Neurobiology of Interpersonal Experience.* New York: Guilford Press, 1999.

Simner, M. L. "Newborn's response to the cry of another infant." *Developmental Psychology* 5 (1971): 136–150.

Smith, Ann. "An analysis of altruism: A concept of caring." *Journal of Advanced Nursing* 22 (1995): 785–790.

Smith, J. R., and L. Brooks-Gunn. "Correlates and consequences of harsh discipline for young children." *Archives of Pediatric and Adolescent Medicine* 151 (1997): 777–786.

Smith, Roger. "The Timing of Birth." *Scientific American* 280 (3): 68 (1999).

Smith, Susan M. "Alcohol-induced cell death in the embryo." *Alcohol Health & Research World* 21 (4): 287–296 (1997).

Somerfeld-Ziskind, Esther. "Recollections of Trauma: Scientific Evidence and Clinical Practice."*American Journal of Psychiatry* 156 (1999): 183.

Sonne, John C. "Prenatal Preparation: Suggestion for Modification." *Pre- and Perinatal Psychology Journal* 1 (3): 208–222 (1996).

———. "Interpreting the Dread of Being Aborted in Therapy." *International Journal of Prenatal and Perinatal Psychology & Medicine* 8 (3): 317–339 (1994).

Sontag, Lester. "Implications of Fetal Behavior and Environment for Adult Personalities." *Annals of the New York Academy of Sciences* 134 (1965): 782–786.

Southwick, Thomas McGlashan, and Dennis S. Charney. "Neural Correlates of Memories of Childhood Sexual Abuse in Women With and Without Post-traumatic Stress Disorder." *American Journal of Psychiatry* 156 (1999): 1,787–1,795.

Spielrein, Sabina. "Destruction as a Cause of Coming into Being." *Jahrbuch für psychoanalytische und psychopathologische Forschungen* 4 (1912): 465–503, Vienna.

Spitz, Rene A. "Anaclitic depression." *Psychoanalytic Study of the Child* 2 (1946): 313–342.

———. "Hospitalism: An inquiry into the genesis of psychiatric conditions in early childhood." *Psychoanalytic Study of the Child* 1 (1945): 53–74.

———. "Autoeroticism reexamined." *Psychoanlytic Study of the Child* 17 (1962): 283–315.

Sroufe, L. A. "The coherence of individual development: Early care, attachment, and subsequent developmental issues." *American Psychologist* 34 (1979): 834–841.

Standley, J. M. "The effect of music and multimodal stimulation of physiologic and developmental responses of premature infants in neonatal intensive care." Presented at the International Society for Music in Medicine Symposium in San Antonio, October 1996.

State of California Commission on Crime Control and Violence Prevention. "An Ounce of Prevention: Toward an Understanding of the Causes of Violence." Sacramento, California, 1982.

Staub, Erwin. "Cultural-Societal Roots of Violence." *American Psychologist* 51 (2): 117–132 (1996).

Stern, Daniel N. *The Interpersonal World of the Infant: A View from Psychoanalysis and Developmental Psychology.* New York: Basic Books, 1985.

Stewart, D. E., and A. Cecutli. "Physical Abuse in Pregnancy." *Canadian Medical Association Journal* 149 (1993): 1,257–1,263.

Stott, D. H. "Follow-up Study from Birth of the Effects of Prenatal Stress." *Developmental Medicine & Child Neurology* 15 (1973): 770–787.

Straub, Mary F. "A Theory of the Psychophysiological Consequences of Umbilical Cord Manipulation by the Fetus." *Pre- and Perinatal Psychology Journal* 7 (1): 61–71 (1992).

Straus, M. A. "Hitting adolescents." In *Beating the Devil Out of Them:*

Corporal Punishment in American Families, edited by M. A. Straus. San Francisco: Lexington, 1994.

———. "Spanking and the Making of a Violent Society." *Pediatrics* 98 (4): 837–842 (1996).

———. "Spanking by parents and subsequent antisocial behavior of children." *Archives of Pediatric and Adolescent Medicine* 151 (1997): 761–767.

Straus, M. A., and D. Donnelly. "Violence and Crime." In *Beating the Devil Out of Them,* edited by M. A. Straus, op. cit.

Straus, M. A., and C. L. Yodanis. "Corporal punishment in adolescence and physical assaults on spouses in later life: What accounts for the link?" *Journal of Marriage and Family,* 1996.

Sullenbach, William B. "Claira: A Case Study in Prenatal Learning." *Pre- and Perinatal Psychology Journal* 9 (1): 33–56 (1994).

Sulloway, Frank. *Born to Rebel.* New York: Pantheon, 1996.

Suomi, Stephen L., and C. Rijyr. "A history of motherless monkey mothering." In *Child Abuse: The Nonhuman Primate Data,* edited by M. Resto and M. Caine. New York: Alan R. Liss, 1983.

Suomi, Stephen J., Stephen F. Seaman, et al. "Effects of Imipramine Treatment of Separation-Induced Social Disorders in Rhesus Monkeys." *Archives of General Psychiatry* 35 (1978): 321–325.

Susser, Ezra B., Alan Brown, and Thomas D. Matte. "Prenatal Factors and Adult Mental and Physical Health." *Canadian Journal of Psychiatry* 44 (May 1999).

Swett, C., and M. Halpert. "High rates of alcohol problems and history of physical and sexual abuse among women inpatients." *American Journal of Drug & Alcohol Abuse* 20 (1994): 263–272.

Taddio, A., J. Katz, et al. "Effect of neonatal circumcision on pain response during subsequent routine examination." *The Lancet* 349 (1997): 599–605.

Taylor, David C. "Oedipus's Parents Were Child Abusers." *British Journal of Psychiatry* 153 (1988): 561–563.

Toch, Hans. *Violent Men: An Inquiry into the Psychology of Violence.* Chicago: Aldine, 1969.

Tonkin, Roger. "Sorting out the 'bad apples.'" *Medical Post,* 2 April 1966, 30.

Tremblay, R. E., R. O. Pihl, F. Vitaro, and P. L. Doblin. "Predicting early onset of male antisocial behavior from preschool behavior." *Archives of General Psychiatry* 51 (1994): 723–739.

Triffleman, E. G., C. R. Marmar, K. L. Delucchi, and H. Ronfeldt. "Childhood trauma and post-traumatic stress disorder in substance abuse inpatients." *Journal of Nervous and Mental Disease* 183 (1995): 172–176.

Trivers, R. L. "The evolution of reciprocal altruism." *Quarterly Review of Biology* 46 (1971): 35–77.

Tronick, E. Z. "On the primacy of social skills." In *The Exceptional Infant: Psychosocial Risks in Infant Environment Transaction*, edited by D. B. Sawin, L. O. Walker, and J. H. Penticuff, 144–158. New York: Bruner/Mazel, 1980.

———. "Affectivity and sharing." In *Social Interchange in Infancy: Affect, Cognition and Communication*, edited by E. Z. Tronick, 1–6. Baltimore: University Park Press, 1982.

———. "Emotions and emotional communication in infants." *American Psychologist* 44 (1989): 112–128.

Tronick, E., H. Als, and L. Adamson. "Structure of early face-to-face communicative interactions." In *Before Speech: The Beginning of Interpersonal Communication*, edited by M. Bullowa, 349–372. New York: Cambridge University Press, 1979.

Tronick, E. Z., and A. Gianino. "Interactive mismatch and repair: Challenges to the coping infant." *Zero to Three* 6 (3): 1–6 (1986).

Trout, M. D. "The optimal adoptive launch." *Pre- and Perinatal Psychology Journal* 11 (2): 93–99 (1996).

Tuteur, Werner, and Jacob Glotzer. "Further Observations on Murdering Mothers." *Journal of Forensic Sciences* 11 (3): 373–383 (1966).

Uvnas-Moberg, K., A. M. Widstrom, G. Marchine, and J. Windberg. "Release of GI Hormone in Mothers and Infants by Sensory Stimulation." *Acta Paediatrica Scandinavia* 76 (1987): 851–860.

Van de Carr, Rene. "Enhancing Early Speech, Parental Bonding and Infant Physical Development Using Prenatal Intervention in Standard Obstetric Practice." *Pre- and Perinatal Psychology Journal* 1 (1): 20–29 (1986).

———. "Prenatal University: Commitment to Fetal-Family Bonding and the Strengthening of the Family Unit as an Educational Institution." *Pre- and Perinatal Psychology Journal* 3 (2): 87–102 (1989).

Van de Carr, Rene, and M. Lehrer. *The Prenatal Classroom: A Parents' Guide for Teaching Your Baby in the Womb.* Atlanta: Humanics Learning, 1992.

Van den Bergh, B. R. H. "The Influence of Maternal Emotions During Pregnancy on Fetal and Neonatal Behavior." *Pre- and Perinatal Psychology Journal* 5 (2): 119–130 (1990).

Van der Kolk, Bessel. "Trauma, neuroscience and the etiology of hysteria." *Journal of the American Psychoanalytic Association* 28 (2000): 237–262).

Van Gelder, Nico M., Roger F. Butterworth, and Boris D. Drijan, eds. *Malnutrition and the Infant Brain.* New York: Wiley-Liss, 1990.

Van Heusen, Josephine E. "The Development of Fears, Phobias, and Restrictive Patterns of Adaptation Following Attempted Abortions." *Pre- and Perinatal Psychology Journal* 2 (3): 179–185 (1988).

Van Houwelingen, A. C., J. D. Sorensen, G. Hornstra, M. M. Simonis, J. Boris, S. F. Olsen, and N. J. Secher. "Essential fatty acid status in neonates after fish-oil supplementation during late pregnancy." *British Journal of Nutrition* 74 (5): 723–731 (1995).

Verny, Thomas "The Scientific Basis of Pre- and Perinatal Psychology, part 1. *Pre- and Perinatal Psychology Journal* 3 (3): 157–169 (1989).

Verny, Thomas, and John Kelley. *The Secret Life of the Unborn Child.* New York: Dell, 1986.

Verny, Thomas, and Pamela Weintraub. *Nurturing the Unborn Child: A Nine-Month Program for Soothing, Stimulating, and Communicating with Your Baby.* New York: Delacorte Press, 1991.

Verrier, Nancy Newton. *The Primal Wound: Understanding the Adopted Child.* Baltimore: Gateway Press, 1997.

Wade, Jenny. "Two Voices from the Womb, Evidence for Physically Transcendent and a Cellular Source of Fetal Consciousness." *Journal of Prenatal and Perinatal Psychology and Health* 13 (2): winter 1998.

Wadhwa, Patrick D. "Prenatal stress and life-span development." In *Encylopedia of Mental Health* ed. Howard S. Friedman. San Diego, Calif: Academic Press, 1998.

Wadsworth, M. E. J. "Delinquency, Pulse Rates and Early Emotional Deprivation." *British Journal of Criminology* 16 (3): 245–256 (1976).

Wahlbeng, Karl-Erik, C. Wyne Lyma, et al. "Gene-Environment Interaction in Vulnerability to Schizophrenia: Findings from the Finnish Adoptive Family Study of Schizophrenia." *American Journal of Psychiatry* 154 (3): 355–362 (1997).

Wakschlag, L. S., B. B. Lahey, R. Loeber, S. M. Green, R. A. Gordon, and B. L. Leventhal. "Maternal Smoking During Pregnancy and the Risk of Conduct Disorder in Boys." *Archives of General Psychiatry* 54 (1997): 670–676.

Walbach, Helene. "Prenatal Preparation: Suggestion for Modification." *Pre- and Perinatal Psychology Journal* 1 (3): 208–222 (1987).

Wang, Z. X., C. F. Ferris, and G. H. L. De Vries. "The role of septal vasopressin innervation in paternal behavior in prairie voles." *Proceedings of the National Academy of Sciences* 91 (1993): 400–404.

Watkins, Helen A. "Treating the Trauma of Abortion." *Pre- and Perinatal Psychology Journal* 1 (2): 135–142 (1986).

Watson, John Broadus. *The Psychological Care of Infant and Child*. New York: W. W. Norton, 1928.

Wayne, Francesca, and Iltar Frith. "Theory of mind and social impairment in children with conduct disorder." *British Journal of Developmental Psychology* 14 (1996): 385–398.

Weiner, Marcia. "Child Abuse." The Survivor Monument Project, Summer Update, 1997. 274 Rhodes Ave., Toronto, On. Canada, M4L 3A5

Whaley, Lucille F., and Donna L. Wong. *Nursing Care of Infants & Children*. St. Louis, Mo.: Mosby, 1999.

Widom, Cathy Spatz. "The Cycle of Violence." *Science* 244 (1989): 160–166.

Will, Jerry, Patricia Self, and Nancy Dratan. "Nursery Stereotypes." Paper presented at the American Psychology Association Meeting, Atlanta, Georgia, 1974.

Wilson, Lynn M., et al. Antenatal Psychosocial Risk Factors Associated with Adverse Postpartum Family Outcomes." *Canadian Medical Association Journal* 154 (6): 785–799 (1996).

Wilson, Matthew, and Bruce McNaughton. "Memory Building." *The Economist*, 29 August 1998.

Winafred, B. Lucas. *Regressive Therapy: A Handbook for Professionals*. Vol. II, *Special Instances of Altered State Work*. Deep Forest Press, 1993 (P.O. Drawer 4, Crest Park, CA. 92326).

Winberg, J. "Do Neonatal Pain and Stress Program the Brain's Response to Future Stimuli?" *Acta Paediatrica Scandinavia* 87 (1998): 723–725.

Winnicott, D. W. *Human Nature*. London: Free Association Press, 1988.

Winokur, M. A. "The use of music as an audio-analgesia during childbirth." Master's thesis, Florida State University, Tallahassee, 1984.

Winslow, J. T., and T. R. Lisel. "Social status of male squirrel monkey determines response to central oxytocin administration." *Journal of Neuroscience* 11 (1991): 2,032–2,038.

Wolock, Isabel, and Bernard Horowitz, "Child Maltreatment as a Social Problem: The Neglect of Neglect," *American Journal of Orthopsychiatry* 54 (1984): 530–543.

Woolett, A. D. White, and L. Lyon. "Observations of fathers at birth." In *Fathers: Psychological Perspectives*, edited by N. Beail and J. McGuire, 72–94. London: Junction, 1982.

Yarrow, L., J. Rubenstein, and F. Pederson. *Infant and Environment: Early Cognitive and Motivational Development*. New York: Wiley & Sons, 1975.

Zahn-Waxler, Carolyn, E. Mark Cummings, and Ronald Ionnotti. *Altru-*

ism and Aggression: Biological and Social Origins. Cambridge: Cambridge University Press, 1984.

Zigler, Edward. "Infants at Physical/Psychological Risk in Day Care." *Behavior Today* 16 (15): 1–3 (15 April 1985).

Zulueta, Felicity de. *From Pain to Violence: The Traumatic Roots of Destructiveness.* London: Whurr Publishers, 1993.

Index